RAKAPOSHI

by MIK

RAKAPOSHI

By the same author:

COMMANDO CLIMBER

HIGH ARCTIC

Mike Banks

RAKAPOSHI

Foreword by Field-Marshal
Sir Gerald Templer

A. S. Barnes and Company, Inc.
New York

Published in the United States 1960 *by*
A. S. Barnes and Company, Inc., New York

Library of Congress Catalog Card Number: 60-11347

Printed in the United States of America

TO OUR FRIENDS IN
PAKISTAN

CONTENTS

ILLUSTRATIONS

[*Names in square brackets refer to photographers other than the author*]

MAPS

ACKNOWLEDGEMENTS

I AM much indebted to General Moulton, Brigadier Sultan Mohammad and Surgeon-Lieutenant Patey, all of whom helped me in the production of this book.

To my expedition colleagues I would like to express my thanks for letting me use some of their photographs, but most important of all, for creating, by their actions, the substance of this book.

We all share a quite unrepayable debt of gratitude to the Mount Everest Foundation, the Nuffield Trust, and many public-spirited British firms, whose support made this adventure possible.

The members of the British-Pakistani Forces Himalayan Expedition have, in addition, good reason to be deeply grateful to the Fighting Services of both Britain and Pakistan for the unstinted co-operation and kindliness we encountered everywhere, from Service Departments as well as from many individual officers and men.

FOREWORD

by

FIELD-MARSHAL SIR GERALD TEMPLER
G.C.B., G.C.M.G., K.B.E., D.S.O.

RAKAPOSHI is among the most familiar and best known of the mountains of the Karakoram. In this respect indeed it comes second only to K.2, the second-highest mountain in the world. Below its immense northern face passes one of the ancient trade routes to Kashgar and Central Asia. And it has for years been one of the glittering prizes most coveted by mountaineers from many nations. Nevertheless despite all these attractions, and the challenge it has offered to mountaineering courage, skill and endurance, Rakaposhi had remained inviolate in all its splendid beauty.

This book is the narrative of two expeditions, each led by the author, to this great Himalayan peak. The second expedition, which was successful, besides being a stirring mountaineering exploit, was also in itself a true Combined Operation. One of its most heartening aspects was the sense of harmony and concord which welded together into a team officers not only from all the British Fighting Services, but also from the Pakistan Army. And it was the strength of this team spirit which carried two of those men finally to the summit—one of the highest in the world to be climbed without the aid of oxygen. I sincerely trust that this will not be the last expedition of this kind that will take place in collaboration with our brothers in arms of other Commonwealth countries.

It has always been a Service tradition to support exploration. We do this for a variety of reasons, not the least of which is the fact that the organization and execution of an expedition pose physical, mental and administrative problems seldom encountered except in war. Expeditions, therefore, put to a stern test a man's character and his organizing ability. There are few beter forms of training in its broadest sense.

The story of the ascent of Rakaposhi, told here with humor and directness, should serve as an inspiration and encouragement to anyone, Serviceman or civilian, who nourishes a sense of adventure. And who doesn't?

Book One

The British-American Karakoram Expedition 1956

I

PEN PAL PLANNING

Beware of all enterprises that require new clothes—Thoreau.

SOME years ago I conceived a twofold ambition: to explore the polar regions and to be a Himalayan mountaineer. Obviously a man does not just wake up one morning with such a ready-made ambition clear in his head; the notion is nurtured gradually, fed on experience and whetted by the literature of the subject. Although I cannot personally identify the specific morning I promised myself that I would explore these two snowy and remote regions of the earth I do know that by 1951 I had formulated and crystallized this twin polar and Himalayan project. The blame for it, I fear, can only really be apportioned to my regiment, the Corps of Royal Marines. This needs some explaining. My job in the Corps was to help train Commandos (who are raised by the Royal Marines) and I had further specialized by becoming an instructor in rock-climbing, mountaineering and snow warfare.

Whether it was in the mountains, on the snow-fields, or clinging to the steep faces of the granite cliffs of Cornwall with my young Commando trainees, I found, immediately after the war, a new zest in life. I climbed on duty and spent my leaves mountaineering in the Alps, rock-climbing in Britain or ski-ing. Almost inevitably I became associated with a group of naval officers (the Marines are part of the Navy, remember) who were endeavoring in this post-war era to revive the great naval tradition of polar exploration. I was well equipped to join this circle of enthusiasts for my Commando training had not only developed my sense of adventure but it had even taught me the necessary basic techniques of the snow explorer. Thus my polar opportunity came first and my Himalayan dream lay fallow.

We hatched our plans and in 1951 I boarded an R.A.F. Sunderland flying-boat and flew to Greenland, spending the summer exploring an unknown area of the north-east coast. This expedition, which was a reconnaissance expedition for a larger and longer one to follow, involved a great deal of hard mountain and glacier travel. A year later I returned to the same area as a member of the British North Greenland Expedition where I spent two long and cold years in the Arctic as leader of one of the expedition's snow-tractor teams. My winters were spent in a congested base hut cooped up with twenty explorers who were a mixed bag of servicemen and scientists. This taught me much about people. The rest of the year I spent in travel and scientific research on the vast Greenland ice-cap which, with the Antarctic plateau, is surely one of the coldest, bleakest and most featureless tracts on the face of the earth. My final journey was an east to west crossing of the ice-cap at its widest, a distance of a little under 800 miles. This is just about the longest journey between uninhabited points that can be accomplished in the northern hemisphere. From the ice-cap I learned the deeper meaning of cold and of travel.

On the ice-cap I also had ample time in which to think. As the expedition dragged through its second year I found my Arctic curiosity, which had lured me to Greenland, well and truly satiated. I had run the gamut of polar emotions from the fear of death to abject boredom and began to look elsewhere for mental and physical adventure. I did not really have to search very hard, for on that utterly flat and apparently limitless ice-cap I found my mind dwelling more and more on the mountain world of my heart's desire. Perhaps this was mere love of paradox or the unattainable, but my imagination was haunted by great processions of giant snow-capped Himalayan peaks calling out to be climbed. And in the valleys there would be friendly people. People! On that sterile, uninhabitable ice-cap human society was the one thing most dreadfully lacking. The Himalayas would not be so lonely, probably more exciting (although in retrospect I could hardly grumble at the lack of thrills in Greenland!). In consequence, even before I left Greenland I was plotting a Himalayan expedition with my friend and brother mountaineer, Lieutenant-Commander Richard Brooke, R.N. We even arranged that Himalayan Club Journals should be air-dropped to us with some mail to assist in our planning. The desire was there and that was the important thing for, as is well known, anything may be achieved by a man provided he wants it badly enough—or is ordered to do it by a sufficiently senior officer. Sooner or later something was bound to turn up.

In the event, Brooke and I had been over-optimistic in trying to organize a Himalayan expedition while we were still completely cut off from civilization on a polar expedition and, not unnaturally, our plans failed to materialize. A year later, however, a most significant letter arrived. It had been typed and posted by my old friend Hamish MacInnes at the Hermitage, Mount Cook, New Zealand, which is a famous mountaineering center in the Southern Alps. Now Hamish is the only friend I have whose typewriting is, for some inscrutable reason, even harder to read than his handwriting, and therefore it took me some time to decipher his letter. Hamish usually wrote to me (or anyone else, I imagine) at times of stress, such as from hospital after his most recent climbing or motor-cycling mishap, or perhaps if he had to interrupt his full-time mountaineering activities for a few weeks to acquire money by so sordid an occupation as work. Whatever its portent his letter was bound to be interesting. From it I gleaned that Hamish had befriended an American mountaineer in New Zealand and they had discovered in each other a common desire to go on a Himalayan expedition. The idea, propounded in the letter, was that the American should invite some of his American friends and Hamish would similarly invite some of his British friends. Hamish himself had been on the verge of joining Brooke and me on our projected expedition the year before when our plans fell through. He therefore invited me to join his expedition, being well aware that it was merely a matter of time before I, like the good Hindu, cleansed my soul by gazing on the everlasting snows of Himachal.

I accepted gladly knowing that nothing associated with Hamish could ever be dull—or over-serious. The American with whom Hamish had teamed up, Pete Robinson, was a geologist who was studying at Otago University with the aid of a Fulbright scholarship. His object for visiting the Himalaya was therefore scientific as well as sporting. He quickly proved himself to be an energetic organizer and bombarded us all with letters and even with a periodical document called *The Karakoram Courier*[1] which contained all the up-to-date expedition news. Pete invited three other Americans to join the party. First there was Andy Kaufmann, a well-known and very experienced climber who would have been an enormous asset to the party and would, no doubt, have been leader. However, Andy made the proviso that, being a family man, he would not be able to afford to come along if the venture involved heavy expenditure. Eventually, and to the regret of us all, this consideration forced him to withdraw. The other Americans were Bob Swift and Dick Irvin, both Californians, both holding scientific degrees. Dick decided to make a world tour of the expedition and sailed to join Hamish in New Zealand to help with the organizing and to try a few climbs in the New Zealand Alps. He would then travel to the Himalayas and back to America via Europe. Bob Swift remained in California and planned to go by sea to Pakistan, picking up some of the expedition equipment in Britain on the way. By this time we had a name and called ourselves the British-American Karakoram Expedition. (Note the "British" and not "Anglo" in deference to our Scots member, Hamish.) We then had some writing-paper printed, both in New Zealand and in the States. Bob's paper, however, used the spelling "Karakorum" instead of "Karakoram" and someone wrote and asked him if he was going on the same expedition. Bob's answer was brief:

Ewe like Ram,
I like Rum

Hamish's letters to me always contained at least one dreadful pun and a few peremptory commands such as "get a doctor"; "see that we make a film" or "raise lots of money, we're broke". I therefore asked Dr. Tom Patey, a very talented young Scottish climber, to join us. He was keen to come but just having finished his medical training he was very hard up and, like Andy Kaufmann, to our regret had to withdraw. I therefore became the expedition quack and soon evolved a simple working method. I took two sizes of pills, very

[1] The Karakoram Range is the western extension of the main Himalayan chain. Throughout the book I use the word "Himalayan" in its broader sense, to embrace the Karakoram Range. The purist would differentiate between these two mountain systems.

large and very small (actually they were diarrhœa and anti-malaria pills) and gave the big pills to people with serious ailments and the small pills to those with small ailments. None of my patients died on me—which is more than many a Harley Street man can claim—and I had many satisfied customers.

I also asked my very old friend Jeff Douglas to join us. Jeff had joined the Marines with me on the same bleak January day in 1941 and we had remained close friends ever since. He had left the Corps just after the war and by the time I asked him to come to the Himalayas he had been in a special and rather daring unit of the Royal Marines during the war when he was wounded, and was also a frogman, canoeist, paratrooper, lobster-fisherman in Lundy Island in the Bristol Channel and, at one stage, on the verge of going to the Gilbert Islands in the Pacific. It was then that he suddenly joined the Arab Legion and founded the Jordanian Navy in the Dead Sea. His expert knowledge of the operation of small boats stood him in excellent stead and he had achieved the rank of major by the time my invitation reached him. In fact he styled himself the First Dead Sea Lord. He had obtained leave of absence to come along when, out of the blue, he was sacked by King Hussein with Glubb Pasha and several other British officers who were in key operational jobs. He then had to drop out in order to look for a job, and I was very sorry to have missed his company. He made amends the next year when, with Hamish MacInnes, he spent a winter in the Himalayas hunting for the yeti, or Abominable Snowman.

Our final shrinkage came when Pete Robinson became involved with study, woman and impecuniosity at the last moment and he too fell by the wayside. He had been a founder-member and had worked hardest of all so it must have been a bitter blow to him to have to drop out. He was a rugged mountaineer and we felt his absence when the going got tough. We therefore ended up four strong: Hamish MacInnes and Dick Irvin who were meeting up in New Zealand; Bob Swift in California and myself in Britain. We were all certain starters and the British-American Karakoram Expedition was in being. We now needed a mountain.

We sought a mountain that was technically very difficult to scale but not so high as to be a labor of Hercules due to altitude alone.

We did not consider, therefore, attempting a 26,000-ft. peak and neither did we want the expense, weight and complication of oxygen apparatus. It did not take us very long to settle upon the Mustagh Tower, which, at a shade under 24,000 ft., was the subject of a spectacular photograph taken by the famous mountain photographer, Sella, just after the turn of the century. From this photograph the Tower epitomized unassailability, a sheer-sided spire cutting into the sky. Other photographs, however, were more revealing and disclosed the fact that the Mustagh Tower was a thin wedge-shaped mountain which looked like a church spire when viewed end on, as in Sella's photograph, but, when viewed from its broad flank, offered two ridges running down at a reasonable angle. We consulted air photographs taken by Professor Desio, decided that the Tower was a suitable and worthy objective, and planned our assault to go up the south ridge via Younghusband Glacier.

An agony of planning now ensued. However attractive the cosmopolitan aspect of the expedition appeared the difficulties of mondial planning, whereby every problem had to be settled by airmail, with its attendant delays, made this stage an absolute nightmare. It became a veritable "pen-pal expedition". Although none of us had any eventual regrets concerning our experiment in international co-operation, I feel we will never again indulge in such an orgy of letter-writing unless we have two clear years in which to plan the expedition.

Money, of course, is the thing you most need at this stage of an expedition, and it is the common misapprehension that this may be obtained very easily from newspapers and film or television companies. To the amateur this is dangerous ground, as I found out to my cost. On two occasions I received offers from television or film companies which in my military world I would have assumed to be definite, suggesting they should finance the expedition in return for exclusive rights; but in each case I was informed, some weeks later, that they had changed their minds. It soon became apparent that we would have to pay our own way. The moral of this, it seems to me, is that the healthiest way to launch an expedition is to plan it within your means and then expand in the event of any unexpected windfalls. Like many British expeditions, we received considerable help from the Mount Everest Foundation, for which, together with many other aspiring but impecunious explorers, we have good reason to be very grateful. Like most expeditions, we received open-hearted assistance from many public-spirited firms. I kept a list of these firms in a file which, with more honesty than tact, I marked "Scrounge". I remember with embarrassment one day discussing with a Managing Director exactly what he was prepared to give us, with this "Scrounge" file laid blatantly on the desk. I hope he couldn't read upside-down.

About this time, when plans were nicely advanced, I received a letter from John Hartog, inviting me round to his Earl's Court flat to have a chat about objectives. I gave a short broadcast on the B.B.C. about how we intrepid mountaineers were going to scale our impossible mountain, and then went round to Hartog's. On walking into his drawing-room, an enormous enlargement of Sella's photograph of the Mustagh Tower stared me in the face. It transpired that he also was taking an expedition to the mountain and had applied for permission ahead of us. He added to my misery when he informed me that a French party, too, had designs upon the Mustagh Tower that same year. Never before in Himalayan history had three parties set off for the same mountain in the same season. We felt that any form of competition or suggestion of a race would take most of the pleasure out of the venture and we decided, as fast as airmail would permit, to alter our objective. The little-known and mysterious peaks of the Hispar and Batura glaciers were particularly appealing and we also thought of Rakaposhi, a virgin, but well-known giant, which had the added advantage of being extremely accessible. By the time these developments had had time to take effect, most of us were about to converge on Karachi, so we decided to alter our objective by direct negotiation with the Pakistan Government on our arrival there.

Bob Swift arrived in London with the tents and vapor barrier boots which were about the only non-standard equipment we took. He was a big, tall, slow-speaking Californian with an unerring sense of humor and a liking for beer and sports cars; I took an immediate liking to him. We soon discovered that when our grandiose financial and publicity plans fell down, we had both been obliged to sell our Austin Healey sports cars in order to raise funds. Bob, carrying the bulk of the expedition stores with him, went by sea to Karachi. At about this stage, when our finances were at rock bottom and our plans quite chaotic, there came a letter from Hamish announcing that he and Dick Irvin, who had joined him in New Zealand, were disappearing into the outback, quite out of touch, where they were collecting sea-shells which he was confident they would be able to sell at a vast profit; we later found out that they did in fact collect a quantity of valuable sea-shells, but spent all the profits on hiring a seaplane to fly them back to civilization.

At about this time also, Hamish, who was responsible for planning our diet, told us all that we must be prepared to live like peasants in the interests of economy. Hamish was a member of the famous and tough Creagh Dhu mountaineering club of Glasgow, who, even in most prosperous circumstances, live at a standard of austerity insupportable by the average mountaineer. I mentally tightened my belt, borrowed two cine-cameras, bought thousands of feet of color film, and boarded an aircraft for Karachi.

On the plane I sat next to a fat passenger who had a youthful face but grey hair—a strange mixture. He wore an expression of artless innocence and read the *Memoirs of Casanova* with unparalleled intensity. I had not been to India since 1945, and as I drove from the aerodrome into the city of Karachi the hot air and pungent smells of the East brought back vivid memories of wartime days in Madras or Calcutta. Karachi is the last big town before Pakistan turns from a lush land into the arid desert of the Middle East; camels sailed along with slow dignity, being overtaken by fussy little donkeys.

I located Bob, who told me that the others had agreed by letter that we should go for Rakaposhi, and he had notified the Government of Pakistan accordingly. Changing the objective at the eleventh hour was a complicated and lengthy business, involving, as it did, negotiations with several separate Pakistani ministries. One has only to recall the sedate pace of our own bureaucratic workings, to gain some impression of our predicament. Precious days began to pass. Hastily we asked for a copy of George Band's book *Road to Rakaposhi* to be air-mailed out to us, and set to work, for there was much to be done to accommodate this change in plan. The Customs in any country present a major problem, and I would recommend any mountaineer whose job it is to pass an expedition's stores through Customs to take with him as reading matter the Book of Job. For instance, once I was entreated by our shipping agent to accompany him to the Chief Appraiser in the Customs Office; when I had been there several hours, eventually I met the Chief Appraiser himself, a pleasant young Pakistani. I asked him what I had to do, and he told me with a smile that nothing was required of me; I had merely been brought along by the shipping agent to lend face. Bureaucratic affairs are difficult to arrange quickly in Pakistan, particularly when you are doing it for the first time and don't know the ropes. It is an unbounded asset if you have heaps of time to spare, so as not to fall into the folly against which Kipling warns: that of trying to hurry the East—it is a sure way of getting ulcers, and most mountaineers are in a regrettable hurry.

Pakistan continues to show a high and kindly regard for things British and we are remembered there with a certain affection, especially by the Pakistan Army, which has inherited the traditions of the fine old Indian Army. Old soldiers are always pleased to meet a British Serviceman, and I used to receive a most impressive salute from the hotel porter, who was an ex-Subadar Major. A driver from the Embassy had driven a tank with Skinner's Horse in Italy during the war with the 4th Indian Division and he remembered with gratitude his solicitous subaltern, who always came around to see that the *sowars* had their correct food, drink and sleeping accommodation. However, our work in Karachi was impeded by the fact that it was Ramzan (Ramadan), the Moslem period of fasting, during the forty days of which it is forbidden to eat or drink between dawn and dusk. Not only does this bring work to a halt at midday, but the strain of it puts everybody into a fairly frayed state of nerves. Bob then caught his first bout of dysentery and lay for several days suffering on his bed. It is a sound idea to land in Karachi with a pocketful of anti-dysentery sulpha tablets.

By now it was mid-May, and high time that one of us moved up to Rawalpindi to make arrangements with the Army for our flight to Gilgit. Development of air transport has taken the bite out of travel in the Himalayan foothills, where a series of small airstrips deep in the heart of the hills has made the long trek from the towns in the northern plains to such places as Gilgit or Skardu a thing of the past. A journey that used to take ten days is now accomplished in an hour and a quarter. It was our intention to fly from Rawalpindi to Gilgit, which is only a few miles from the foot of Rakaposhi, making it probably the most accessible great mountain in the world.

I flew to Rawalpindi via Peshawar, stopping there for a couple of hours. The famous Khyber Pass, that favored sniping-ground of unruly Afghan tribesmen, was visible a few miles away. A hospitable Englishman took me for a beer in the Peshawar Club, which at that time in the morning looked deserted and forlorn with its walls hung with countless prints of successive Masters of the Peshawar Hunt whose quarry was a jackal instead of a fox.

Peshawar was the nerve centre of the pre-war frontier fighting, and in the old days the bar was usually six deep with officers from the regiments who had just got back from frontier duty. Now our footsteps rang hollowly.

We took off again and soon I was in the garrison town of Rawalpindi, with its wide green avenues; it houses the headquarters of the Pakistan Army. Colonel Goodwin and his brother Bill, with the generosity that one so often receives from fellow-countrymen in the East, put their bungalow at the disposal of the expedition. Our stay there, waited on by soft-footed Pathan servants, and in an atmosphere redolent of Caruso and Kipling, was extremely pleasant and restful. There also we met our liaison officer, Captain Fazal-i-Haque of the Pakistan Army Education Corps, who would accompany us on the expedition as the representative of his Government: and there Dick and Hamish (sea-shells now having faded into history) joined us.

It was some five years since I had seen Hamish, when we had climbed together in his native Highlands: in the meantime he had led an adventurous life. With a fellow-member of the Creagh Dhu, he had been on an enterprising and extremely lightweight expedition to the Himalayas, where they had attempted the formidable peak of Pumori, near Everest. Since then he had been knocking around New Zealand uranium-prospecting and, on odd desperate occasions, even working. He was just as I remembered him: tall and broad-shouldered, athletic and always cheerful, his head full of wild and wonderful plans, his pocket usually empty! He borrowed from Dick, Bob and myself socks, gloves and various other essential items which he had forgotten. We more or less expected this. Dick Irvin (like Bob, from California) was a short, squarely-built man, also with a typically dry American sense of humor, who had climbed above 20,000 ft. on a mountaineering expedition to Peru. Hamish and Dick, therefore, were two proven high-altitude men. Bob's experience as a climber was chiefly in the Yosemite, in the Sierras, and in Canada. My own mountaineering experience was mainly Alpine, but I had in addition my two years in Greenland, which would stand me in good stead on the frigid higher snows of the Himalayas.

We took stock and found, somewhat to our surprise, that we had money and equipment in judicious proportions: considering the difficulties of the organizing stage, this was most remarkable. We made a few last-minute purchases and were ready to fly to Gilgit.

On May 22nd the Colonel drove us to Chaklala, the airport of Rawalpindi, where we awaited the return from Skardu of a plane which would then take us to Gilgit, only to be told that we could not fly because the plane was not fitted with passenger seats. However, we waited until the plane landed, and duly observed nine passengers disembarking. A peep inside the aircraft revealed that they had been sitting on perfectly normal seats. Confronted with this evidence, the airport official relented and said that we could go. At this moment the chief pilot of the airline stormed into the office, declared that it was too late in the day to fly, and hinted very roundly that we were not V.I.P.s (Not that we had claimed we were!) I made frantic overtures and almost wept on his shoulder until he took pity and allowed the plane to take off.

The flight to Gilgit is accurately described as the most impressive and hazardous scheduled air flight in the world. The route follows the gorge of the River Indus and crosses over the Babusar Pass (13,690 ft.). Emergency landing-grounds are non-existent and navigational aids scanty. Normally there must be perfect weather at both ends before a flight is undertaken.

The old Dakota was heavily loaded with stores and took a very long take-off before it growled its way into the air. As we flew steadily north, gaining height, our perspiration ceased and soon we were delightfully cool, and a little later somewhat uncomfortably cold. The ground below us became rugged and undeveloped by man, and presently a ribbon of white appeared out of the haze away to the north. The details in this white ribbon became clearer and resolved themselves into snow peaks, one white hump growing larger and seeming to stand out above the others—it was the great massif of Nanga Parbat (26,620 ft.). The size of the hills increased until we were flying along valleys with the tops of surrounding peaks above us. We literally scraped over the Babusar Pass with the aircraft very near to its ceiling. An engine failure at this stage would have been catastrophic. The view was now dominated by Nanga Parbat, its vast ice precipices being on a scale beyond my Alpine experience, and it was difficult to comprehend that this facet of the mountain was perhaps 15,000 ft. In proportion it looked no larger than Ben Nevis. We followed the Indus Valley towards Hunza with immense peaks cutting into the sky all about us. As we approached Gilgit first Haramosh took pride of place and then, looking a little later, Rakaposhi dominated the landscape—high, elegant and immense—but I cannot justly claim that ecstasy which more emotional mountaineers like to think they experience on first viewing their objective.

We lost height, made a steep and sudden turn, skimmed over a gorge with a river foaming through it, and touched down in a world utterly different from Rawalpindi: different in climate, different in landscape and different in people. We were surrounded by smiling olive faces and were fanned by a refreshingly cool breeze. I had always thought of Gilgit as the end of the trail, and was almost prepared to tie on the mountaineering rope as I stepped out of the plane. However, we were whisked away in a jeep to the Residency, where the Political Agent lived. The Residency, a relic of the old days of British India, was set among lawns and green trees and made beautiful by bird-song. Along the veranda, typical of the East, an impressive row of antlers was arranged. We were shut in on all sides by towering valley walls, just as I had imagined it. Mr. Kiani, the Political Agent, and Major Chowdry, who was in command of the Northern Scouts, were both extremely helpful, and very soon we had arranged jeeps to take us and our stores up the Hunza valley to Nomal.

That evening we were invited to a buffet dinner at the Residency, which we duly attended in our best climbing clothes; Dick Irvin appeared in shorts, which were more respectable than his long trousers. To our horror a dozen or so guests turned up in dinner-jackets. The Pakistanis were maintaining our old "outpost of Empire" etiquette with a vengeance. We, of course, should have known better. The apparel, I regretted that evening, oft proclaims the man.

That same evening we met the four high-altitude porters who had been sent to us by the Mir of Hunza. The head porter, or sirdar, was Issa Khan, a veteran of the German expedition to Nanga Parbat and the Italian expedition to K2. On both these mountains he had carried sturdily and high and was one of the most famous of the Hunza porters, who boasted the title of "Hunza Tiger". He had an alert, expressive face and was obviously wise in the ways of expedition, for he immediately asked us if we had had Rakaposhi medals made for the expedition porters—which, not being Germans, we had not. Next came Dilap Shah, a charming weather-beaten old shikari, or hunter, who had spent most of his life roaming the glaciers and foothills of Hunza. He looked simple (in its nice sense) and unsophisticated. Then came Qambar, a hulking man who was introduced as having "killed many Hindus". He had a malevolent look about him, except when he smiled, and I do not doubt that if he were so inclined, he was capable of killing not only Hindus but probably his whole family as well. These three had all served in the Gilgit Scouts and, on hearing that I was a Captain Sahib, rained incessant salutes upon me. Last and youngest of the porters was Nadir Aman, who could easily have been mistaken for a Greek.

On the lawn of the Political Agent's house we distributed the equipment to the porters, who accepted it gratefully with much trying on and exchanging of items; we had managed to guess more or less correctly their boot sizes. We also explained to them very carefully, and repeated several times, which of the items we were giving them and which we were lending them. Despite our efforts to make it crystal clear, this differential between gift and loan was later to cause us trouble. In practice, once you have given an article to a porter he regards it as baksheesh, and it is fruitless to try to retrieve it.

II

RAKAPOSHI

Northward we then beheld Rakipushi, lifting high her silver spear—Martin Conway, 1892.

GILGIT is an important nodal town. It stands athwart one of the more important trade routes at that very strategic point where Russia, China, Afghanistan and the old British India, now Pakistan, come close together. Its main trade used to be north over the border into Sinkiang, but this has been sealed off by the Iron Curtain. The economy of Gilgit is now dependent on the Government-subsidized airlift, which has changed the nature of the bazaar and reduced the picturesque caravan trade.

We would approach Rakaposhi by travelling up the Hunza valley to Nomal (see Map 1), crossing the river and following the Jaglot nullah to its head. Although mechanization may be decried by the purists—"the sight of a jeep makes a horse go lame", as the sage Tilman might well have said—we were not sorry to be able to drive the seventeen miles from Gilgit to Nomal, for this stretch has the reputation of being as dry and dreary as any march in the whole Indus Valley.

Loaded into three jeeps, we started placidly along a wide road. As we turned into the valley of the Hunza River the country became steeper and starker. Soon the route was clinging to the rock face of the gorge, built out here and there on dry walls. In addition, and usually at the worst places, it dipped frighteningly.

There's a wheel on the Horns o' the mornin'
And a wheel on the edge of the pit
And a drop into nothing beneath you
As straight as a beggar can spit.

1. General view of Rakaposhi (25,550 ft.) from the west. The S.W. Spur and Ridge form the right skyline.

2. Mike Banks.

3. Hamish MacInnes.

4. Bob Swift and Dick Irvin.

Only the driver appeared to me to be relaxed and enjoying the journey. Soon we ran gently downhill into the greenery of Nomal, where we stopped at the Rest House. Fruit was shaken down from the trees into blankets; eggs were soon frying.

The rope suspension-bridge had not yet been erected at Nomal, so we were spared that particular Himalayan hazard. But we were not to be let off an ordeal by water. A crude and ramshackle *zakh* made of four inflated cowskins, literally tied together with bits of stick, was produced. It looked utterly inadequate to cope with the turbulent Hunza River, which was here seventy yards wide and obviously in a desperate hurry to reach the sea. The craft was rowed by an ancient Charon using a pair of dilapidated oars, but what he lacked in equipment he made up for in skill. However violently he bobbed about in the heaving water, however quickly he was whisked downstream, he maintained a perfect rhythm and always managed to keep his craft correctly pointed. He was using an hereditary skill handed down by centuries of incomparable watermen. River-crossing in the Karakoram must always be treated as a major problem of travel, for the glaciers which feed the rivers are the greatest in the world outside the polar regions and produce an immense volume of water as they melt. Needless to say, we crossed in safety if not with composure. I personally unlaced my boots and took my rucksack off my shoulder, all ready to swim for it. In gathering darkness we walked a few miles to the village of Matum Das. There we had supper, and, during the meal, and afterwards as we prepared for bed, our every small move was watched with rapt attention by a circle of villagers: enough to satisfy the most egocentric.

Rakaposhi, at 25,550 ft., stands among the mammoth peaks of the world. Rising so close to Gilgit, it is therefore a very familiar but curiously unexplored peak. The reason for it being unexplored is quite simple: it is too difficult. Consequently, when its brothers in height, Nanda Devi and Kamet, fell in the thirties, it was still inviolate in the late fifties. It is best viewed from Baltit, the capital of Hunza, where it is often ringed by a belt of cloudlets, and prettily named Dumani, "The Necklace of Clouds". In Gilgit it is crudely and unromantically called Rakaposhi. The origin of this name is doubtful, but might well be because, to the earthy but practical

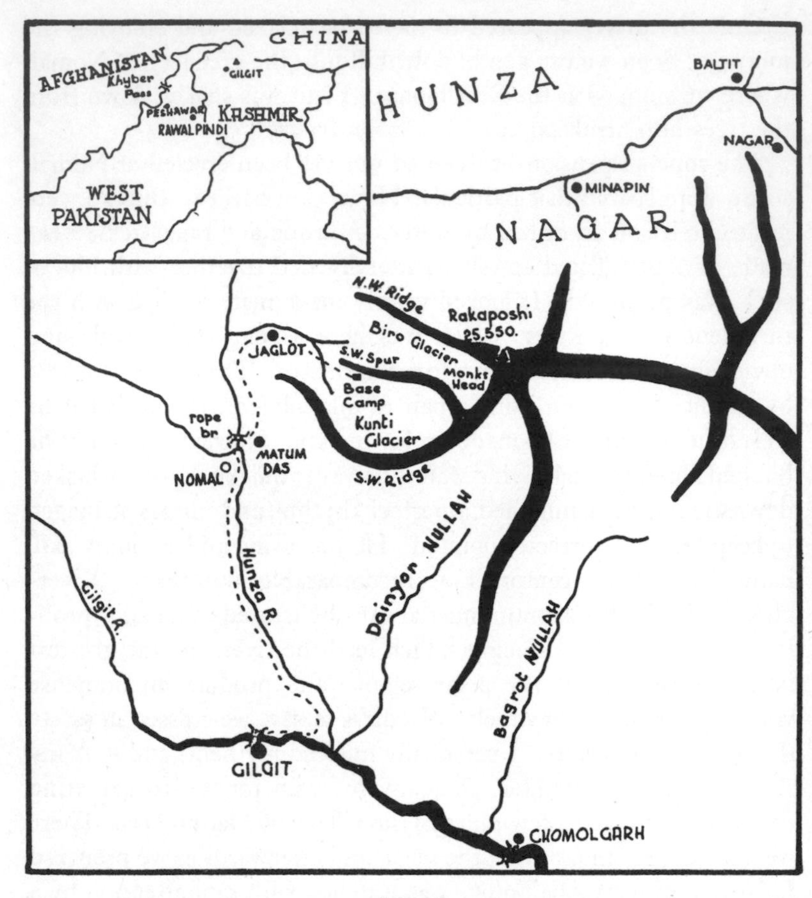

Map I

Sketch map of the approach and ridges of Rakaposhi.

inhabitants of Gilgit, the streamer of snow which trails from its summit was reminiscent of pus squirting out of a boil. I am sorry to have to tell this to the armchair idealists who like their mountains to be called "Goddess Mother of the Clouds", etc.

The mountain was first visited by Martin Conway (later Lord Conway) in 1892, when he penetrated the Bagrot nullah, which was the southern approach. Although he surmised that the high summit slopes were climbable, he observed that the ascent to the crest of

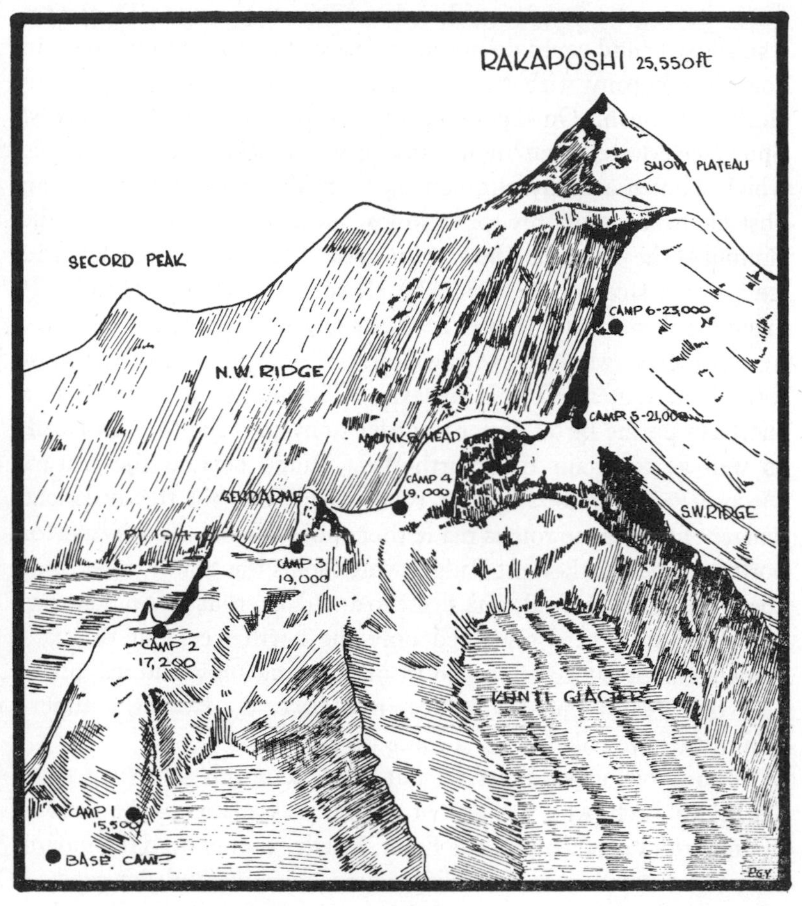

MAP II

Sketch of the S.W. Spur of Rakaposhi, showing the main features and the camps of the British-American Karakoram Expedition, 1956.

any of the approach ridges was sufficiently difficult and dangerous for him to rule them out as impossible. Other parties have visited the Bagrot nullah since, but have only tended to confirm Conway's original opinion. Nearly forty years elapsed until in 1938 Campbell Secord and Vyvyan approached the mountain from the west. They gained the foot of the North-West Ridge and climbed the peak on it—some 19,000 ft., which they thought was 23,000 ft., but which, in fact, was merely a small incident in an immense ridge. They were a small party and could do no more. Secord returned to the peak in 1947 in company with two Swiss and the celebrated Himalayan climber, Tilman. On this occasion they tried out the South-West Spur (see Map 2), but their passage was blocked by a gendarme which Tilman actually climbed but considered too formidable an obstacle to lie across his route so low on the mountain. From the summit of the Gendarme he saw the great 2,000-ft. wall of snow and ice set at a steep angle which he christened "Monk's Head". It extended from about 19,000 ft. to 21,000 ft. This great obstacle, he considered, would make the South-West Spur one of the most formidable routes in the Himalayas. Tilman also tried to make a short-cut up the Biro Glacier in order to by-pass the Monk's Head, as well as to attain the North-West Ridge beyond the feature (Secord Peak) climbed by the 1938 expedition, but the avalanche danger of both these routes made them unjustifiable as highways for porters. The South-West Ridge, which joins the South-West Spur above the Monk's Head, was so steep and dangerous that no one has ever tried it. There remained only the north face, but this is a stupendous precipice of 19,000 ft. of plunging snow and ice, probably the greatest mountain face in the world. Even the super-optimistic have failed to see a route up there.

In 1954 two expeditions set out for Rakaposhi. A strong team led by Rebitsch, who was one of the early assailants of the famous but notorious north face of the Eiger, briefly reconnoitred the mountain, but decided it was too difficult an objective and departed. I often wonder what became of the special Rakaposhi medals they had had stamped for the porters. The other expedition was from Cambridge University, led by Alfred Tissières, and included George Band, who was to scale Kangchenjunga the following year. They were six strong, among them being several very stalwart young Alpine climbers. They considered seriously, but dismissed as dangerous, the short route up the Biro to a point on the South-West Spur beyond the Monk's Head, as Tilman had done before them; they repeated Secord's climb on the North-West Ridge, but considered the continuation of the ridge far too difficult to be followed by porters; then they concentrated their attention on the South-West

Spur. They pushed beyond the Gendarme to the foot of the Monk's Head, which itself was then scaled by Tissières, Band and Fisher. Their attack, however, had insufficient impetus to establish them above it. It now looked as if the South-West Spur were the only route feasible to the summit of Rakaposhi. George Band, in his book *Road to Rakaposhi* wrote: "We had proved that the climb was possible to the top of the Monk's Head and beyond that seemed reasonable easy terrain. Before us, the mountain had almost come to be considered as impossible . . ." But to sober us Band went on to write of that "terrific wall" the Monk's Head, and asked: "In the Alps it would have seemed a serious problem. Had anything like it ever been tackled in the Himalayas before?"

When we chose the South-West Spur as our route in our attempt on the summit of Rakaposhi, we were under no illusion as to how tough a nut it would be to crack. The main question, perhaps, was whether our small party of only four climbers was justified in tackling so large a mountain over so long and difficult a route. If, as so often happens on climbing expeditions, anything went wrong when we were high up on the mountain and beyond support of our porters, we might well find ourselves in a predicament from which we lacked the mutual strength to extract ourselves. We were willing to take the risk, however, and made towards our spur of the mountain.

In Hunza there is a strong coolies' trade union which permits the villagers to carry only from one village to the next in order to share out more equally the visitor's obviously inexhaustible fund of rupees. The next day, therefore, we could not go farther than Jaglot, the nearest village, barely half a day's march distant; a pleasant walk along the bank of the Hunza River, on the far side of which the jeep route was visible, clinging to the rock face. The scenery was grandiose but barren, unrelieved by even a touch of green; dull brown cliffs plunged down from the heights. We turned suddenly into a gully of loose earth and rotting rock up which a track zigzagged its unattractive course, thereby breaking out of the Hunza valley. We supposed that we had left the last sparse patch of greenery at Matum Das and that from now on we would be faced with the screes, ice and soaring rocks of the Karakoram. At the top of the gulley we passed beneath a wooden arch, almost Japanese in its elegance, and to our amazement entered a different world. In a single step we left behind us the cruel immensity of the Hunza valley and found ourselves in a miniature landscape of chattering, bubbling rills running through and irrigating brilliantly green fields. Fruit trees and willows gave us shade. Such a surprise banished in a twinkling the sweaty grind up the penitential gully—a mountaineer's compensation.

We entered Jaglot through a maze of six-feet-wide alleys made of dry stone walls. Why the village was so walled-in and so secretive, like a Kasbah, I could not fathom. We meandered through these alleys, glimpsing side passages and carved doorposts, until we emerged on the far side and were directed to what has no doubt become "Expedition Orchard". Here, like the expeditions before us, we camped under a great and sheer cliff. Hamish, who was fairly pulsating with surplus energy, immediately gave a demonstration of rock-climbing up this face, letting out an occasional yodel. Rakaposhi was just in view, very high and distant, peeping above the intervening shoulder of a subsidiary ridge.

Whatever flights of inspiration this first close view of our goal should have induced in me were most regrettably dulled by the lethargy that accompanies a mild bout of dysentery.

The next day, May 26th, while the main body slowly trundled a day's march up the valley, Hamish and I decided to push ahead and obtain a preview of our future base camp. We enlisted as a guide a Jaglot man called Sadi Kali, who had been with Tilman and Band and was reputed to be a good hillman. All day we followed his twinkling feet as he moved with lithe certainty over the steep and rough hill track. The Jaglot nullah is delightful. Above the village we passed waterfalls and met cheerful, sturdy young shepherds. The fields then gave way to pine forests, and we could easily have been in the Tyrol or Norway. As it cut in from the Hunza gorge towards the heart of Rakaposhi, the valley mounted in steps of alternate pine forest and old dry lake beds, now a wilderness of earth and rounded stones. We passed under the caudal end of the South-West Spur, and there I came to a juddering halt due to the combined effect of diarrhœa and altitude. Hamish and Sadi Kali were still going like a pair of steam-engines, so they ascended a further thousand feet of scree until they found the Tilman/Band base camp. In this one spot, amidst the apparent desolation of scree and ice, grass grew, small flowers bloomed and a stream trickled. Tent platforms were already made. In fact, "One Base Camp, All Mod. Con., Suitable Small Expedition. Immediate Occupation." Good enough for us!

Hamish, Sadi and I returned and met the others camped in a pine forest called locally Darbar. After a forest bivouac, campfires were crackling at dawn, and after eating the *chappattie* the Jaglot men (there being no intermediate trade union village) carried to base camp, taking seven hours and frequent rests. The last thousand feet or so was a grisly haul up loose scree, which was very trying to the heavily-laden villagers; as they staggered in, one by one, and suffering from altitude as badly as we were, we gave them a packet of cigarettes. On the Naib Tessildar's advice (he was accompanying us as the Political Agent's representative) we also gave them a rupee backsheesh, for they had carried uncomplainingly and well. In addition to their loads, each man had carried up to base camp about twenty flies, which they considerately left with us. The flies, however, seemed as much affected by the altitude as we were, and were so sluggish that they fell easy victims. Later they appeared to acclimatize, and next day they were to be as nimble as ever.

As we paid them, half the coolies were unable to reckon either what they had earned or what we had given them. They accepted the money and cigarettes either with a smile and salaam, or with a half-baffled, half-suspicious glance. They were good sturdy carriers, but always ready to ask for more or make one march into two: they took everything cheerfully, carried well, and had the inestimable attribute of honesty—during the whole expedition there was no pilfering. They were also fine-looking types, strong and fair-skinned; some had abnormally long, fang-like incisors.

That night we set up base camp roughly and felt very content. The Pen-Pal expedition had arrived; it had arrived, somewhat surprisedly, with a reasonable fund of money and equipment. There had been no losses or untoward delays. We were camped, in good health and order, at the foot of a reputedly climbable ridge.

It was now up to us—and Rakaposhi.

Six tents and a couple of tarpaulin shelters comprised base camp.

We found ourselves hemmed in on all sides by the plunging flanks of the South-West Ridge and the South-West Spur. At the head of the dry and shabby ice of the Kunti Glacier we could see the upper ramparts of Rakaposhi; nearer at hand, the elegant peaks of about 19,000 ft. which rose from the continuation of the South-West Ridge gave us some beautiful mountain forms to look at and over-photograph; immediately above our heads great rock walls rose sheer to the crest of the South-West Spur. Our near views were, therefore, spectacular enough to please the cragsman's eye. Only a far view over the battalions of blue mountains was lacking.

Dick undertook an irrigation project to prevent the stream from running amongst the tents; food and climbing gear were separated into orderly piles and a wireless aerial ran across the scree; climbers' and porters' kitchens were made by building stone walls and stretching tarpaulins above them as a roof. The business of acclimatizing and sorting out continued. Although the altitude was only a little over 14,000 ft., rather like camping on top of the Matterhorn, we all felt deathly sluggish and suffered from headache. Hamish appeared to be less affected by altitude than the remainder of us, and even managed to walk with Issa Khan up to Camp I of the previous expedition, but he caught sunstroke on the way, and next day he too was immobilized with a throbbing head and a raw-burned face.

The weather was peerless—delightfully cool by night, so that a crust of ice formed over the stream, and blazing hot, almost too hot, by day. To cope with these conditions I wore lightweight pyjamas by day and put on my warm day clothes at night.

On Thursday, May 29th, I carried a light load of about 25 lb. up over the moraines and *névé* patches to Camp I with Bob. The way led out of base camp and up about 800 ft. of boulders among which sprang edelweiss and wild rhubarb. The route then flattened for a while as it followed the bank of the glacier before it turned uphill towards the South-West Spur, which then came into full view. About a further 800 ft. higher a convenient scree platform, on which we found the tent platforms of earlier expeditions, offered a site for a camp. We decided that it was too near to base to be useful as a camp, but would make an admirable advance depot for stores waiting to be carried up to the South-West Spur. As I felt reasonably fit,

I plodded on up the hill towards Camp II, which would be situated on the crest of the South-West Spur. The mountain-side facing me was a mixture of rock and snow, either of which could be followed. Usually it is best to climb up on rock, where the feet can be placed firmly and carefully, and to descend on snow, when great lunging paces can be made, particularly when the snow is soft. I started up on snow, which was littered with lumps of avalanche debris. A rock section followed to an upper gulley, or couloir, which then wound its way through the rock buttresses above me to the crest of the spur. I found the rock to be deceptively difficult, and I soon started traversing back into the snow couloir. Unfortunately, I had to pass under a small waterfall, which drenched me. However, the searing heat of the sun soon dried me off and after a total of two hours' snow trudging I attained the ridge at about 17,300 ft., still wearing only pyjamas. I am sure there is something in the Alpine Club rules about this sort of thing! I located the tent platforms and an old cheese tin of the 1954 team and then descended to base camp in little over an hour.

The stage was then set for the build-up along the South-West Spur. We set aside the food and fuel we should require above the Monk's Head and this pile of stores, plainly before our eyes, was our problem and our challenge. Get them above the Monk's Head in good time and then, given the weather, the summit might be attained. But, even foreshortened from base camp, the Monk's Head looked steep and distant, and the pile of equipment large and heavy.

The organization of our food by Hamish in New Zealand had been simple; he took everything and anything that was offered him by kind-hearted manufacturers. Consequently our diet was not perfectly balanced. Meat was one of our worries. I supplied some rather moth-eaten pemmican left over from one of my Greenland expeditions: Hamish produced some dehydrated meat, but only in sufficient quantity for the higher camps; he also produced some "comprehensive food" which, in the form of typical hospital slosh, claimed to provide for the complete nutritional needs of a man for a day—which it probably did, but it tasted like flour and water and was left uneaten. We took the obvious remedy and sent down to

Jaglot for a sheep, fervently hoping that we would murder it and eat it before we nicknamed it "Nobby" and came to like it!

During the night of Wednesday, May 30th, Dick was coughing very badly and feeling seedy. Hamish and I, with Nadir, went up to the rock step above Camp I to place a fixed rope. Even at 8 a.m. the heat on the snowfield was almost unbearable, so that Hamish had to make a mask to protect his face. Our energy was so sapped that we could not attain the ridge. When we got back Dick wisely decided to go down to Darbar, with a pocketful of penicillin tablets to try to clear his chest infection. Fazal-i-Haque went down to stay with him in case he got worse.

On Thursday, June 1st, we sent old Dilap, the only porter in camp, up to Camp I with a load while Hamish, Bob and I sorted out a month's food for our approach climb along the ridge. It was still horribly hot by day, though wind and clouds were playing games around Rakaposhi's head and shoulders, making pretty, ever-moving cloud garlands. My light meter went right off the scale, even inside the tent, so intense was the light. Lack of headaches and an increase in energy indicated that we were beginning to become acclimatized.

On June 3rd we left early to occupy Camp 2. We trudged up on good snow with light (25-lb.) sacks. An under-layer of ice caused occasional bother, but a slight breeze kept us from frying; once again a pyjama job. Bob was feeling a bit off-colour, so he went straight down—Hamish and I lazed about, then ascended a little further up the ridge, climbing the broad snow and scree shoulder above the col where Camp 2 nestled. It was easy going, but perhaps dangerous late in the day when the layer of snow softened on its bed of ice. From Camp 2 we did a sitting glissade (mountaineer's jargon for sliding down snow slopes on one's bottom) almost all the way to Camp 1—a very exhilarating slither.

We used George Band's book *Road to Rakaposhi* much as a climber in North Wales might use a *Climbers' Club Rock Climbing Guide*, a practice which almost ran us into trouble. In certain small respects our head porter, Issa Khan, had displeased us. It will be remembered that he had been on the Nanga Parbat expedition and had also been in the Gilgit Scouts. Now in Band's book we read that his expedition, too, had employed as a porter a Scout called Issa

Khan who had been to Nanga Parbat, and this porter was so bad as to receive a strong reprimand from their Liaison Officer, General Hayaud Din. On this circumstantial evidence, we assumed that the two men were identical and that our Issa Khan was withholding this information from us. We were all too ready to find fault with him. Closer investigation, however, revealed the perfect alibi of his having been on the Italian K2 expedition while Band was on Rakaposhi, and all was forgotten. In fact, he turned out to be a good natural mountaineer and an instinctive leader.

It is usual in the Himalayas for climbers to become acclimatized to great altitudes by devoting a couple of weeks to minor peaks of about 18,000 ft. This quite often provides the most sporting climbing of the whole expedition, and is frequently looked upon as being one of the most enjoyable phases. With so high a peak before us and so small a party to tackle it, we had to forgo this pleasure and concentrate every effort on establishing our camps along the South-West Spur. We would obtain our acclimatization by constant load-carrying journeys between the various camps, employing the well-tried principle of "carrying high, sleeping low". This policy has the added advantage that stocks of food in the higher camps are consumed more slowly.

The immediate plan, therefore, was to transfer some 800 lb. of stores from base to Camp 2 on the crest of the Spur proper. This task would be undertaken mainly by the porters, who showed themselves quite confident and competent to work independently under the surveillance of Issa Khan. While they were doing this, we would prepare the way along the ridge to the Gendarme, even perhaps to the foot of the Monk's Head itself. Now that we were about to occupy the higher camps the weather became more important, and we listened intently on our radio receiver to the special forecasts which Radio Pakistan very kindly broadcast for us. It was on June 5th that, carrying rucksacks of about 40 lb., Bob, Hamish and I set out from base camp to occupy Camp 2 and prepare the way beyond. This involved an ascent of some 3,000 ft. We wended our way slowly out of camp, following the line of small cairns that the porters had erected to lead through the screes above the camp by the easiest route, and along the true right bank of the Kunti Glacier until we came to the foot of the gully which led up to the ridge. We had a rest at Camp 1, which was never an occupied camp but merely used as an advance stores dump. Our way led upwards over snowfields at an easy angle to the foot of the gully. Here we had placed a fixed rope to help to ascend directly the small rock step which led to the gully itself. Alternatively, a detour around to the left could be made, which involved some mild rock climbing. The general angle steepened; the snow was good and hard, so that firm steps were easily kicked. The presence of avalanche debris at the bottom of the gully indicated where some spring avalanches had fallen, but the snow seemed well consolidated and this type of danger appeared small at present. An occasional falling stone would tinkle down on our right, but these were small, slow-moving and easily avoidable. Enclosed as we were by the walls of the gully, heat was our greatest enemy, the radiation sapping our energy beyond belief. It was of an intensity quite beyond tropical or Alpine heat. So fierce was it that we would blister and have cracked lips even despite precautionary application of lotions or protective spirit to exposed spots. The only remedy we could devise was to wear masks completely covering the face, which made us look like members of the Ku-Klux-Klan.

The gully wound its way up through the rock buttresses, never becoming formidably steep but, on the other hand, always at such an angle that one was really climbing and was conscious of the possible result of a slip. About two-thirds of the way up we negotiated a rock island blocking the gully which landed us on to the final snow slope. This always seemed absolutely interminable. Our pace would get slower and slower and our rests more frequent until, with a thankful gasp, we would arrive at the col and throw off our rucksacks.

Coming from base camp in its enclosed cirque of rock, the site of Camp 2 with its splendid views was refreshingly open. Beyond the dark haze of the Indus gorge, and seemingly floating above the dun-coloured foothills, the immense snows of Nanga Parbat gleamed. Nearer at hand Haramosh and Dobani, both fine-looking snow peaks, cut into the air. In the other direction rose the great peaks of Hunza; beyond them the mountains marched in unbroken ranks to the blue distances of the Hindu Kush until the mind boggled at the scale and the extent. They were mountains but roughly mapped and seldom visited by Europeans; mountains fit to satisfy the appetite of generations of explorers yet unborn.

Soon we had three tents erected and a tarpaulin laid out on which we piled snow to melt and provide us with water for cooking. We used the rock platforms constructed by previous expeditions to pitch our tents on and, because we were sleeping on rock and not snow, we were snugly warm on our air mattresses, using only one sleeping-bag. The next morning we awoke to the sound of drumming canvas as snow spatules drove against the tent but, like rain, this always sounds worse inside than out. At 9 a.m. the three of us set out to investigate the ridge, Bob and I taking the opportunity to try out our U.S. Army surplus vapor barrier boots. They resemble a rather compact gumboot, and insulation against the cold is achieved by a waterproof layer of sponge rubber which forms the sides and foot. They are a floppy, spongy fit, but even with only one pair of socks they keep the feet very warm. One of their drawbacks is that the perspiration cannot escape and soon one's socks are wet through. They can be worn with crampons, but are too clumsy for very steep climbing either on rock or ice.

The ridge rose steeply above the col in a combination of scree and snow, taking the form of a broad shoulder. We followed the scree as high as we could until it petered out into a snowfield. At first, steps could be kicked, but after a while the snow thinned out into ice. We could have climbed straight up this in crampons, but we were preparing a regular route for laden and tired men, which meant that large well-cut steps, close together, were required. We fashioned these on assembly-line basis. The man in front would cut a reasonable step with his ice-axe, the second man would enlarge it, and the third man would trim it off and clean it out. This was pleasant airy work, and is there a mountaineer who does not enjoy cutting steps—provided it does not go on for too long—and is not mildly conceited of his prowess? In its upper section the slope became quite steep, perhaps forty degrees; it then narrowed from a broad shoulder into a corniced ridge and we found ourselves traversing hesitantly below some gigantic cornices on our left, with a steep mountain-side falling away on our right. With our axes we hewed a veritable thoroughfare across the flank of the mountain. This we called our "Road to Rakaposhi" in mimicry of the title of George Band's book.

We decided we had had enough step-cutting for the day, so we cramponed along the remaining distance in order to have a look at the continuation of the ridge as far as the foot of the Gendarme, about a mile distant, where our next camp would be. The ridge, crinkled with cornices, stretched from our feet down to a depression marked by a rock outcrop and then rose gently to the foot of the Gendarme. The left flank of the ridge, overhung by cornices, was terribly steep and unclimbable. Our route would clearly lie along the right side, which was still impressively steep, but climbable. From now on, our climb would be of an Alpine standard. The Gendarme itself, viewed *en face*, seemed to present an almost perpendicular face of rock and snow. We considered that along a well-prepared route we could make the journey from Camp 2 to the foot of the Gendarme in one day, thereby dispensing with the intermediate camp that Band had employed. The route to the foot of the Gendarme looked reasonable enough for us to take the porters along it. We returned to Camp 2 happy in the conviction that the next phase should present no insurmountable difficulties.

During that night and all the next day the wind blew and snow fell. The col proved to be a windy spot and drifts of snow began to build up to leeward, obliging us to go out into the storm and dig out the tents and stores. We had had almost perfect weather for the last two weeks and regarded this as a passing squall. How wrong we were! The blizzard blew on and off for the next seven days, imprisoning us in our tents and making us thankful for the luxury of a separate tent each. Several times a day we would shovel away the drift snow which was pressing in the walls. This period enabled us to get to know each other better than we had done previously: Bob tended to be philosophic, Hamish soporific. I was always mildly surprised that Bob, who, like many big men, was inclined to be quiet and gentle, should swear horribly and angrily when small things went wrong—for instance, when he was trying to pull off a tight boot in a confined space, or when a tin was unco-operative. Typical of Bob, though, he would vent his wrath on things and never on people. He had a big, soothing personality, and was a wonderful influence when we were either bored or over-excited.

The days drifted by with Bob reading his books and Hamish singing songs either of his native Scotland or from his considerable I.R.A. repertoire; sometimes he would keep quiet and write poems, and these, a mixture of Kipling and Robert W. Service, would be read to us at regular intervals. Even though I have been tent-bound in blizzards in many different parts of the world, I could never endure it with anything like Bob's philosophy. I tend to champ around with impatience to get on with the job in hand, doze fitfully during the day and find myself quite unable to sleep at night. We all found that at this early stage of acclimatization we experienced fantastic dreams, or rather hallucinations. For instance, I imagined I heard the radio station that broadcast our weather forecasts dinning in my ears, and even when I woke—I knew I was awake because I drank a glass of water and shook my head about vigorously to drive the sleep away—this wretched radio station still went on chanting its call-sign of "Azad Kashmir". Bob, on his part, was plagued by a procession of our particular brand of egg-whisks, which he imagined marching uphill inexorably with little rucksacks on their backs, and he couldn't get rid of them either. Hamish, typically, slept like a log and laughed at us. Bob and I would greet each other at breakfast by asking: "Did 'They' get in again last night?" As we became acclimatized the hallucinations ceased, but they were very real at the time.

There may be some curiosity as to who was the leader of this small international band. I am sorry to say that the other three had ganged up on me in Karachi and foisted the job on me on the score that, first, I was absent in Rawalpindi and therefore could not argue, and secondly, that by quite a few years I was the oldest of the party. Nobody, least of all myself, took this honor seriously, and all decisions were made by democratic discussion if possible, or by argument if that failed. In the event, the mountain dictated the decisions and we for the most part had no alternative but to comply. In the valley it is necessary, however, to have one man nominated as leader to represent the expedition officially to such people as the Political Agent: but on the mountain, when the real work starts, if all the members are of comparable experience and reasonable temperament, a leader is redundant. A leader who takes things too seriously is a disadvantage rather than an asset and can safely be dispensed with in a party as small as ours. When an expedition is so large—say six or above—that people get out of touch with each other, then a leader is needed to co-ordinate activities.

At Camp 2, just over 17,000 ft., the air was very thin and any violent effort would cause frantic panting. This grew less and less noticeable the longer we stayed up there. A further indication that I was becoming acclimatized was that my pulse, which had been racing at about 100 to the minute just after my arrival at base, was now down to a steady 50 at Camp 2, which was 3,000 ft. higher. In fact, although we denied ourselves a certain amount of pleasure by not climbing minor peaks before starting on Rakaposhi itself, our policy of acclimatization by load-carrying on the mountain seemed successful. Feeding was a problem, and even at Camp 2 the food began to appear unattractive as we felt our appetites falling off. We realized, however, that to maintain our strength we must force down our day's ration no matter how unpalatable it tasted, and also drink as much fluid as we could to combat the increased dehydration of the body at high altitudes.

5. The precipitous Hunza Road.

6. The rope bridge across the Hunza river at Nomal.

7. Approach march with Rakaposhi in the background dominating the scene.

8. Base camp at 14,000 ft. Unclimbed peaks in the background.

III

CAMPS AND BLIZZARDS

I therefore perswade my selfe, that the element of the aire is there so subtile and delicate, as it is not proportionable with the breathing of man, which requires a more grosse and temperate aire . . .—Father Joseph de Acosta, sixteenth century.

THE storm began to relent on the seventh day, June 12th. At last the clouds in which we had been living were torn apart, to be pierced here and there, suddenly and dramatically, by the shapely spires of the South-West Ridge across the valley. The sun would shine brilliantly for a period, its radiation warming us to tropical heat; then vaporous clouds would boil up over the col, plunging us into mist and reducing us to sub-Arctic temperatures in a twinkling. It was all very unfair to our poor bodies.

Hamish and I killed time with a session of spectacular rock-climbing practice up an 80-foot fang of rock which stood sentinel over the camp. As the sun sank that evening, the weather became calmer and clearer, and only the higher peaks, Rakaposhi, Haramosh and Nanga Parbat, retained wisps of cloudlets about their heads. At sunset we could see enormous distances in every direction. The stars came out big and frosty, full of promise for the morrow. As ever, the land towards the Hindu Kush, towards High Tartary, seemed to linger in a mysterious blue haze.

The evening did not belie the dawn, which came in clear and beautiful. After our inactivity we needed no urging to be up and doing. We trudged out of Camp 2 at 7.30 a.m., carrying rucksacks of about 30 lb. weight. However, the storm snow was still lying thick on the ice and had not received nearly enough heat from the sun to compact it. It was wearisome to wade through it and dangerous too, because the unstable snow was lying insecurely on the smooth ice beneath—textbook conditions for an avalanche. In fact, exactly these conditions, on this same ice slope between Camps 2 and 3, were later to become notorious. We stuck at it for six hours, painstakingly shovelling away the loose snow that had accumulated on our "Road to Rakaposhi" and cutting big safe steps in the ice thus exposed. Then, content with our day's work and delighted to have been active again, we scooped out a shallow ice cave and cached our loads. On our return to Camp 2 we were met by Dick, who had now recovered from his chest trouble and was ready to play his full part. He told of deep wet snow at base camp and of a tent and rope lost in an avalanche.

The sun had worked wonders with the snow, and when we set off next morning it was much firmer and safer. We followed our tracks of the previous day and progressed beyond our cache until we had a good view of the ridge to the foot of the Gendarme. Here we located an old tent platform, used by Band, on the very lip of the cornice overhanging the Biro Glacier, many thousands of feet below. Rummaging in the snow, we found a jerrican with a little paraffin in it, and two kitbags. Consumed with curiosity, we emptied the kitbags and found odd items of food, notably two tins of baked beans and some tinned *pâté de foie gras*. It is extraordinary how any food which is different to one's own immediately seems more attractive. We feasted on the baked beans that night.

The following day Bob and I, assisted by Hamish and Dick, set out to occupy Camp 3, which we hoped to pitch at the foot of the Gendarme, thereby cutting out the intermediate camp used by Band. In fact, we only got as far as the intermediate camp, which we regarded as temporary and christened "Cornice Camp" on account of its airy position, perched impudently over the sheer drop down to the Biro Glacier. Bob and I spent an uncomfortable and cold night there, trying not very successfully to sleep on a tilted platform, with the uneasy notion at the back of our minds that if the cornice broke off we would find ourselves airborne. A friend of mine once camped, in Greenland, on the snow bridge of a crevasse, which must have been comparable to our camp site on the cornice. Neither could really be recommended.

Next day, in two trips, we transferred ourselves and our camp to our true Camp 3, and Cornice Camp, a cramped and comfortless place, was never used again. Camp 3 was approached along the sinuous length of the South-West Spur, which was massively corniced on its left. It was here that Band's party had had a harrowing time when Wrangham and a porter fell 60 feet as a cornice crumbled under them. Warned by their experience, we steered a course which left a very respectful margin between ourselves and the edge. The cornices were enormous, like icing dripping over the side of a gargantuan cake. The climb itself was steep, over a mixture of snow, ice and scree. Crevasses had to be avoided and a rock island bypassed. At about 19,000 ft. we found a most convenient platform a few yards short of the Gendarme itself, which offered ample flat space on which to erect our tents. We were separated from the Gendarme by a deep and wide bergschrund, which is the name given in the Alps to the crevasse between the moving ice of a glacier and the mountain proper. It was a good day's climbing from Camp 2, and although the ground was difficult, the ascent was nowhere desperate enough to frighten the porters. We knew that two mountaineering obstacles lay before us: the Gendarme and the Monk's Head. Tired but content, Bob and I turned in that night all set to climb on the morrow the Gendarme which was towering, in a sweep of rock and ice, three hundred feet above our heads. The last visitors had been able to cross the bergschrund near the cornice and follow the relatively gentle crest of the ridge. Since that time the approach to the Gendarme had apparently altered, for now a yawning crevasse forced us down the slope, offering only one crossing place. We roped up at Camp 3, walked the few feet to the crevasse bridge, which we crossed, and found ourselves on a traverse with a considerable and steep drop to our right. The snow was hard and granular, and at first a couple of hefty kicks sufficed to make a step. Ice glinted ahead, and soon I had my axe swinging. The gradient became much steeper, perhaps sixty-five degrees, and I settled down to a bout of ice-climbing. The ice was tough and the exertion soon made me tired and breathless. Progress became slow. To make better speed I moved to my right, where frost-shattered rocks of very friable appearance protruded from the snow. With much scraping away of snow and cutting of occasional ice steps where necessary, Bob and I ascended the face of the Gendarme in a series of pitches which provided climbing of a standard which one is lucky to find in the Himalayas. Our enjoyment of the difficulties of the climb was counterbalanced by the thought that the Gendarme would be a tricky place for a tired man to descend in bad weather, perhaps too formidable an obstacle for our porters. Much would depend on what Issa Khan, with his wide experience, thought of it. The other three would always abide by his decision.

The crest of the Gendarme was airy and exposed, with sheer drops on the left and right to the Biro and Kunti glaciers respectively. Bob and I glanced hungrily towards the Monk's Head, which we now saw in its entirety about a mile distant. It was this view which had finally deterred Tilman from the South-West Spur in 1947. Seen *en face*, it looked horribly sheer and I could sympathize with his reactions. But we were looking at it through different eyes, for we knew that the Cambridge men had climbed it: and they, no doubt, had climbed the Gendarme with assurance, knowing that Tilman had done so before them. This is the legacy one expedition leaves the next—the comfort of "what man has done, man can do", so that the members of subsequent expeditions are never climbing quite alone until they get beyond the highest point so far attained. Thus Everest, until its first reconnaissance in 1921, was merely the highest point on the face of the earth. But from then onwards it became invested with the emotions of men and, if the spirit that makes men climb mountains counts for anything, Everest acquired whatever it was that these men took to it, and so became a finer mountain to climb. Similarly with Rakaposhi in its more modest way. From 1892 (surely in the dawn of Himalayan mountaineering) it has been an obvious but curiously unattempted objective. Those parties who did try it failed, through no lack of skill or fortitude, to gain more than a bare lodgement on the mountain itself. Only the Cambridge expedition managed to follow an approach ridge to the towering bulk of the mountain proper, and it was a lightweight reconnaissance and not a siege party that vanquished the Monk's Head. Rakaposhi has never, thank goodness, attracted the heavyweight type of national expedition which, say, Nanga Parbat has.

Modest but competent mountaineers have tried it and failed, without tragedy. Although it became the most often attempted twenty-five-thousand-footer, it is emphatically not a "killer mountain." On the other hand, it has been attempted only by mountaineers, never by "death or glory boys".

Nearer at hand a steep snow slope ran down some hundred feet or so to a snow platform and then swept down again out of sight. Bob and I descended cautiously, avoiding, with much axe prodding, a crevasse which seemed intent on keeping us company down the hill. The snow was soft and deep. To us this meant that, first, there was an avalanche danger, and secondly, that it would be a penitential grind to get back over the Gendarme when the time came for retreat. If anyone got hurt and had to be carried, his chances would be slim. In fact, should things go wrong, the Gendarme could be a worse obstacle than the Monk's Head itself, where at least gravity would help us down (we were even foolish enough to put that to the test later).

We walked across the snow platform and saw that a very steep slope of soft snow led down to a col. Beyond that a rounded dome of snow separated the Gendarme from the Monk's Head. The route could either go over the top or wind its way through some seracs at a lower level. It was hot and we were tired, so we decided to return to camp, content with having climbed the Gendarme and spied out the lay of the land to our next camp, which would be at the foot of the Monk's Head. Cautiously we descended the rocks and ice, leading through—that is, one person would descend to the extent of the rope, tie himself to the rocks, and then the second person would climb down to him and descend a rope's length beyond. We returned to camp happy that another obstacle had been overcome.

The glittering face of the Monk's Head held the promise of a steep and exhilarating climb. It was an altogether less worthy reason, however, that urged us to camp at its foot as soon as possible: food. We read in Band's book that his expedition had left forty man-days of rations, with stoves and paraffin, in a cache at the foot of the Monk's Head. We turned up the relevant index and studied Band's daily diet with intensity, gently watering at the jowls when we came to the items "Sardines, 1 oz." and "Baked beans, 2 oz." There were certain praiseworthy features of our own ration, such as the Weet Bix cereal, with some quite excellent New Zealand powdered milk, which formed our staple breakfast. What we mainly lacked was a good protein meal at night, which should have contained the chief calorie intake of the day. The pemmican and comprehensive food had proved uneatable. We had only a small amount of dehydrated meat, and this took a lot of soaking and pressure-cooking to make it even barely palatable. It is of interest that great strides have recently been made in the technique of dehydrating meat. The other night for supper I ate a dehydrated steak which was not compressed into a tin. It was as light as a sheet of cardboard, re-hydrated in a few minutes when soaked in water, and when fried tasted excellent. If only I had found out earlier!

It was decided, now that we had pioneered the way up the ice of the Gendarme, to try to reach the foot of the Monk's Head on the morrow. We were keen on climbing and on finding the food in roughly equal proportions.

Such was our intention. "The best laid plans o' mice and men gang aft agley." Next morning a blizzard was blowing. It blew the morning after, and the morning after, and so on for ten days.

Weathering out storms is just as much part of a Himalayan expedition as the climbing, and sometimes much more! As usual, on the first day of bad weather we were quite content to take a rest day —but only one. When the weather thickened, we resigned ourselves to the minimum of four days which it seems to take for a Karakoram storm to pass. This particular one brought considerable snowfalls, which slowly submerged our tents. Moreover, during the first night, we heard the loud swoosh of an avalanche sweeping down from the slope of the Gendarme above our heads. We were perched right beneath the Gendarme, and it would not need much of a snow slide to bury our little tents completely. That evening at seven we peered through the torn clouds towards the distinctive spike of rock above Camp 2 where Hamish and I had practiced rock-climbing. Three flashes of a torch told us that Dick had listened to the radio down there and was signalling that a storm was forecast. We turned in, but slept somewhat coldly, for Camp 3 was pitched on snow and therefore chillier than Camp 2, which was pitched on scree. We conformed to a rough routine imposed on us by conditions. We still enjoyed the luxury of two tents. Bob was in the American Gerry tent and I was in the Black's Mountain one. The Gerry tent was of an advanced design and had much to commend it: it was double-skinned, which made it better insulated against the cold and therefore much warmer than a single-walled tent, and at either end it had a "vestibule", small compartments in which rucksacks or cooking things could be stowed. Its shape or "belly" was maintained by curved fibreglass wands which kept the canvas walls pulled out and allowed the maximum space within. And, most important on high mountains, it was light, weighing only eleven pounds. The Black's Mountain tent was a very adequate, robust, single-skinned tent of traditional British design, costing something in the region of $50 against the $120 of the Gerry. We used the Gerries for all the highest camps.

We had few distractions during our ten days' imprisonment, and these were usually unwelcome. First, Bob experienced a vague general pain in breathing, and we immediately feared pneumonia. Pneumonia is badly aggravated by lack of oxygen (patients in hospitals are often put into an oxygen tent) and one can die very quickly if caught at a high altitude. It would have been almost impossible to evacuate Bob in the prevailing conditions. He therefore took large quantities of oral penicillin and achromycin, hoping to disperse any inflammation. The pain slowly resolved itself into a toothache which became so sharp that he asked me to have a go at removing the tooth. He was about as keen on my pulling it out as I was on pulling it. Fortunately, perhaps, I had left my evil-looking pair of dental forceps down at Camp 2, and the best I could do was to wind a length of nylon thread round the tooth and give a tug. The pain proved too much, and Bob decided that he would rather suffer the toothache than my tortures. This was just as well, because next day an abscess burst from the tooth into the mouth, and he was soon well again.

So the days followed on one another. My diary reads: "*Another featureless day of intermittent snowfalls—a day passed with such minor excitements as losing, and later finding the pot-holder in the snow at the bottom of the tent, and yet once again digging out the tent. We endeavor to keep awake for as long as possible during the day to make sleep easier at night.*" We found that we were eating far too little, which was probably just as well, as we had insufficient rations to last us, anyhow. We felt cold, particularly at nights, when I used to put on all my clothes before getting into my double sleeping-bags. Later (speaking as the tough outdoor type!) I am ashamed to relate that I used my polythene flask as a hot-water bottle, and found it quite effective in warming up feet that until then had stubbornly remained as lifeless as a pair of herring on a fish-monger's slab. I remember, one night, losing my sleeping-pill in the depths of my sleeping-bags. I struggled and contorted for five minutes trying unsuccessfully to find it, but the effort made me so warm and tired that I dozed off at once. I am sure there is a moral somewhere.

One day, while we were having breakfast, a hiss of snow above us turned into a rumble and we quickly felt the tent being buried. It took us several hours to dig it out and re-pitch it. In so doing I accidentally broke one of the poles. It required all the rest of the day and all my ingenuity to repair it, using a tent-peg as a splint, an ice-axe as an anvil and an ice-piton as a hammer. But it helped pass the time. A little later my tent sustained a small rip which widened as the wind rose. I managed to stitch the madly drumming canvas as the storm worsened.

Even though it lasted longer, I found the storm at Camp 3 more tolerable than the one at Camp 2. Perhaps I had learned a rather more philosophic attitude. Tutored by the porters, we had come to dismiss most setbacks with a shrug and a mutter of "In sh'Allah", which means "If Allah permits". This is the convenient stratagem of the Moslem to shift responsibility for action, or lack of it, on to the infinitely broad shoulders of the Prophet. Bob's company, too, went a long way towards making the time pass harmoniously. He had a wonderful capacity for work when there was any, and a commensurate ability to hibernate happily when we were riding out a storm. He was as big mentally as physically, and would dismiss a setback on the mountain or an act of non-co-operation by the porters with Olympian aloofness. His humor was ironical yet kind. I have endured many storms with many different companions, but of them all I would choose Bob.

On the tenth day I poked my head out of my tent at 5 a.m. to see a clear and beautiful dawn. Escape was at last possible. I blew my whistle repeatedly to waken Bob, whose job it was to get breakfast, but I could not rouse him. I squirmed back into my sleeping-bags, ate a bar of chocolate, then put my head out again and shouted in my best American:

"Bob, you lazy sonofabitch, wake up! It's a clear day. Wake up, you lazy basket!"

This must have taken him back to his Army reveilles, for with a few expletives he woke up and prepared a miserable breakfast of tea, dry biscuit and a slop made from jelly and powdered milk, which was about all we had left. With food supplies so low, it was high time we were away. Carrying only our sleeping-bags and air mattresses, we roped up at camp and started down the slope below. The deep and unstable snow did not look as if it needed much to make it avalanche. Just in front of us, a large lump of cornice suddenly broke off and slid silently down to the Biro Glacier many thousands of feet below. A little later we heard that familiar crack which is often the noise an avalanche makes as it starts and is often the last noise a mountaineer ever hears. We didn't like the look of it at all.

"Ruddy dangerous, Bob. D'you think we ought to go back and wait another day?" I said.

"Guess we ought to, Mike," Bob answered.

Pause.

"Oh, hell! Shall we bash on?" I suggested.

"Might as well!"

So we went on, moving very carefully. One of us would make a belay by ramming his axe into the snow as far as it would go and taking a turn of the climbing rope round it. The other would then go to the full limit of the rope. By keeping the maximum distance between us, we hoped that thus we would not both be caught in the same avalanche. It took us three hours to reach our temporary site at Cornice Camp, a journey which should only have taken three-quarters of an hour. Just beyond, we looked directly down to Camp 2, where we saw someone moving. I blew my whistle and received an answering wave. This assured us that if we were caught in an avalanche a rescue party would quickly be organized. We made the reverse traverse along the "Road to Rakaposhi", climbed down the ensuing steep section with care, and finished with a joyous sitting glissade right down to Camp 2.

Camp 2, in reality a bleak camp pitched on a windy col, had all the sophistication of a metropolis to Bob and me. Our reunion was a happy one; gossip and goodwill overflowed. Hamish had cooked an exotic sweet which Bob and I, with our jaded palates, relished. It was a mixture of milk powder, jelly, pudding mix and Weet Bix, which might sound revolting at sea-level, but at an altitude where everyone was sugar-hungry this sort of thing tasted like heaven. We had a pleasant evening, with more eating, and then Hamish read us some of the poems he had written during the last three weeks which he had spent at Camp 2. They were his usual blend of Service and Kipling, and made a strong appeal to the "beyond-the-blue-ranges" yearning which every embryo adventurer usually has somewhere in his make-up. In our sleeping-bags we lay and listened to the commercial radio station in Ceylon broadcasting alternate program of record requests and hot gospellers. When you have been starved of it any music, however lowbrow, sounds attractive.

Dick and Hamish were now to take over the assault, enabling Bob and me to rest up after our period of storm and under-nourishment at 19,000 ft. Dick was a great weight-carrier, like many Americans who habitually climb in undeveloped mountain tracts devoid of huts and other such Alpine luxuries. A 100-lb. load was therefore not an unusual burden for an approach march on his mountaineering holidays. In contrast to Hamish, who always went like a bomb, Dick moved very slowly and deliberately, usually with a heavier than average pack, and he invariably delivered the goods at the end of the march. He was a skilled photographer, and in general a practical and scientifically minded man. Again in sharp contrast to Hamish, whose constitution seemed immune to the ravages of the altitude or the tropics, Dick was an avid pill-swallower. Almost as a ritual, before going to bed he would place his special aluminium drug tin on his sleeping-bag, and extract and swallow half-a-dozen or so gaily colored pills. The irony of the thing was that both Hamish and Dick succumbed to illnesses: Hamish contracted dengue fever and Dick infective hepatitis of the liver, neither of which complaints could have been cured by any of our pills. We would pull Dick's leg about this, but he had a sharp wit and usually got the better of the raillery.

If the weather remained co-operative and were prolonged into a fine spell, the plan was for Hamish and Dick to place fixed ropes on the Gendarme and work out the route over to Camp 4 at the foot of the Monk's Head. They would also look for the cache of rations left by the Cambridge expedition, which, if found, would not only provide us with a welcome change of diet but would save us a considerable amount of carrying over the Gendarme. Bob and I were to supervise the porters over the long and exposed mountainside between Camps 2 and 3. Most of the food and stores required were now at Camp 2, and the time was convenient for the porters to relay most of these stores over to Camp 3. We had not tested the porters on really difficult ground so far, but we were confident that they would be capable of this climb.

On June 28th Bob and I accompanied Dick and Hamish to Camp 3. I was still weak from my long, undernourished immobilization at Camp 3 and could only just stagger along through the new snow with a mere 20-lb. rucksack. That same day the porters moved up to Camp 2 in readiness for the carry to Camp 3. At supper that night, intent on getting as much good food in me as I could manage, I did my best to eat a bowlful of pemmican. Although I used to eat it very happily on my Greenland expeditions, I found that at an altitude of 17,300 ft. I could only just get it down, and then it was done as a duty rather than a pleasure. Time and time again I yearned for a tin of humble bully beef. For the very highest camps we had a few blocks of dehydrated meat mince prepared by the Ministry of Supply for certain Army lightweight rations.

The next day we made a trip to Camp 3 with our four porters, who carried about 35 lb. apiece. Bob came along to take movie photographs—not so cushy a job as it might sound, because the photographer has to keep dashing ahead, or out to one side, to get into a good position. The porters carried well, doing exactly as Issa Khan told them and politely distrusting our advice. Issa Khan, I am glad to say, proved most adequate. Although I offered him the rope several times he disdained it on the ascent, but wisely used it on the descent, when the snow had become softer in the sun. Old Dilap carried very well, his creased face running with perspiration and his deep-set eyes gleaming with excitement and humor. Whatever the temperature, he never adjusted his clothes. He wore windproof trousers and a tattered but elegant hacking-jacket of home-woven tweed. Only under duress would he wear climbing boots and crampons, much preferring his home-made sheepskin footwear, which looked rather like moccasins.

This porterage continued for three days. At Camp 3 Hamish asked us to exchange his rather scratched sun goggles for Issa's. This we did, with the immediate result that Issa suffered from sore eyes which confined him to his tent. We wondered how Hamish had stuck it. So Bob and I escorted the three porters towards Camp 3, but without Issa they were slow and listless, making difficulties where they had moved with speed and confidence the day before. We roped them for safety, but something was wrong, and they continued to lag. It is on occasions like this that the ability to speak to them in their own language (Brushuski) is so important. My fragmentary Urdu was quite inadequate to the situation, and we had to stop and dump the loads at the site of Cornice Camp. Strangely, old Dilap was the most unhappy of the three, and I would have given a lot to know what was worrying them.

On July 1st, after we had been working on the mountain for a month, Bob and I moved up to Camp 3. On arrival there, we found that Hamish and Dick had roped the Gendarme from top to bottom and also cut convenient steps along the line of the fixed ropes. They told us that they had embarked on a ten-hour slog through soft snow over the Gendarme, over the whaleback and towards the Monk's Head, Hamish on one occasion falling into a crevasse but being held on the rope by Dick. They had also carried all the loads for use above the Monk's Head over the Gendarme. From what they could see of the great snow basin below the Monk's Head, they were very pessimistic about our chances of finding the Cambridge food.

"Don't reckon you'll be eating those sardines," predicted Dick. "We'll just have to go on chewing this dehydrated leather."

I thought of the few meat bars we possessed, and reckoned that at least we might have something just eatable when we got really high on the mountain.

A day of ferrying gear over the Gendarme followed. The porters, who had agreed to move up to Camp 3, duly arrived, and for some inscrutable reason handed back some rum we had given them. They had professed to be very fond of *Hunza pani*, the local firewater, so this action remained somewhat mysterious. They might just conceivably have thought that our need was greater than theirs.

We asked Issa Khan what he thought about carrying for us over the Gendarme to our Monk's Head camp.

"K2 *thik hai*, Nanga Parbat *thik hai*, Rakaposhi *bote crab*," he replied, which, loosely translated, means: "K2 and Nanga Parbat were not too bad, but damn Rakaposhi for a lark." He added that there was nothing of this steepness on either of those two other great mountains, and the Gendarme was beyond the prowess of the porters. Further, he was not prepared to live at Camp 3 unless he was provided with an air-bed, an extra sleeping-bag and three blankets. As we had not really expected them to go beyond the Gendarme, we accepted the fact that from now onwards it would be "coolie-sahib" all the way. We said good-bye to the porters, thankful that they had achieved what they had.

On July 3rd we moved into Camp 4. First we made a double journey over the Gendarme, thereby depositing all the necessary loads on the far side of it. The descent on the far side was a steep one down a slope of deep, soft snow, and fell about 350 feet in two steps, each of which was provided with a fixed rope. We had rightly surmised that the reverse journey over these slopes back to Camp 3 would be a horribly penitential snow slog. Our way now led through a feature we nicknamed the Notch—a narrow passage through a corridor between great overhanging seracs. The route had to be chosen carefully to dodge the numerous crevasses, and at one point our path lay directly beneath a giant cornice. We would glance nervously up at the several tons of poised ice just above our heads and hope fervently that it would not choose that exact instant to break off. A level walk then carried us to Camp 4, which was beautifully situated. We could see back through the Notch towards the

Gendarme. The complete grandeur of the North-West Ridge was in full view on our left, and we could follow it right up to the point where it joined the final cone of Rakaposhi. We also had the opportunity of examining a suggested short-cut up the Biro Glacier which would then follow a corridor leading to the South-West Ridge beyond the Monk's Head. The route looked attractive and quite feasible until we heard an enormous rumble and saw tons and tons of ice avalanche down on to the Biro Glacier, sweeping the alleged short-cut.

But the Monk's Head dominated the scene, soaring nearly 2,000 feet above the camp across an intervening snow basin. It looked very like the famous north face of the Aiguille d'Argentière in the Alps, though perhaps a shade less steep and long. The line of least resistance fairly obviously ran up its extreme left edge, where an ill-defined ridge was formed. The face looked climbable by Alpine standards, but was it possible with a heavy rucksack, and what would it be like on the descent, particularly if the climbers were exhausted? These considerations seemed to make the face look steeper and altogether more formidable. So far it had been ascended only by an unladen party. We had to carry two tents, camping equipment, and about fourteen days of food and fuel above the face. We reckoned that we might achieve this by making three journeys each, with individual loads of 40 lb. It was therefore essential to fix ropes over the steeper sections.

Camp 4 consisted of one Gerry and one Logan tent, the latter being a large, single-skinned tent which would sleep three quite roomily. From camp we scanned the snow basin at our feet for anything which might mark the Cambridge food depot. But no marker, no hump or unnatural undulation broke the even surface of the snowfield. The area was far too large and featureless for it to be of any use roaming round prodding the snow with our ice-axes in the hope of finding the food that way. We could not even judge with any accuracy, despite much discussion, how deep the dump would be buried after a lapse of two years. Sardines became a wistful memory.

IV

SUMMIT BID

Disparate, numbed, through silent centuries,
move the explorers,
and inward, in each microcosm,
burns the small dying flame
of separate time—Michael Roberts.

ON July 4th (there was a certain amount of Anglo-American raillery on that Independence Day) Hamish and I attacked the Monk's Head, equipped with 550 feet of rope. We contoured round the snow basin, occasionally prodding with our ice-axes where we suspected crevasses or, with the eye of hope, saw on the surface of the snow some irregularity which we construed as the buried food. Plodding through soft snow, we reached the foot of the slope which steepened above us into the broad white face of the Monk's Head. After stopping for a breather and to fix our crampons (ice-claws) on to our boots, we started to climb on granular snow, moving to the left towards the ill-defined ridge. We crossed a bergschrund where it was narrow and consequently easy to step up over, but a few yards beyond the general angle of the slope sharpened abruptly and the soft snow gave way to hard-frozen granular ice. We could have climbed over this section without cutting steps, for we were both wearing twelve-point crampons—that is, crampons with two of the ice-claws sticking straight out in front. These two extra claws are particularly useful on steep snow or ice, where a good kick sticks the two front prongs into the wall one is climbing. However, we were less intent on climbing the face than on making a safe route for laden men. From camp 4 I had suspected bare ice on this section, and had borrowed Bob's extra heavy ice-axe to use on the expected long session of step cutting. The ice splintered well under a rain of blows and I worked patiently, warming up and enjoying the exercise. Hamish was armed only with his short *marteau-piolet*, which means "hammer-axe". Athough unsuitable for this type of step cutting, it would be useful for hammering in the ice-pitons which would be needed for anchoring the fixed ropes, but it also afforded Hamish a cast-iron excuse for watching me do the hard work: an excuse he did not lose.

"Get cracking up there!" he would shout when I rested. "If I had a great big axe like that I'd be going twice as fast. You're a cream puff!" (Cream puff, it should be explained, was the general expression used by the Creagh Dhu Club to describe those lesser mortals who used ice-axes, for instance, and not hammer-axes; or reactionaries who still had some use for a climbing rope and its attendant safety.)

With Bob's good heavy axe arching through the morning air, I rained rhythmic, walloping blows on the brittle ice. Fragments the size of soup-plates flew out and hissed down the slope. With the wholesome joy of the decent craftsman I advanced steadily, leaving behind me a diagonal of ample steps which would offer a safe staircase of descent even in mid-afternoon, when the heat of the sun would have made the ice slushy. I arrived near some rocks at the left-hand edge of the face and, stopping there, I hewed out a square platform large enough for both Hamish and me to be able to stand on comfortably. He then joined me and drove in an ice-piton. This is a metal spike about ten inches long, specially designed to hold firmly in ice. Next he climbed directly upwards for about 150 feet, jabbing his twelve-point crampons into the face, and trailing the thin rope behind him. He reached an isolated rock, tied the rope to it, and called to me to come up and join him.

Climbing directly upwards, I found the ice face exhilaratingly steep. It was a delightful angle for climbing: had it been any easier it would have been dull; had it been steeper it would have been frightening. The surface was really *névé*, that is, rough granular snow which has very nearly turned into ice. It offered a firm support to the two forward-pointing prongs of my crampons. After climbing a further sixty feet over fairly easy snow and rock, we arrived at another isolated boulder to which we could attach a rope. We were now on the true crest of the ridge.

The ice face swept grandly up above our heads until it met some large seracs high above us. I led up two more pitches, one of 150 feet and another of 200 feet, and we were then out of rope. The angle was uniformly steep, and the twelve-point crampons (as opposed to the more usual ten-pointers, which do not have the two forward-pointing claws) were an undoubted asset. It is remarkable to recall that a famous pre-war mountaineer of great experience pronounced that crampons were a waste of time in the Himalayas. They were seldom off our feet and we felt we could have achieved little without them.

Hamish joined me and we hammered in the top ice-piton to secure the fixed rope. There was little point in our climbing any higher and expending precious energy; we could see that the route was quite feasible as far as a large serac which blocked our view. We would jump that fence when we came to it. We must have attained a height of a little over 20,000 ft.—quite an event for me, as that height has a special significance for British climbers, just as 6,000 metres has for Continental climbers. I had subconsciously expected something dramatic to happen, rather like going through the sound barrier. But all I noticed was that each step took just a little more effort than it had done previously.

We scampered down the 550 feet of fixed manila line, climbed down the staircase of steps I had cut and, taking off our crampons when we reached the soft snow, walked back to camp, keeping a sharp eye open for any sign of the Cambridge food dump. We saw nothing, and to this day the food reposes in its spectacular refrigerator. Having rested a while in camp, we made one final relaying journey to collect the last of our loads from their cache at the col below the Gendarme.

The next morning Bob and Dick, who had been watching Hamish and me carefully from camp, set off at eight o'clock to contribute their share by fixing ropes on the upper half of the Monk's Head. Hamish and I, shouldering loads of about 40 lb., followed a couple of hours later and caught the others up a hundred feet or so below the serac we had all noted blocking the route. Here the angle eased slightly, but the snow was soft and deep, and Bob had all our sympathy (though little else to help him) as he ploughed a way upwards.

We congregated on a snow ledge under the overhanging bulk of the serac as Bob climbed out round an icy corner with a dizzy drop beneath it. Very slowly the rope paid out. Then Hamish, realizing that Bob was wearing the somewhat sloppy vapor barrier boot and ten-point crampons (the vapor barrier boot is not much firmer on the foot than a well-fitting pair of gumboots) climbed up to him and took over the lead. Two more lengths of fixed rope, totalling about 220 feet, led us to the gently rising summit slope of the Monk's Head. It was a great moment for us: the most formidable obstacle on our route was now well and truly subjugated, garlanded with fixed rope from top to bottom, and quite safe as an avenue of retreat.

The weather had been moody and suddenly the view was blotted out by swirling clouds as the wind came up. We were tired and the snow was soft. Taking it in turns to go out in front and do the donkey work of step-kicking, we groped upwards through the storm. Hampered by weariness and the glutinous snow, it was possible only to kick thirty steps at a time before stepping aside, gasping, to allow the next man to lead through. We must have been very near the summit when the wind rose to a higher pitch and we were enveloped in a seething, stinging turmoil of driven snow. Retreat was the only prudent course before our footsteps became obliterated and we found ourselves lost in a white and dangerous world. We made a dump of all our loads, marking the spot carefully with tent poles stuck into the snow. With heads bent against the blizzard we followed our fast-disappearing steps, located the top of the fixed rope, which we had wisely marked with a bamboo pole, and descended the Monk's Head to the roomy comfort of the Logan tent at Camp 4.

We estimated that we each had to carry two more loads over the Monk's Head before we could safely occupy Camp 5 with sufficient food and stores for the final camp and an adequate reserve of food in case of a long storm. Consequently, on the following day (July 6th) we made another ascent, this time in perfect weather. As usual, we found the steep face of the Monk's Head very tiring, yet so exhilarating as to keep lethargy at bay. Above the face, on the long slope of soft snow, the absence of danger and the increasing heat of the sun as it rose higher sapped what small reserves of energy we had. It was important, however, to get Camp 5 established at the foot of the final cone of the mountain, where the South-West Spur was joined by the South-West Ridge. This entailed climbing over the gentle dome of the Monk's Head, descending to a snow col, and then walking over a long but gentle whaleback hump to another broad col at the foot of the final slopes.

This proved a long and tiring carry, and one by one, as we arrived at the site of Camp 5, we collapsed in a heap. We now stood directly beneath the lowest of three great steps which led to the summit. Thenceforward the way, according to all the previous expeditions, should have been a pleasant if somewhat airy stroll. We looked upwards, and as my diary notes:

The upper slopes of the mountain gave us a rude shock. Instead of the easy slope we had been led to expect, we were confronted by a second Monk's Head! A great upsweep of snow and ice, split by seracs. We have no more fixed rope, and route-finding will be ticklish. What a mountain for a party of only four!

The sun had been playing full on the face of the Monk's Head, and we were very grateful for the fixed ropes when we came to the sections of *névé* where the granular snow had so softened as to give the impression of climbing down over a surface of ball-bearings. The day, our tenth day of continuous exertion above 19,000 ft., had been a tremendous effort, and rest was an obvious need. The next day, therefore, we lay in our sleeping-bags, scarcely twitching. The stage was now set for our bid for the summit.

On July 8th we all made our third ascent of the Monk's Head, carrying our personal gear, which consisted mostly of sleeping-bags, spare clothing, photographic equipment (including the heavy cine-camera) and a variety of those "essential" oddments which insinuate themselves into one's rucksack at the beginning of an expedition and remain there. Our loads were in the region of 25 lb. Another perfect day greeted us, and we noted that the intense sun of yesterday had warmed the ropes and made them sink into the ice. Some of the ice-pitons were wobbly, and these we secured by hammering them in and then covering them with loose ice to keep the sun from warming the metal. The climb up the Monk's Head in the early morning was, as ever, enjoyable if strenuous. In contrast, the snow plod from the top of the fixed rope through the soft snow over the dome of the Monk's Head and over the whaleback to Camp 5 was ghastly.

The heat of the day increased and we became extremely lethargic —"we just went soggy", in our jargon. There was not a breath of wind, and the achievement of each step was a painful and ponderous effort. We had to pick up an extra 20 lb. apiece at the cache we had made when the bad weather halted us on our first ascent, and this additional load completed our misery. The sweat ran down our faces, the snow became white-hot, and the warm air that we sucked desperately into our lungs refused to be transmuted into energy. With aching and protesting bodies and befuddled minds, we literally staggered across the easy ground to Camp 5, and as we arrived we collapsed onto our rucksacks with a gasp or oath of relief. Before permitting us to camp triumphantly on its pate, the Monk's Head had taken its toll in work and sweat. More than ever we came to realize the sheer size of the mountain and the almost impertinent smallness of our party.

We had above the Monk's Head two tents and about fourteen days' supply of food. Therefore we had only one tent which we could move up to use as Camp 6. To make up for our lack of numbers we adhered rigidly to the very sound practice that at every camp below us there should be a tent, food and fuel. This is a golden rule of great mountaineering and is the only safe insurance policy in the event of retreat in tempest. Add to the list of minimum camp amenities a team of four tough and cheerful Sherpas waiting for their sahibs to come down from the uppermost camp, and you have reduced risks to rock bottom. We were limited both in numbers and equipment. Camp 5 was at about 21,000 feet, which meant that the summit was still 4,550 feet higher up. The fact remained that we had to establish one higher camp, which could be occupied by only two men, and launch our assault from there. On a mountain of the stature of Rakaposhi it would have been prudent to pitch the top camp within 1,000 feet—at most 1,500 feet—of the summit to be reasonably sure of "knocking the bastard off" (to borrow Hillary's Everest aphorism). Two very long days would obviously be necessary to gain the summit. We were even then very tired.

The summit altitude of 25,550 must be very near the reasonable upper limit for a climber without oxygen, particularly if the ground is difficult. Men who have been higher than this without oxygen (e.g. Nanga Parbat, Annapurna) have been members of considerably larger parties, with far better support and prospects of retreat, and even so have achieved their goal only by staring death in the face. In our perverted climbers' fashion we were still enjoying ourselves, and none of us would have lavished on the mountain more than a very sober gamble of our lives. We had come to climb, not to conquer. Neither was there any rivalry between the British and American factions.

We had to select our summit pair to occupy Camp 6 the next day. Hamish, who had been going noticeably the strongest, was a unanimous vote. Bob, Dick and I were performing very much on one level. It was decided that if any two were to stand on the summit it would be most in keeping with the spirit of our international venture if one man came from each nation. This meant that an American should accompany Hamish, and Dick was chosen. Bob and I would help carry for the other two to Camp 6 and then descend to Camp 5 again the same day. On the following day, if the weather were fine, Hamish and Dick would make their summit bid; Bob and I would climb again to Camp 6 to be there to support them if they were exhausted after a victorious ascent, or, if they had failed, to try ourselves the day after, perhaps using the steps they would have kicked or cut on their attempt. Feeling mildly excited, we turned in.

The next day, July 9th, was cloudy and depressing but suitable for climbing, so we set off up the hill. We plodded wearily at first through deep snow, but as the mountainside steepened we encountered hard snow, ice almost. We crossed some crevasses and zigzagged up a long ice slope which was seamed with small crevasses and potholes. Hamish described it in his doggerel:

The cracks were so frequent, so deep, so wide,
We thought the mountain was hollow inside.

A band of rocks and scree led directly upwards, so we climbed over to these and followed them for several hundred feet. The weather was steadily worsening and we were shrouded in cloud. The hours were flying past and as we pressed on up into the white blanket, cold and tired, we stared into the mist, always hoping to see an easement in the angle of the ridge which might offer chance of a camping site. Above the rocks, in a high wind which had made us cold, we traversed leftwards and landed on a steep and dangerous ice surface. We gained the safety of some rocks and huddled together in a miserable little group. We had been laboring for about five and a half hours. Hamish seemed to possess the reserve of optimism of the whole party.

"Wait here and I'll just go up a bit higher and have a look around," he said, and slowly ascended until he was lost in the swirls of cloud.

We sat on our rock, dumbly thankful but not very hopeful. Suddenly a whistle and a shout rose above the soughing of the wind.

"Come on, lads! A camping-place!"

We hauled our rucksacks onto our shoulders and set off towards the voice. After a couple of hundred feet the ridge narrowed and then eased. We followed Hamish's footsteps and then saw that he had stopped at a wide flat platform. Camp 6 at last, after the hardest six and a half hours we had so far spent—and full marks to Hamish! The tent was pitched, and Bob and I wished the others good luck on their summit assault and left them to sort their camp out. We estimated that the height of Camp 6 was 23,000 feet. (It will be noted that we did not carry those pessimistic, mechanician height-guessers, altimeters. This figure, though, must have been reasonably accurate, judging from our impressions of distance between Camps 5 and 6 and from longer views of the mountain.)

I regret to say that although the climbing that day had often been exposed, sometimes steep, we had been negligent and had not used the rope. It is a nuisance to be all tied together, and annoying for the others when one man wants to stop. It also prevents people from making their own speed and local route, and from stopping when they want to. Bob and I started to descend as we had come up, unroped. On an icy section of the ridge, not far below Camp 6, he slipped. He applied the brake in the approved mountaineering manner by pressing the pick of his ice-axe into the ice, but although this stopped him accelerating, it did not stop his fall. I stood, silent and aghast as I watched Bob fight his personal battle. He was falling towards the steepening mountainside which dropped abruptly away thousands of feet right down to the Biro Glacier. But Bob's luck was in that day, for he slid towards some rocks which were surrounded by soft snow where they protruded through the ice. Here he stopped, and I climbed carefully down to him. He was unhurt, but a little shaken by his narrow escape. We had left the rope up at Camp 6, so we had to continue our descent without it.

Lower, below the rocks, we decided to try a short-cut. (Has anyone ever made a successful one? Has anyone ever resisted the temptation to?) We found our way blocked by a long curving crevasse. Forced at last to cross it, we tied two waist slings together and I stepped gingerly forward, only to drop out of sight at once. Luckily I landed on an ice ledge about seven feet down and managed to scramble out the other side. A great leap carried Bob across. Lower down again, on the broad slopes above Camp 5, we found that our crampons were "balling" in the sun-warmed snow—that is, the snow was sticking under our feet, like mud on your boots in a ploughed field on a wet day. This makes the boots very slippery and it can be dangerous. So we took our crampons off and then, on that perverse hillside, found that the snow gave way to ice, on which crampons are necessary. I went on a few paces and lost my footing and fell, executing several neat somersaults before I came to a stop in soft snow. On both my falls my hat had stuck securely on my head. Bob and I were very tired indeed when eventually we reached Camp 5.

We awoke next day to a clear dawn, and conjectured how the summit pair might be faring. For the second day in succession we climbed the two thousand feet between Camps 5 and 6. For some reason, perhaps because we knew exactly what was in store, the ascent proved easier than the day before. When we reached Camp 6 we saw ice-axes stuck in the snow outside the tent and immediately deduced that Hamish and Dick had not attempted the summit, despite its having been a good day for climbing. We crawled into the tent and learned that Dick had woken to feel pains in his legs and, fearing phlebitis, which had virtually killed an American climber on K2 quite recently, he decided not to risk the all-out exertion of a summit bid. This was a piece of straight bad luck but although we were not to know it at the time, it probably cost us the summit, or at least the chance of having an honest go at it. Dick was now feeling much better, and we determined to set out all together the next dawn and go as high as we could. It meant all four of us cramming into the diminutive two-man Gerry tent, and we had no illusions as to how uncomfortable the night would be. We were not disappointed: it was ghastly! No one had enough room to stretch out. Those lying near the side of the tent were chilled down one side of their body; Hamish kicked me to death and I spent half the night shoving him back into his chilly tent-wall position; Dick and I clanged skulls every time we moved; only Bob managed to adopt an Olympian attitude, and he sank his great bulk down on the floor, or us, and gave a clever impression of sleeping, or at least resting. It was, we all agreed, worse than being benighted, or as Shakespeare put it:

> *O, I have pass'd a miserable night,*
> *So full of ugly sights, of ghastly dreams,*
> *That, as I am a Christian faithful man,*
> *I would not spend another such a night.*

At 3.30 a.m. we "got up", if that is the expression. Dick manfully coped with breakfast, and produced a meal which our jaded palates could scarcely accept. Weak, cold and tired after our miserable night, we emerged to a clear but blowy dawn. We roped up almost immediately and I led off, ferreting a way across a broken, half-open crevasse. A snow ridge led to an abrupt little snow bulge about fifty feet high. It was as steep as the Gendarme, but the snow was excellent. I cut up it, fashioning both hand- and foot-holds, but moving far too slowly, I fear, for the other three who, standing motionless, were getting very cold. Urged on from below, I moved as quickly as I could, and soon we were all above the snow wall. Hamish then took a turn at leading and was faced with the task of finding a way over some truly enormous crevasse bridges. Above them the angle increased and, still roped, we plodded slowly towards the next band of crevasses. After several forays Hamish pronounced that the bridges were too insecure and that we would have to go down and round to find an alternative way. Disgruntled at having to lose height so painfully gained, we made our detour. Then Bob stopped.

"I think my feet are going numb," he called out.

9. Hunza porters carrying ration boxes in a snow storm.

10. Shovelling drifted snow off tents at Camp 2 after a storm.

11. The snow slope above Camp 2 (visible on snow col left of figures) on which Banks and MacInnes were later avalanched.

2. Heavy going on the snow traverse nicknamed "The Road to Rakaposhi". The Hindu Kush range can be seen in the distance.

13. View through the tent flap, Camp 3 (19,000 ft.).

14. Camp 4.

"Let's go across to the sunlight where you can take your boots off," suggested Hamish.

It was a good idea, for quite close the sunlit snow of early dawn was gleaming. Bob, who was wearing vapor barrier boots which were a shade on the tight side, took them off and hammered some life into his feet.

After half-an-hour or so we moved off up the slope again, this time managing to dodge the crevasses. The wind was rising and blown snow was hissing over the ice. It was very cold. The slope was now quite reasonable, so we took off the rope. My legs were chilling even though I was wearing long underpants and battledress trousers. To remedy this I stopped and put on my windproof trousers. Tired and apathetic, I laboriously pulled my windproofs on over my crampons, a slow and fiddlesome business. I was reluctant to get my fingers cold in removing the metal crampons. Once the windproof trousers were on, my legs warmed up, and slowly I joined the others, who were huddling in dejection beside a boulder. Feeling dulled mentally and very tired, I walked over to them with weary and ponderous steps and slumped down, grateful for the rest.

We "reviewed the situation", if that is the way to describe the staccato conversation of four pathetic mortals crouching round the purely hypothetical shelter of the boulder. We were cold, heart-wearied by our long weeks of high tussle, and exhausted by our more immediate exertions. I was, as I have said, happy to rest awhile before we forged on.

"We're going down," someone said. I accepted the news dully. Hamish, who must have been colder than the rest of us, was keenly aware of the danger of frostbitten feet. I must admit that my own feet, on which I was wearing one pair of socks, were comfortably warm in my vapor barrier boots. Dick was convinced, as he had been all along, that Camp 6 had been pitched too low to give us a reasonable chance of the summit. Bob was very tired and fell in with the general wishes. I myself, though quite as tired as the others, felt rather bewildered by their decision. Having struggled so hard for the 500 feet we had gained, it seemed inhuman to waste the effort. Before I consented to go down, we reached the agreement that Hamish and I would remain at Camp 6 to make a second attempt the following day, while Bob and Dick would go down to Camp 5, where there was some spare food. None of us could face the prospect of another night with four in a two-man tent. Surely the morrow would be fine? And we had steps ready-cut up the snow wall; our route-finding puzzles through the crevasses had been solved. Yes, Hamish and I would have a good rest (can one rest at 23,000 feet, with the body deteriorating?) and the summit would surely fall to us.

We found the descent to Camp 6 fairly effortless, as is usual at great altitudes. Bob and Dick had a brief rest and then continued on down to Camp 5. Hamish and I lounged about for the rest of the day, desultorily going over our plans for the next day's climb. I noticed that I could eat only about a quarter of my full ration. For instance, I could stomach only half a Weet Bix cereal biscuit for breakfast, whereas at base I could easily eat four, washed down with milk. I could manage only a quarter of the army meat bar. I did my utmost to force this food down, but, like a small child told to eat up its pudding, I rolled the stuff round my mouth and swallowed it only slowly and after considerable mental effort. Hamish managed a little better, but he too was slowly starving himself. On reflection, also, I am not sure that we were drinking enough. Physiologists attribute much of the high-altitude lassitude to dehydration, which in turn is caused by increased sweating through the lungs, which are continually and rapidly being filled with very dry air which absorbs a lot of the body's moisture. As usual, I took my sleeping tablets that night and enjoyed some good rest, if not uninterrupted sleep, in sharp contrast to the previous night. Hamish, as ever, scorned the use of pills and yet seemed to enjoy a better night than I did.

The next morning, to avoid the deathly cold of pre-dawn, we rose a little late and struggled into our pullovers, down jackets (a modern Himalayan "must"), windsuits and gloves. We squirmed out through the tubular sleeve entrance of the tent and put on our crampons, and, having roped up, looked about us. Great torn clouds were blowing above and below us. There was no blue sky overhead. As we plodded away up the initial snow slope, the clouds enveloped us.

"Let's give it half an hour to clear up," Hamish called into the wind.

"Suits me."

We returned to the tent, but within the agreed half-hour not only had the cloud thickened and the wind risen, but peals of thunder had started to boom out.

"It's not on today," said one of us.

"And we've only got a day and a half of food," replied the other.

That was our dilemma. If the storm blew itself out during the day, without leaving the mountain unclimbable under a blanket of new snow, what should we do on the morrow?

"Hamish, with so little food we daren't risk the long flog up to the summit tomorrow. We'd get back here completely whacked and with only about one meal in reserve. If a storm came up we'd be dead."

"Aye, you old cream puff, you're right. We'll have to go down," agreed Hamish. "But we'll come back," he added.

"Of course."

"We can either go down to Camp 5 and get some more food, or go right down for a rest," he said.

We therefore agreed to give Rakaposhi best for the moment, but to return to the onslaught without delay. At Camp 6 we would leave certain articles of which we had no immediate need. They included my camera and some spare clothing.

It has been asserted by veteran mountaineers that thunder and lightning are rarities in the Himalayas. Our experience, then and later, indicated otherwise. For all that afternoon we crouched in the tent with thunder crashing about us, horribly conscious that our camp, perched on a ridge and full of metal objects such as tent-poles and ice-axes, would be an obvious point for the electricity to discharge. I have to admit that I am frightened by thunder, and never more so than on that day. Hamish, to my envy, seemed to maintain an "In sh'Allah" attitude of indifference to the turmoil without.

The day passed slowly, and we were relieved to observe that it did not snow. We wondered where Bob and Dick might be during the storm. We supposed they were sheltering at Camp 5, probably waiting to see us safely down on the morrow. Unbeknown to us, they were in fact descending the Monk's Head on this stormy day; and drama was being enacted.

V

HIGH TENSION

They warred with Nature, as of old with gods
The Titans; like the Titans too they fell,
Hurled from the summit of their hopes . . . —A. G. Butler.

WITH a cheery "Good-bye and good luck", Bob and Dick had left Hamish and myself at Camp 6 to make our final attempt on the summit. They must have been very tired after the "sardine night", followed by the climb of some five hundred feet. None the less, they descended successfully to Camp 5 that same day, and, like us in the camp above them, revelled in the comparative luxury of having only two men in a two-man tent.

Next morning they pondered whether to wait for us at Camp 5 and help us if we were very spent after our second summit bid, or whether to go on down. They realized that if they waited, we would all be obliged to cram into the solitary two-man tent and make another "gruesome foursome". Rather than face a repetition of this, they elected to go on down, leaving us to look after ourselves. Consequently, although the weather was thick and menacing, they left camp next morning and set off for the Monk's Head. They found the bamboo marker at the top of the fixed ropes and started, hand over hand, to swarm down them.

As they descended, so the storm built up. Thunder began to crash about them; lightning flashed. Being thus caught in a thunderstorm is one of the most frightening experiences that can befall a mountaineer. Nothing can make you feel more puny or impotent. In the Alps the usual procedure is for the party to leave their ice-axes, and any other heavy metal objects, on a ridge and then to descend down the flank of the crest to a spot where the lightning is less likely to strike. This is all very well if you are on a ridge, but Bob and Dick were on the broad bland face of the Monk's Head with not a vestige of shelter anywhere. Furthermore, they were acutely aware that on that unbroken snow face they, with their ice-axes, cine-camera and tripod, and sundry other metal articles about their persons, were the obvious points of discharge for the lightning.

They scurried down the ropes, urged on by the rather too impressive tympani of the electric orchestra. When they were about half-way down Bob suddenly felt himself being charged with electricity.

"It was just like my head was in the electric-light points," he described it afterwards. "I put my hand over my head and this relieved me for a moment, but soon I felt the electricity running through my hand as well. I got hell-scared!"

He realized that an electric potential was probably building up to discharge and that he was in imminent danger of being fried and electrocuted simultaneously.

"I shucked off my rucksack, hoping it would fall to the bottom of the Monk's Head where I could pick it up later, but the sonofabitch rolled thousands of feet down onto the Biro Glacier instead." Cine-camera and tripod followed, but these luckily did fall to the foot of the Monk's Head.

The charge built up; Bob could stand it no more. He stumbled and fell. Very fortunately indeed for him, he had taken the precaution of clipping his waist-line to the fixed rope, so that as he fell he was supported by the fixed rope and merely hung head down for a few seconds, having tumbled a short distance. Feeling terribly groggy, but thankful and surprised to be alive, he followed the ropes to the bottom of the Monk's Head. Dick, who had not been very far away, for some reason had remained relatively unaffected. But Bob could never quite figure out why that particular cloud had not discharged!

Bob's rucksack was quite irretrievable, and this put them in a predicament. They had now only one air-bed between them and a light sleeping-bag apiece. They passed a chilly night at Camp 4, hoping perhaps to see us on the next day. However, Hamish and I were now two days behind them, so we did not appear as two tiny dots slithering down the ropes of the Monk's Head opposite them.

They spent one more miserable night and then decided that we must work out our own salvation. They packed their kit and made back to Camp 3. The ascent of the reverse side of the Gendarme, thigh deep in steep, soft snow, was exhausting in the extreme, and they were very tired when they reached their goal. The next day they descended to Camp 2 and continued without pause down to base.

Hamish and I, blissfully unaware of all these happenings, passed the day, July 12th, in our tent listening to the storm outside. Ragged clouds enveloped the camp, visibility was down to fifty yards, and it looked as if it might snow at any minute. All thought of a final desperate foray for the summit, in the style of Hermann Buhl on Nanga Parbat, was banished. Hamish and I, like most ordinary, reasonable folk (sorry to call you ordinary and reasonable, Hamish!) ultimately prefer to be live mountaineers rather than dead heroes. So we went down.

We were able to follow the rough crest of the ridge, taking care to rope up over the ice slope where Bob had so nearly fallen to his death on the Biro Glacier below, and located the ribbon of rocks when they loomed up as dark shadows against the universal whiteness of the snow and cloud; they would guide us down for several hundred feet. The wind was tearing at us and Hamish began to feel very cold. His resistance to cold is normally far better than mine (he slept in only one sleeping-bag; I needed two), but on this, and one other important occasion, he was almost crippled with cold whereas I was reasonably comfortable. I think I must have learned my lesson in Greenland and consider that it was purely a question of clothes. I would pile on all my clothes in the tent and emerge hermetically sealed against the wind. Hamish often would not, and later, in the middle of a climb, he would not be bothered. We accomplished the climb down with difficulty, all the elements combining to make things worse for us, and finished with a long and carefree sitting glissade which carried us almost to Camp 5.

We noticed a deserted look about the place and assumed that Bob and Dick had descended the Monk's Head to await us at Camp 4, which boasted two tents and would therefore accommodate us all without a repetition of the sardine-packing of Camp 6. Next day the weather was still a bit cloudy, which made it difficult to differentiate between snow and sky. We could just discern the trail of footprints in the snow left by Bob and Dick. As we neared the steep snow slope where the face of the Monk's Head plunged down out of sight, we were thankful for our foresight in marking the top of the fixed ropes with a bamboo marker. This loomed out of the whiteness and guided us to the ropes, which we descended safely. On the wide and featureless snow basin below, the tracks grew more indefinite, and we spent some time walking around in the blank landscape trying to locate our tents. (There is nothing more frustrating and worrying than groping around in a world that resembles the inside of a gargantuan ping-pong ball.) After a time, and not before it had caused us some concern, we found the two tents of Camp 4 and made towards them, hoping to meet Dick and Bob. Instead, we found the following note scribbled on a piece of paper tied to the tent-pole:

Mike and Hamish.

We are leaving for lower camps. Bad electrical storm descending Monk's Head. Bob got charged and lost his pack, which went down to the Biro. Recovered movie camera (broken) and cup. We spent the last two nights here with only one sleeping-bag, and it is too cold to wait longer for you. We are taking the stove to Camp 2 in case we have to stay there. We hope to get to Camp 2 today. Bring what you can. Good luck.

Dick and Bob.

This was our first intimation of their near escape. Hamish and I had been toying with the idea of replenishing our supplies from our reserves at Camp 4, reorganizing the party there, and then setting off again for the summit. We were now concerned that Bob might be in worse shape than he led us to believe (it would have been typical of him to minimize his troubles). We therefore decided to return to base, where we could all enjoy a long overdue rest and discuss our next assault.

Hamish and I, anxious not to bring down the mountain a single item, however light, which we would need again, had left our climbing rope at Camp 5. When we left Camp 4 next morning, therefore, we were faced with the descent of the Gendarme without the assistance of rope, the fixed ropes having been removed in order to place them on the Monk's Head. The snow was soft and we made sluggish progress up the steep slopes on the reverse side of the Gendarme. When we came to the crevasse, which had been so easy to jump down over, we found that we had to climb it by trusting ourselves to an insecure-looking snow bridge. I demanded a rope. Hamish reckoned that this confirmed his suspicion that I was a cream puff. Even so, I still demanded a rope. We improvised, tying together a spare pair of nylon bootlaces, a spare tent-guy which happened to be in someone's pocket, the bit of nylon cord which normally connected my two gauntlets, and two slings. And I a member of the Alpine Club! At best it was a gesture, perhaps of some psychological value.

I was not honestly looking forward to the descent of the other side of the Gendarme over a mixture of very steep ice and rotten rock. By this time the rope had ceased to be of even psychological worth. I stubbornly demanded that the tatty thing be employed, mostly to support the canons of sane mountaineering. Hamish, equally incensed, held it at finger's length, obviously regarding it as an insult to the Creagh Dhu! We descended slowly, Hamish tending the "rope" above me. The rocks were clear of snow and reasonably easy to negotiate, but the bottom pitch gave us some trouble. In fact, I think it was one of the most difficult ice pitches I have climbed down. I could not have done it without the twelve-point crampons I was wearing, and I had to cut hand- as well as foot-holds. There was a dizzy drop to the Kunti Glacier far below, and the spaghetti-thin rope merely served to mock me. I was determined not to fall off and thereby give Hamish the satisfaction of shouting to me as I went that he knew the rope would break! The difficulty of climbing down on ice of this steepness is such that one is stuck to it like a fly to a wall, and it is both hard and tiring to cut the necessary steps. Climbing very carefully, I reached a safe anchorage at a rock and called for Hamish to come down. After a brief survey of the ice and a final disdainful glance at the "rope", he said he would rather risk his neck on a nearby rock face which offered an alternative method of descent. He managed beautifully, moving very fast, but equally sure-footedly. We then climbed down to Camp 3.

The next day we climbed back along the corniced ridge to Camp 2 and continued down the gully towards base without pause. We had the brilliant idea of bundling up in a kitbag such soft articles as a tent and sleeping-bags and letting them bounce down the gully, thereby saving ourselves the effort of carrying them. It worked well until they became jammed in some rocks under a waterfall. We then paid for our laziness by having to carry them down for the remainder of the way saturated with water and about five times heavier than usual.

We arrived back at base camp on the afternoon of July 16th. For six long weeks we had been toiling on the ridge, and we were all in a terribly weakened state. The first assault on Rakaposhi was over.

VI

COUNTER ATTACK

It is best to keep the nerves at strain
To dry one's eyes and laugh at a fall
And baffled, get up and begin again—Robert Browning.

WE badly needed three things: oxygen, food and rest, none of which were available high on the mountain. We therefore bundled a few essential belongings into our rucksacks and set off down to the valley, intent on buying the first sheep we saw. Acting on Fazal-i-Haque's advice, we did not stop at the attractive pine forest of Darbar, but continued down to a village called Barit, where, he assured us, we could gorge on as much fresh meat, fruit and vegetables as our emaciated bodies could consume. This was true within limits, and that night we demolished the better part of a sheep. But there is usually a snag somewhere, and this became apparent the following morning. Flies! Flies by the hundreds of thousands. Flies thicker than I had dreamed possible. They were so numerous, and settled in such legions on every exposed square inch of skin, that it was obviously futile to swat them. When preparing meat for the pot, the mutton would be quite literally black with flies.

We gained a brief respite from the scourge when we went down to the river to enjoy our first bath for nearly two months. The swift stream brought down with it a cool breeze which discouraged the pests. As we stripped, we were amazed at the sight of our own bodies. All our fat and a lot of our muscle had just vanished. We must each have lost at least 20 lb., and my figure was slimmer than it had been in my teens. Legs had become thin and spindly; ribs could be counted through the taut skin.

While I was finishing washing, a very pleasant villager came and watched me curiously as I soaped my feet. He had probably never seen soap before and, being barefoot himself, obviously thought it the height of sophistication to wash one's feet. When I had finished I solemnly handed him the soap. He smelt it with approval (I think it was the brand that every famous Hollywood star is alleged to use). He then gave his feet a thorough rinsing in river water, after which he applied some soap to them as if it were scent. He returned the soap with a smile and we felt like brothers.

The flies and the heat between them made our stay at Barit the mere simulacrum of a rest period, so, having procured some "meat on the hoof", we walked it and ourselves up the valley to the arboreal shade and coolness of the pine glades of Darbar. We lounged along the wooded tracks plucking small, sour gooseberries, and made camp with the scent of pine needles in our nostrils. The pressure cooker hissed over a wood fire, which we later built up into a camp bonfire worthy of a Boy Scouts' jamboree.

By now we had, after considerable discussion, evolved a plan. Bob and Dick intended to accompany us as far as base camp, send the porters up to Camp 3 to collect certain personal belongings they had left there, and then leave the mountain. They proposed to take a trip to Baltit, the capital of Hunza and the seat of the Mir, and then return to Karachi to catch a boat. Bob had lost some of his vital kit (though we could have replaced this from Fazal-i-Haque's), and they both considered a further attempt would be fruitless. Hamish and I, who did not share their viewpoint, were undisguisedly disappointed. We would not concede that the mountain had won unconditionally, and contemplated another attempt. We could count on our porters to carry for us to Camp 3: it was the situation above this camp which would need very careful assessment. Camp 4 consisted of two tents and was well stocked with food, lacking only a primus stove, which we could easily carry over from Camp 3. Camp 5, above the Monk's Head, consisted of a tent, stove and about eight days' food. Camp 6 lacked food, but held a stove with some paraffin. Establishing these camps had been the labor of weeks, and Hamish and I were reluctant to abandon them. The Monk's Head was still roped and we were splendidly acclimatized. We were, however, underweight and weak through our steady physical deterioration high on the mountain. Given a fine spell, the pair of us had a game chance of rushing our objective.

On the debit side, Rakaposhi was really too big a mountain for two tired climbers to tackle without a high degree of risk. If one of us fell sick or had an accident there would be little hope for him. Those who lead adventurous lives are inevitably faced with comparable situations. If the gamble comes off, the participants are acclaimed as showing enterprise and resolution of a high order. They are branded New Elizabethans these days. Failure can only be regarded as foolhardiness. Hamish and I, who both conceal caution beneath a certain panache, thought over the situation carefully and together decided to take a calculated risk. We had one priceless asset: each trusted and respected the mountaineering competence and integrity of the other. But we also agreed to be very conscientious in the use of the rope!

Thus we two British parted ways with our American friends. We had had a fundamental disagreement on tactics: nothing more. Our friendship was, I think, proven by our ability to disagree cordially.

"You're nuts!" Dick would declare.

"There it is. Come with us!" I would say, pointing to the summit of Rakaposhi, just visible above the Monk's Head.

So, on July 23rd, Hamish and I, accompanied by Issa Khan and Qambar, set out on our second attempt on the peak. We wound our way up through the now familiar screes above base, rested as usual at the cairn and stores dump which we called Camp 1, and then climbed the two-thousand-foot gully which led to the crest of the ridge and Camp 2. The scintillating snows of May had melted and the hillside was now a wilderness of screes. The gully was a ribbon of ice or *névé* scoured down the middle by a stream whose water came from the melting snowfields above. I was feeling fit and optimistic. Hamish, for a reason soon to manifest itself, felt sluggish.

We were carrying fresh mutton and a supply of fresh eggs, and so enjoyed an outdoor supper in perfect weather that evening. Our by now old friends Nanga Parbat and Haramosh stood out proudly on the horizon. Far, far away to the north-west a triangle of golden light shone. Could this be Tirich Mir standing sentinel above the hazy peaks of the Hindu Kush? Could these be the same serried battalions of great ranges through which the young Alexander had marched his armies centuries ago? What courage that man must have had, in those days before maps existed and when geography was the hearsay of the caravan master! There is something irresistibly romantic in the blue mountain distances of Central Asia; in the way that names roll off the tongue, such as Kashgar, Tashkent, Samarkand . . . And you cannot dispel the dream by telling me that the caravan route is now a jeep road and that the bazaar is now a Russian industrial town.

We got up and away early the next morning, for we had noticed the night before that our ice steps had all melted away on the slope above us and would have to be recut. This is usually a slow business, for whereas snow steps can usually be kicked or cut with a few light slashes of the axe, ice is far tougher and takes many well-aimed blows to fashion an adequate step. In Himalayan books one frequently reads of a morning starting cheerfully at some unearthly hour as the grinning Mongolian face of a Sherpa appears through the tent flap, closely followed by tea and porridge. As an experiment that morning, we tried this system of hotel service with our Hunzas. Never again! The egg was an indescribable, cold mess and the tea was brewed Hunza fashion—that is, immensely strong by our standards, and well stewed. The part of the tea that the Hunza most enjoys is eating the leaves afterwards.

We climbed up the scree above Camp 2 to the familiar boulder on which we had so often rested and which had come to be regarded as a milestone. Above us was pure ice, so we sat on the boulder and waited while Issa Khan hewed a stairway of steps. His ice-craft was good, and his balance confident and easy as he swung his axe. Big, hulking Qambar standing behind him gave more the impression of uncoordinated strength as he too wielded his axe, enlarging the steps. The weather was fitful: cold and cloudy. Hamish, who better than any of us had demonstrated an ability to assume the horizontal and doze during any hiatus in the activities, suddenly said that he was feeling seedy and ought to go down. True, he had climbed up to our milestone very sluggishly; all the same, I did not take this statement very seriously and continued to concentrate my attention on the dim figures of Issa and Qambar, who were just visible through the curtain of cloud as they slowly worked on the ice steps. But Hamish's complaints became more insistent and I was forced to pay heed. He had been markedly the toughest and healthiest so far, and I was most surprised to hear him advocate retreat. At about the same time Qambar was beginning to feel somewhat unhappy on the steep mountainside, so Issa wisely tied him on to a climbing rope and they descended.

We climbed down the screes to camp, where Hamish immediately turned in while I made tea. After this we rested. Hamish was still feeling very unwell; furthermore, there was an unpleasant reek in the little tent which (for once) was not attributable to the usual base reason. Hamish's breath was smelling horribly, so much so that I lay in my sleeping-bag with my head out of the tent door. He had other unquieting symptoms: his joints ached; his eyes hurt when he moved them, his head ached, he had a temperature, and he felt weak and lethargic. He had a general condition of fever. In our English/Urdu gabble I tried to discuss his symptoms with Issa, and from our somewhat indeterminate conversation Issa inferred that Hamish's fever was both dangerous and contagious. My diagnosis was that it was not malaria (which I had had during the war in Burma), but might possibly be dengue fever. This shot in the dark, we found out later, proved to be accurate. At the time, however, Hamish was feeling utterly wretched and Issa was being downright morbid. Convinced by Issa that Hamish had contracted some dreadful, incurable and contagious tropical disease, I let him pass the night alone in the comfort of his tent (which I now privately suspected might also be his coffin) and I slept out on the scree under the stars. It was a calm night and I was agreeably surprised to discover that a night in the open at over 17,000 feet can be both warm and pleasant.

Next morning the patient was weak and ill, but not noticeably worse.

"I'm not goin' t'die just so you can get my wrist-watch and camera," he announced, mustering a smile.

"If you did, at least I'd get my gloves and socks back," I countered, offering him an egg. He must have been genuinely ill, for he was unable to eat what was for us very much of a luxury.

"Hamish," I said, "you've got to try to make base while you still have the strength to walk. We'll never be able to carry you down from here, but we could rig a stretcher at base and carry you down to the road if you get worse."

"I'll try, but I feel rotten."

In the early morning, before the snow softened in the heat of the sun, and before the stones started buzzing lethally down the couloir, we set off from camp. I gave Hamish the security of a rope and we started down. He did all right at first, and soon we were well down the gully. But his reserve of energy was very small, and each time he rested it took him an immense effort to regain his feet. We offered to try to carry him but, wisely perhaps, he said he would keep going as long as he could. At last we reached the bottom of the couloir and attained the safety of Camp 1. Now that he was out of range of falling stones, he rested. All his strength seemed to have been sapped and it took him over two hours to complete a fifteen-minute walk.

Base was dismal. Bob and Dick were just leaving, and the place was almost out of food. We parted somewhat dejectedly, with me imploring the Americans to send the porters, whom they were taking down, back to camp as soon as humanly possible with some fresh food. We seemed to be living on potatoes and porridge, which was no sort of food either for an invalid or a Sassenach.

With our American friends obliged to go to catch their boat, with Hamish still weak and feverish, and with a stomach heartily fed up with combinations of porridge and potatoes, I felt depressed, but not beaten. The camps were there, the mountain was there. I turned to Issa Khan and I tempted him cruelly. Did not Rakaposhi, I said, cleave the sky above his village home? Would he not become the most famous porter in the Hunza valley, and favored by the Mir, if he trod the summit with me? Had he not already been higher than Rakaposhi on the Italian K2 expedition? If, with me, he climbed Rakaposhi, would it not be the highest summit a Pakistani had climbed, and would he not be the Tensing of his country?

Issa was sorely tried, but his native common sense made him refuse my offer. The climbing was too difficult for him, he said. He did agree, none the less, to give Hamish and me a flying start, if we made a third attempt, by going ahead of us and completing the steps he had already started on the ice slope above Camp 2, and continuing these along the "Road to Rakaposhi".

Consequently, early on July 28th Issa and Qambar climbed up to Camp 2 to start on this task. We were surprised to see them coming down the scree back to camp that same evening. As they neared, we saw that they were still wearing crampons, and they must have been walking over the broken rocks with these on for the last couple of miles. Crampons are most unsuitable for scree travel, and we wondered what on earth made them do it. We were soon to find out when the two very shaken men walked into base.

Apparently they had arrived up at Camp 2 in good time that morning and, keen to start, had immediately set about cutting steps on the ice slope above—steps they had been working on when Hamish fell ill. All had been going well until Qambar, who was the biggest, strongest, but clumsiest porter, slipped and pulled Issa Khan with him. The slope was bare ice and they slid for a good four hundred feet. They must have travelled fast on the smooth surface of granular ice, and to them it must have felt like sliding down an enormous sheet of sandpaper. Issa had sustained a cut hand and a bruised head, while Qambar had a pain in his chest. The worst damage, however, was to their morale. They were badly shaken, and although we made them soup straight away, all they wanted was sleep.

The position now was about as gloomy as it had ever been. The two other porters were still away assisting Bob and Dick down to Gilgit; Issa, our best man, and Qambar, our strongest, were out of action and it seemed very doubtful if they could ever be persuaded to set foot on the mountain again; Hamish was still weak with fever: and to cap it all, our diet was still a dreary choice of porridge or potato powder. The summit, which looked so tantalizingly close, was now further away than it had ever been.

VII

AVALANCHE

White snow on the cold hill above has blinded me and soaked my clothes. By the blessed God! I had no hope I should ever get to my house.

Welsh englyn; Gwerfyl Mechain; fifteenth century.

OFTEN there is a simple remedy for a complex situation. Our troubles were solved merely by Dilap and Nadir turning up from their trip down the valley. How glad I was to see old Dilap, his smiling face, as ever, running with sweat, his deep-set eyes gleaming with life and kindliness, and on his back, as on Nadir's, a great bundle of food! The two men who had had the fall were delighted to see their friends, and Hamish soon gained strength as he ate enormous meals of good fresh food. Nadir and Dilap were quite prepared to carry for us, but we decided that they should not go beyond Camp 2, as we did not like to trust them alone on the ice slope. After a short period of recuperative rest we were all set for a third attempt on Rakaposhi; and was not the third time proverbially lucky?

On July 29th Dilap and Nadir carried our light rucksacks up to Camp 2. Although we normally encountered sections of ice on this route, old Dilap on this occasion disdained his expedition climbing boots and crampons and set off in his soft sheepskin bootees, which somewhat resembled sloppy moccasins. Also, he preferred his fawn homespun jacket, which with its full-skirted cut and single vent looked very "county", to his expedition windproof. This weathered individualist then made his own way to Camp 2, dodging all ice and following his own route over the rock. He did not go his separate way out of bravado or conceit, it was merely that he had spent a solitary life hunting in the high valleys and glaciers, and was just not used to following people around. Later that evening at camp he splashed a pan of boiling water in his face, which only made him smile. We also noticed how he peeled the potatoes that night by the ancient method (as old as potatoes) of rubbing them against a rough stone.

Hamish had not quite recovered his full strength, but each meal and each hour of sleep produced an almost visible improvement. By then my own leave was beginning to near its end, and it was remarkably game of Hamish to set out on what was our third attempt on Rakaposhi so soon after his illness. But, as I have said before, Hamish has, I suspect, tremendous resilience.

As we left the camp and started to ascend the screes the next morning, we realized that the mountain was at its iciest. The long spell of good weather had melted a great deal of the snow, and much of the lower route would now be over ice instead of snow. We hoped that we might move fast over this, using crampons. One point is worth bearing in mind when ice-climbing in the Himalayas: whereas in the Alps in summer the ice remains much the same all day, in the Himalayas the almost unbelievable heat of the sun will turn ice slushy by early afternoon. Dilap and Nadir accompanied us, carrying our rucksacks as far as the now familiar boulder which marked the upper limit of the screes. Until then we had always cut steps on the ice slope, but now we decided, due to the iciness of the surface, to put on our crampons and dispense with the labor of step-cutting all the way over the "Road to Rakaposhi". This would have been unsafe for porters with their lack of mountaineering skill, but was suitable for us.

We moved quite fast to begin with. The day was still cold and the ice hard as we attained that part of the ridge where it levelled out into a corniced switchback. We were surprised to see how much snow had melted, exposing great fields of dun-coloured scree where previously there had been glistening white snowfields. Feeling tired, we enjoyed a long rest in a scorching sun at an island of rocks before the final slog up to Camp 3. When at last we dragged ourselves to our feet we found that the ice had become very treacherous. The top layer was composed of slush, which had to be removed by a horse-like pawing motion of the foot before the crampon could bite into firmer ice underneath.

As the slope steepened on the final drag to camp, we encountered quite the worst breakable crust I have ever experienced. Breakable crust is a layer, or crust, of granular snow on the surface, and is formed by the surface of the snow melting and then refreezing into a hard, icy crust. Unfortunately, it is seldom strong enough to bear the whole weight of one's body, and has the infuriating and tiring characteristic of giving partial support and then suddenly collapsing, whereupon the mountaineer lurches forward, thrusting his leg deep through into the soft snow beneath. This, obviously, breaks the rhythm and, in addition, an effort is needed to extract the embedded leg. On the next step the other leg then breaks through. The man in front is almost certain to get tired and angry, and it is the etiquette of the sport that when this occurs the rest of the party offer to take spells at trail-breaking—an offer which the leader accepts by stopping with a gasp, wiping the sweat off his face, and saying, in a voice vibrant with relief: "O.K. Would you like to have a go now?" "Of course I would," lies the man behind.

This particular stretch of breakable crust let me through to the thighs (I am honestly not exaggerating), so that I had to place the flat of my hands on the snow in front of me and squirm out of the holes I was making, only to plunge through again. Seven hours after our departure we reached camp. I have seldom been so played out in all my life, and all I was capable of doing was to flop down on some old sacks. Of course, the correct thing to do when you feel tired is to busy yourself in the tent brewing cups of sweet tea. But theory is one thing . . .

We turned in that night grateful to think that our trek to Camp 4 the next day would be mercifully short and flat in comparison with our recent toils. After the heat and exertion of the day we were very thirsty and drank mugfuls of warm lemon crystals to counteract dehydration.

That night I felt pains in the lower part of my chest every time I moved, and could think of one reason only—pneumonia. This illness is particularly dangerous at high altitudes, where it is greatly aggravated by the lack of oxygen. I recalled the story of a friend of mine who had been camping with a companion at about 19,000 feet. The second man, a botanist, had been feeling somewhat off form during the day, but was well enough in the tent that evening to arrange the specimens he had just collected. During the night he began to feel worse, and had died of pneumonia before the dawn. Pneumonia patients in hospital are sometimes given extra oxygen to help them; high altitude camping is obviously the worst possible condition. I also remembered that our achromycin (antibiotic) supplies were either, over the Gendarme at Camp 4, or down at base, and we had none with us.

When it was time to get moving at 5 a.m. I suggested to Hamish that it might be wise for me to remain on the right side of the Gendarme in case I got worse, when my only hope would be to make a dash for base with its lower altitude and achromycin. After breakfast, however, I felt much better, and Hamish and I did a little careful diagnosis. We came to the unanimous decision that my "pneumonia" had been caused by my drinking a mugful of very strong, acidic lemon crystals. It was nothing more serious, in fact, than a mild acid burn of whatever the pipe is called that conducts food to the tummy.

But it's an ill wind . . . By the time our diagnosis was complete the weather had worsened. By midday a full blizzard was blowing. It snowed and it blew furiously all day; and again all the next day. In fact, it was the worst, although not the longest, storm that had so far smitten us. Apparently it was general all over the Himalayan range, for, we learned later, it flooded the roads and railways in the plains where the great Indus and Sind rivers burst their banks. The only way to get from Rawalpindi to Karachi then was to fly. In the foothills bridges were washed out, and near Gilgit a village built in a nullah, which for years had been considered safe, suddenly found itself in the midst of a foaming watercourse.

On the first day of the storm Hamish and I were mildly disappointed that the weather had worsened, but were none the less quite glad to have a day of rest in order to recuperate after the unexpectedly heavy slog up to Camp 3. On the second day we began to have doubts concerning the condition of the mountain and whether it would remain climbable after so heavy a snowfall. When by the third dawn the blizzard had not abated one jot, we began to feel troubled. We peered outside into a seething white turmoil. Almost with a start we both realized that our adventurous two-man assault on the twenty-five-thousander would now be unjustified. In such conditions a strong and large party, let alone two weak men, would have found it a stern task to plough a furrow up to the summit through the deep soft snow.

"Hamish, we've had Rakaposhi for keeps this time."

"It was worth trying. What about getting down, though?"

"We've hardly any food left here, so we've got to get down. And pretty quickly too. This storm might go on for days. The snow'll be getting deeper all the time."

"We ought to be able to follow the bamboo markers even in this rotten visibility. Let's get moving, Mike."

We broke camp and packed our rucksacks. These were heavy, for besides our personal gear—sleeping-bags, air-beds, crampons and the like—we had the tent and two cine-cameras, which brought the weight of the rucksacks up to, or perhaps a little above, the sixty-pound mark. The weather was still vile, and was to remain so all day. Only once before had I been rash enough to travel in such weather and that was in Greenland, when, as the outcome of my folly, the snow-tractor which I was driving plunged into a deep crevasse and came to rest in a chaos of torn metal. On this present occasion we had to move in the interest of self-preservation. Wind was driving the falling snow slantwise into the ground and visibility was down to about twenty yards, with occasional clearings up to seventy yards or so. In this blank white world we had to follow the line of the ridge, knowing that if we went a few yards too far to the right we would be walking out on to the dangerous overhanging cornices which, if they broke, would hurl us down the sheer mountainside to the Biro Glacier many thousands of feet below. If we went too far left, crevasses were lurking to swallow us.

We found that the driven snow tended to blur our sun-goggles, and were obliged to take them off. We discussed the possibility of getting snow-blindness from the ultra-violet light from the sun which is known to be able to penetrate cloud. Hamish theorized that the light would be diffused by its reflecting from every particle of falling snow and would be so broken up as to be harmless. We had to take our goggles off, anyway, to see where we were going, so his argument remained academic.

When the going was good, it would take a quarter of an hour from Camp 3 to gain an island of rock where the ridge dipped to its lowest point. That day it took us an hour and a quarter of hard going, even though it was downhill. We passed bamboos here and there which assured us that we were on the correct route, but between markers we were constantly straining our eyes into the featureless white world, trying to make out the dim line of the cornices on our right or the seracs and crevasses on our left.

As I have remarked, it took us four or five times longer than it should have done to reach our island of rocks. There we had a rest and talked things over. The snow was most unstable and prone to avalanche, so that we were very apprehensive about climbing back over the "Road to Rakaposhi", which led across steep ice which in turn was above a steep and rocky mountainside. An uncontrolled slip here could have only one outcome.

On our way up to Camp 3 Hamish and I had stopped for some time at the island of rocks, spying out a short-cut down to the glacier which seemed to avoid very successfully the whole long and tiring climb over the subsidiary snow peak on which the "Road to Rakaposhi" lay. This short-cut we considered the lesser of two evils. We climbed down the snow, but had gone only a short way when Hamish's legs suddenly broke through a crevasse bridge. I pulled on the rope and he thrust his axe into the snow and somehow he was extricated. This put paid to our short-cut and made us "rather bear those ills we have than fly to others that we know not of". From somewhere Hamish found the energy to turn round and plough his way up the steep snow we had just descended, and we reached the site of our old Cornice Camp.

In front of us now the ridge rose slightly and then flattened out along the traverse of the "Road to Rakaposhi". We came to the last protruding patch of rock and I climbed out on to the fluffy snow which was covering the ice. I did not like it at all, so I called to Hamish to make sure that he was well secured and could arrest my fall with the rope should I slip. Actually this was a fairly impossible request, for he had no firm rocks to which he might have tied himself, only loose fragments of scree. Instead, he thrust his axe into the loose snow and took a turn of the rope round the shaft.

The surface on which I found myself was a mountaineer's nightmare. It was the steepest section of the route between Camps 2 and 3, and was normally ice. On this occasion the fresh storm-snow, fluffy unstable stuff, was covering the surface to a depth of a foot or so. It was equally impracticable either to sweep away the masses of loose snow and cut steps in the ice beneath or to fashion firm snow-steps by the alternative method of step-kicking. I felt reasonably safe so long as Hamish remained belayed on the scree, but the traverse went on for several hundred feet and soon we should have to forsakc this security. As it happened, I had progressed only some few feet out onto the snow when a clean-cut section stripped off the surface and avalanched. I started to fall, or rather slide, down the steep slope. I called out to Hamish and at the same time tried to arrest my fall by applying the usual brake—pressing the pick of my ice-axe into the snow. This had no effect and, partly incapacitated (and obviously made heavier) by my sixty-pound rucksack, I swooshed down the ice face. Hamish, seeing what was happening and rcalizing the shortcomings of his belay, lay right back in anticipation of the strain which would come on the rope. When it did come, it whipped the axe clean out of the snow, and Hamish then performed the feat of holding me merely with one hand, round which he had taken a turn of rope. I was then moving fast towards the rocky mountainside, and had he failed to stop me we would both have gone to perdition. He held me and once again I thanked my lucky stars that my friend Hamish was made of spring steel. I regained the scree, found some sort of a belay, and called to Hamish to join me, which he did.

We were in a serious predicament: although we had a tent with which to make a camp, we had neither food nor fuel. A camp site would have been difficult to find on so steep a hillside. In any case, the wind and snow had not abated, and conditions were quite likely to be the same the next day and the next. We took Hobson's choice.

Hamish climbed out over the section down which I had recently fallen. He moved out on to the rotten snow, kicking each foot hard in until the snow seemed to have stopped sliding and to have compacted into a passably sound step. Then, his already drawn and ascetic face fixed in worried concentration, he slowly transferred his weight and started kicking the next step. He moved out about thirty feet, burrowed into the snow with his axe, and fashioned an ice stance on which to stand while I moved. Then I quitted my rock belay and launched myself out on to that inimical snow.

We both tacitly understood that we had renounced our last surety and that if one fell his companion had only a slim chance of holding him. What use was the rope, then, other than a suicide pact? For me it was the moral prop which enabled me to remain safely on that mountain face. Hamish and I had complete trust in each other's snowcraft and sense of balance. As one climbed, the other was able to relax mentally and think: "If he can do it, then so can I." In that sense, we leaned heavily on each other. I do not think I could have made that climb alone. There is no one I would rather have made it with than Hamish.

Pitch by pitch we defeated the obstacle, kicking with the feet, scraping the snow off with the axe, cutting ice stances at the end of each pitch. I think it lasted at least ten years before we attained the rounding of the ridge at the end of the "Road to Rakaposhi".

Slowly, oh, so slowly, the angle of the ridge relented until we knew we were approaching the broad ice slope leading down to Camp 2, about 1,500 feet below. By then we were physically and mentally nearing the end of our tether. All this time it had been snowing and blizzing mercilessly, wetting us to the skin, penetrating our windproof outer garments and our down jackets. Again I think I must have been wearing warmer clothing on the lower part of my body, for Hamish was positively shuddering with cold and advocated camping. But it was an impossible place to camp, and we had to force our weary, overladen bodies on. Time was advancing and confirmed our judgement that, even had we had the strength, we would never have had the time to hew out ice steps all the way across that hair-raising traverse. Without regret, we turned our backs for the last time on the "Road to Rakaposhi".

The snow was still driving stinging spatules into our eyes so that

5. Mike Banks, snowblind.

16. Hamish Mac Innes climbing th difficult step on th Monk's Head, a about 20,000 ft.

17. Gilgit scene.

18. At the War Office (l. to r.) Major-General Moulton, General Ayub Khan, Captain Banks, Field Marshal Templer.

we groped on crabwise, peering into the storm trying to catch a glimpse of an identifiable feature or a bamboo marker. I was in front, and suddenly noticed a crevasse running parallel to our course, but on my left, where there should have been only the unbroken surface of a snowfield.

"Hell's bells, Hamish! We're standing on a ruddy great cornice!"

I think at that stage Hamish was almost too cold and tired even to care. Anyhow, we scuttled back to safety. We had, in fact, wandered on to the lip of an enormous double cornice, thereby maintaining the Rakaposhi tradition which seems to insist that climbers at some stage or other should court death on these dangerous snow overhangs.

At last, and with undisguised relief, we found the bamboo marking the top of the final steep plunge which led to the snow or scree set at an easier angle above Camp 2. I led down, kicking steps as best I could in the creaking snow. After the traverse it seemed child's play.

"Mike!" came a bellow from above.

I looked up to see Hamish whizzing down the slope in a heap of avalanche snow. A couple of seconds and the strain would come on the rope. I kicked my crampons into the snow as hard as I could, but I do not think they bit into the ice beneath. I jammed my ice-axe into the snow, but it did not meet much resistance in the soft, newly-fallen stuff. I leaned in towards the slope and waited. The rope tightened and stretched, and then I was jerked over backwards and felt myself sliding rapidly down the slope. I tried to stop, or at least control, my fall by ramming my axe into the snow, but it merely dragged through without effect. I recollect somersaulting madly, quite out of control. I had a vivid conviction that we were heading straight for the Biro Glacier and was afraid of the injuries we would sustain as we bounced over the scree and down the mountainside. Finding myself the right way up, I tried again to apply the ice-axe brake, but I had not the strength. I somersaulted again, and then very gently came to rest. At first I could not believe it and thought that I was still sliding, but cushioned in avalanche snow. I wiped my face and looked around.

We were opposite the isolated boulder which marked the top of the screes and was our customary resting-place. We must have fallen about three hundred feet. We were now resting on loose avalanche snow and at some stage I must have leap-frogged past Hamish, because he was now above me. Most of the avalanches which we had seen coming down this slope had hissed right down the mountainside past Camp 2 and headed along the gully towards Camp 1, a distance of a couple of thousand feet. I still do not understand why this particular one was so considerate as to stop just when it did.

I saw that I was nearer the edge of the avalanche debris and nearer the boulder than Hamish, but was dreadfully afraid that the least twitch might set the loose mass of snow moving again.

"Keep quite still and I'll try to climb across to the boulder," I shouted up to Hamish.

I moved very delicately, but could not make the distance in one rope's length. Hamish climbed towards me, treading like a cat. A little later we gained the security of that boulder where we had rested with thankfulness so many times—a benign hunk of rock. We were both surprised how extremely exhausting, physically and mentally, the fall had been. However, we had now reached the safety of the scree, and we descended to Camp 2 without further incident. Night was then approaching.

The tents at Camp 2 were, as usual, drifted over with snow, so while Hamish crawled inside and set about preparing a meal, I shovelled snow. When I crawled into the tent Hamish announced that he could not get the stove to work at more than a flicker. It needed pricking and, for the first time on the expedition, there was no instrument to be found either with the stove or within the recesses of our rucksacks. We were sopping wet to the skin, so we crept miserably into our sleeping-bags and waited an interminable time for the water to warm. Darkness fell and we lit a candle. It seemed to me to be burning very brightly. But it was a perfectly normal candle. It began to burn so brightly that it hurt my eyes to look at it.

"Hamish, I think I'm going snowblind!"

And so was Hamish. For sorrows come not as single spies but in battalions.

We first felt the pain only when looking at the candle, but soon it became general and we began to weep copiously. We suffered agonies, just as if our eye-sockets were filled with hot and burning sand. Of snowblindness Whymper had said: "The pain is acute and sometimes makes strong men howl." This was our unlucky camp, for so confident had I been of regaining Camp 4 that I had left my medical kit there. Hamish, who claimed immunity to all diseases and ills (we did not quite see that his bout of dengue fever bore this out), carried no medical supplies and depended on his robust constitution and hypochondriac friends. Thus we had tubes of cocaine eye ointment above us at Camp 4 and below us at base—and a fat lot of good it was to us at Camp 2. We tried the well-known remedy for "welder's eye"—pressing tea-leaves against the eye—but it was ineffective. I also took a mouthful of sedatives, but we remained awake and in pain most of the night, unable to open our eyes for more than a second or so at a time, and listening to the gale tearing at the canvas and piling ever more snow over the tiny tent. Neither of us knew how long the blindness would last, but we realized that we must wait till we were at least partially recovered before we could negotiate the gully down to Camp 1.

Next morning I could only keep my eyes open for about five to ten seconds before I had to close them in pain. Hamish was slightly better, due, I think, to the fact that he had been wearing a cap with a small peak which had shielded his eyes a little. Tearfully I held the Primus while he worked wonders with an ice-piton and managed to change the nipple of the stove. We were at least assured of a hot meal. The storm continued to blow all day as we lay in our sleeping-bags, letting the warmth of our bodies help to dry our clammy clothing. We listened to avalanches hissing down the slope above and continuing along the gully. But ours had stopped half-way. Why?

Again we slept. Next morning our eyes were much better and, with goggles on to cut down the light, we were able to keep them open. Hamish's vision was more or less normal, but mine was blurred. We forged down the gully through deep new snow, still fearful of avalanches. In fact, as we were just debouching from the gully we heard a hiss above us and raced to one side to let an avalanche pass to our left. A few moments later another passed to our right—Rakaposhi's final parting shots to shoo a couple of impertinent trespassers from her sanctuary.

On arrival at base camp we found the place deserted. Surely they were just a little hasty in giving us up for dead! Later the porters appeared: they had been sheltering from the storm down the valley at Darbar, where they could enjoy plentiful food, a fire and a shepherd's roof over their heads. They were carrying eggs, fruit and some joints of mutton. We feasted and relaxed. All around the great cirque the rocks were snow-spattered, just as they had been in May, and it was now August. Rakaposhi would remain unmolested at least until the following spring.

We prepared for departure. The porters went up to Camp 2 and collected the bits and pieces which remained there; Issa ostentatiously cleaned one of the Primuses, dropping heavy hints that: "Wood very scarce my home, Sahib. Paraffin stove better." He had done well and he received a Primus as baksheesh. We sent another porter down to Jaglot to recruit five coolies to carry our baggage out—it had taken fifty-six to carry it in.

After a couple of days the coolies appeared, trudging slowly up the hill and apparently suffering just as badly from the altitude as we ourselves had done when we first arrived. Our base camp had been dismantled and all that remained was a couple of dry stone walls, an enormous tapered cairn which Bob and Dick had made and which resembled a Buddhist chorten, and a pile of discarded packing-cases. When the five new arrivals spotted the abandoned wooden cases they pounced on them, pulling out all the loose nails. Apparently nails are valuable in Hunza and Nagyr and, like all metal objects, have to be flown in, which makes them both rare and expensive. We produced a pair of pliers to accelerate the process, and Issa went out of his way to help one of the coolies who was fairly obviously the village idiot. The altitude and the mechanical problem of extracting nails were together just a bit too much for him to cope with.

We turned our backs on the mountain and walked down the screes. In the Jaglot Nullah we gained some impression of the fury of the recent storm. The rivers were in spate, the log bridges swept away; where there had been unbroken forest, the rush of flood-water down the hillside had carved out channels up to seventy yards wide, blocked by mud and tree roots. Even the more permanent-looking bridges had gone. Above Darbar we had to cross three turbulent streams, and a fall into any one would have been very dangerous. Old Dilap, who had obviously done this sort of thing since his youth, forded them all with his ice-axe holding him against the stream and the foaming water up to the top of his thighs. Hamish and I, after much casting about, managed with the aid of two long jumps and a tree which had fallen across the third stream. Issa, in charge of the coolies, was obliged to indulge in some rough field engineering, spanning the water by dragging uprooted trees across and using them as bridges. Even so, the village idiot jibbed, and Nadir had to carry his load across. I wish I could have understood the local dialect so as to follow the rather rich line of persuasion they used to coax him across.

As darkness fell, we hurried through the pines of Darbar to gain a meadow on the far side. Issa, his already prodigious energy heightened by an end-of-term feeling, pelted ahead and had a great roaring campfire going to light us and the porters in. We ate a good meal and then stretched out round the blaze listening to the alternate radio requests and hot-gospelling program from the commercial Radio Ceylon. I watched the strange shadows of the pine trees cast against the hillside by the dancing flames. It was warm and windless; the stars were big and a comet (or was it a meteor?) went trailing across the sky. In sharp contrast to our bitter and taut foray into the upper snows, this relaxed and homely moment comes back to me as one of the most enjoyable of the expedition. I expect Hamish and I were even then talking of our next.

Rain and thunder at dawn sent us fleeing for the Hunza valley. At Barit we saw that whole houses had been washed away, but as a small compensation there were no flies as we demolished a chicken for breakfast. At the larger village of Jaglot the main street had become a seething river and furniture was to be seen stacked on roofs, away from the flood-water. The vines were heavy with grapes and there were apples on the trees. Thenceforward we gorged continuously on some of the best (and cheapest) fruit I have ever had in the tropics. Next day we walked down to the Hunza river, which was lashing itself into a mad turmoil in its haste to race down and join its senior partner, the Indus. No matter how skilful the oarsman, no *zakh* could have crossed that river in its spate.

River crossing in the Karakoram can be guaranteed to provide excitement: either it entails fording with the freezing water up to your stern, trying to tear your feet from under you; or it is a perilous crossing on a *zakh*; or it may be by means of a *jhula*, which is perhaps the most refined torture of all, and was the method we were to employ to get back across the river.

A *jhula* is a home-made suspension bridge used when the river is too deep to ford and too swift to allow the use of a *zakh*. It consists basically of three ropes which form the cross-section of a V; your feet go on the single rope at the vertex and a hand on each side is used to maintain balance. The ropes themselves are as thick as a man's leg, too thick really to permit the sort of "life or death" grip you soon feel you need. You are always told with a smile that such a bridge is never repaired until it breaks; on the other hand, seldom or never is one known to break. You start confidently enough, but as you get out over the flood the bridge begins swaying, the roar of the torrent seems to mount up with your nervousness, and finally an optical illusion lends sickening unreality to the whole business. You are forced to look down to see where you are putting your feet, but in so doing you look beyond your feet to the water. Soon (as when a train standing by yours starts moving out of the station) you get the impression that the bridge itself is racing upstream. If you tend to vertigo, or are just the nervous type, this can lead to a sort of mesmerized panic. The best thing is, like a tightrope walker, not to look down too much. We admired the way the very sturdy and professional porters from Matum Das walked unconcernedly across with their heavy, ungainly loads on their backs. On the far side we met two German Boy Scouts who had been hitch-hiking for the last fifteen months. One of them, the tougher-looking, had tried the bridge but had been too nervous to cross.

We crossed the river and our feet trod the road—and that is the end of almost any expedition. Twenty years ago we would still have been two weeks' marching from Srinagar; now we were one hour's jeeping and thirty hours' flying from London Airport.

There was little left to do except pay off the porters and go home. Hamish, who has a more sensible attitude to time, and who is normally unencumbered by any binding form of employment, spent a further fortnight travelling to Baltit, the capital of Hunza and the home of our porters. I passed a few days waiting for suitable flying weather and rambling round Gilgit. I saw the Moslem Shia sect festival of Maharam, when for six hours, in a semi-ecstasy, all the men of the village march through the streets in procession, beating their chests in unison. The more devout ones also scourge their backs with chains. By the end of the procession, which includes the richly-caparisoned white horse of the Prophet, backs and chests are beaten raw and bloody, eyes are closed as if in a trance: a very demanding religion.

I also wandered round the Christian graveyard, where lonely tombstones mark the graves of lonely men. There was, for instance, that of G. W. Hayward "cruelly murdered at Darkut, July 18th, 1870, on his journey to explore the Pamir Steppe". In the library a gallery of photographs of sternly whiskered Victorian Political Agents stared down, including such men as Manners-Smith, who won a spectacular V.C. for a brilliant rock-climbing attack in the Hunza war of 1891. There are many of these cemeteries in the East where cows now graze and Moslem and Hindu children play among the stones; pathetic monuments of the British Raj.

My leave was running short, so I flew home, having helped Hamish on to the first horse he had ever ridden in his life and watched him disappear in an unhappy cloud of dust towards Hunza, said by some to be the happiest and simplest land in the world.

VIII

PERSPECTIVE

Happy is the man who has made a good journey.

SOME weeks later, in London, Hamish told us how he had fared on his journey to the now almost legendary kingdom of Hunza, a land still extremely difficult of access and still ruled over by its feudal Mir. Hunza is a place that has been much written about—mostly, unfortunately, by the "flying fortnighter" type of journalist who brings away from the country a superficial understanding which is presented with considerable professional skill to the public via the popular press. In this manner Hunza has gained the reputation of being a sort of Central Asian Arcadia where sufficiency, content and an idyllic climate produce the essential ingredients of bliss. It has been described as "Happy Hunza, the place where they would just hate to find gold"; which is absolute nonsense, for no wise ruler such as the Mir would be so foolish as to ignore any form of natural wealth which would improve his simple, frugal kingdom. It is said that James Hilton also visited Hunza years ago and there found the inspiration to write that masterpiece of escapism, *Lost Horizon*, with its haunting Shangri La hidden from the world behind its Himalayan fastness.

Hamish did, none the less, corroborate the inaccessibility of the country. During his second day of riding he had to walk his horse across those precarious sections where the track was built out from the face of the living rock, with the Hunza river thundering in the gorge below him. He vowed to stick to the relative safety of motor-bicycles thereafter.

So he arrived in Hunza clad in his best clothes—an old pair of pyjamas which must have suffered considerably through having been so recently used as riding breeches. He bore to the Mir the twin gifts of some color film and the open, warm smile of the foot-loose Scot. He then spent a pleasant holiday in this remote land which is overshadowed by the stupendous northern wall of Rakaposhi. He examined this 19,000-ft. precipice, probably the greatest mountain face in the world, for possible routes, but even though he scanned it with the optimistic eye of one who knows he will not have to put his theory to the test, he could trace no imaginary route up the gleaming white wall. One day, inevitably, this bastion will fall, but it will surely be one of the greatest routes in the history of mountaineering.

Hamish then visited the porters in their own homes and learned something of this country where polo was invented and where weddings take place only on one selected day of the year when the Mir throws the party in order to save poor families the expense, and where, for better or for worse, mothers-in-law accompany newlyweds on their honeymoons to see that the domestic side of the house is conducted properly! Having panned for gold in New Zealand, Hamish tried one of the swift-flowing rivers in Hunza but, like the American, Clark, before him, found only low-quality deposits hardly worth the taking. His time running short, he then returned to Gilgit and in easy stages came back to Britain.

Before we dispersed to our several countries, all four of us forgathered in London, where we crammed into my tiny flat in Regent's Park, making a happy repetition of our sardine night at Camp 6. We all vowed that, during this reunion in London, we would have a whale of a party as a finale to our pen-pal venture. In the event, Bob and I, who both professed a devotion to beer, were still so weak and deranged with dysentery that after a pint or so we meekly agreed to call it a day and we went home to bed. Dick did not even make first base! This avid pill-taker felt, and looked, worst of the lot; so ghastly, in fact, that we rushed him round to the Hospital for Tropical Diseases, where they immediately put him to bed, diagnosed infective hepatitis of the liver, and told him that he would not be drinking beer for at least a year. He cannot have wasted his time in hospital entirely, because a month or so after arriving back in the States he announced that he was marrying the girl who had nursed him. Hamish, who when he had visited Dick saw only a jet-black Zulu nurse, sent a congratulatory letter which, if nothing else, was concise. It read: "Ha! Ha!" But things must have turned out all right, because Dick wrote to say that he and his new English wife had climbed some phenomenal number of peaks during their honeymoon—which seems about as satisfactory as the Hunza mother-in-law system!

Bob in due course sailed for the States, after having sampled a week-end of British rock-climbing in Wales attending one of those British institutions, a club dinner. He was caught by surprise when I explained that he would be expected to wear a tie and listen to some speeches. At his last climbing club dinner in California, I learned, the president had barely announced that he had a few words to say when a pie hit him in the eye and the dinner ended in uproar, to the general satisfaction of the members. Hamish disappeared for a day into a jungle area of London and emerged with a "hot rod". This was a dangerous-looking motor-bicycle which had to be pushed to start and was more at home on the track than the road. Hamish, confident that it would go faster than a police car, vanished towards his native Scotland with several brown-paper parcels tied on to the bike. Later he took it to the Continent, having first removed the baffle-plates from the silencers so that it made a truly ear-splitting roar. As he drew out of the French docks he screamed to a policeman over the din of the engine:

"I hope I am not making too much noise."

The policeman gave him a vast smile and replied:

"Monsieur, that is not noise. That is music!"

The bad luck which had dogged our money-raising efforts before the expedition seemed to remain with us after we split up. We sent our story to *Collier's Magazine* and they immediately closed; Hamish sent his article to another editor, who died on receiving it. I obtained a B.B.C. contract to put our film on TV for half-an-hour in February. The Americans had the film on their side of the ocean but promised faithfully to return it by Christmas, which allowed me a comfortable margin of two months. They then proved apparently unable to differentiate between Christmas and Easter, on which latter feast they sent me the film—two months late, and we lost the contract!

I said at the beginning of this book that this expedition to the Karakoram represented the realization of my twofold ambition to explore both in the polar regions and the Himalaya. This is a fairly rare achievement, the only other person I can recollect as having wintered in the Arctic and climbed a major peak being that redoubtable adventurer, Colonel Spencer Chapman. I was undoubtedly the first person to achieve this in the post-war era. In the public mind the Himalayas and polar snows are closely related—indeed, Everest has often been described as "the third pole". It is of interest, therefore, to examine and compare in a modern light these two traditionally British forms of exploratory endeavor.

It is most probable that a person's taste for any particular form of exploration depends largely on his personality, and so it is not my intention to play off the Himalayas against the polar regions. But to illustrate my point, my main job during my two years in Greenland was running a vehicle team in order that a scientist could carry out geophysical research into an abstruse subject called isostasy. Although he tried to explain to me, patiently and simply, what isostasy was all about, and although I became proficient at my job of surveying with a theodolite, I had only a very superficial understanding of, and second-hand interest in, our work on the ice-cap, and had forgotten my calculus anyhow. No, if the theodolite did have a soul, it failed to communicate with me!

The Himalayas I found more exhausting, more dangerous, more exhilarating, incomparably more beautiful and, somehow, more enjoyable than Greenland. Perhaps it was that my companions were more lighthearted, but I think it was principally an overriding feeling of common purpose that really made the expedition for me. In Greenland some twenty-five people were pursuing eight or more different lines of research, often with conflicting requirements. On Rakaposhi, as on any attempt to scale a great mountain, we were almost monomaniacal. Our aim, the summit gleaming in the thin air above us, was material, visible and undeniable. Every struggle we made was in concert to trample that high snow. This one aim was so deeply implanted in our minds that, however undernourished, weary or befuddled by altitude we were, it was the one tangible thing we were able to cling to. This is rather difficult to convey to anyone who has never known the efficiency of his mind and body reduced by about 80 per cent. The only desire then is to go down; it is the only sensible, rational thing to do. Then the voice of this monomania whispers to you to go up. It cannot produce any reasons, except to remind you of the bargain you made with yourself months ago in England. And the spirit always wins—or there would be no sport of mountaineering.

Then there is the question of people. The polar regions—the Antarctic particularly—are often, and rightly, described as pure, clean, and unsullied by man. This is true, and few pleasures can compare with the private conceit of seeing a view for the first time from the crest of a pass that no man (air pilots excepted these days) has ever seen before. The Himalayan valleys, in contrast, have been populated for untold centuries by laughing, almond-eyed Mongols or tall, serious Aryans. The blue haze that blankets the distances seems also to mantle the history of this antique land. Who knows whether, by the side of the caravan route or in a ruin on a hill, you might not find a coin or a fragment left by Alexander's armies, or a relic of some trader who came out from Bukhara when that city was the capital of the known world? Or, to take a more homely instance, Issa Khan (whose name, literally translated, means Jesus Lord), resting for a spell high on the mountain, would point down to the murk of the valley, impossibly far below, and say:

"Baltit there, Sahib. My children there."

At once it made the hill more friendly, for was it not, after all, merely Issa's village mountain? And Issa, with his blue-grey eyes and brown hair, might he not have been a Macedonian whose forebears marched with the armies of the god-man we call Alexander and he Iskander? This question of the feeling of a country is a very personal one, and you will find an affinity either with the poles or with Himachal according as you are moved more by the impact of things or of people.

I learned from the Political Agent in Gilgit and from officials in the Ministry of Kashmir Affairs, that the Pakistan Government was reserving the mountain for her own climbers. I could quite see their point. Each year an increasing number of expeditions takes the field, and the stock of major virgin peaks is rapidly diminishing. The

Pakistanis are keen to develop mountaineering among their own nationals and, naturally, wish to reserve at least one of their own mountains for their own endeavors. In a country which contains such an unrivalled wealth of beautiful mountains, it is entirely wholesome that the sport should prosper; and if we Europeans can pass on something of the technique and tradition of the craft, we will be doing mountaineering a real service.

This is also a fitting moment to examine the reasons for our failure. Briefly, we bit off more than we could chew. It was not so much that the mountain was too high; rather was it that the route was too long. Had we been climbing upwards all the time, I think we would have made it quite comfortably. As it was, the South-West Spur was about four miles long and full of switchbacks. This made us spend too long a period (some five weeks) working too hard too high on the mountain. I cannot think of another oxygenless expedition which ever had to work its members harder. Moreover, I feel we did not pay enough attention to our diet, which was badly deficient in protein. Much of our later weakness might have been attributable to unnecessary undernourishment. It is a thorny problem, and the individual cannot really know what he is able to stomach at a great altitude until he has tried it. I remember longing for ordinary bully beef instead of our dehydrated meat bars.

I know Dick and Bob will disagree with the next point I am going to make. I think our party as a whole was beaten psychologically as much as physically. In fact, after our summit bid Hamish and I felt full of fight and ready to continue the assault as long as we had food to do so. Had we rallied as a team at Camp 5 we might have made it. Even when lack of food drove us down from Camp 6, Hamish and I were so confident of returning that we left there such precious things as my camera, from which I did not even bother to remove the exposed film. Though we did not know it at the time, when Bob and Dick left Camp 6 they had abandoned all hope of attaining the summit, having assessed the chances perhaps with less emotion and more logic than we had. After our retreat, Hamish and I were almost driven frantic at the thought of all the food and camps on the mountain and only lack of manpower stopping us using them in another summit bid. It is arguable that we were over-sanguine in making two further lone attempts, and it is probably fortunate that bad weather eventually put a stop to our adventure. But I think we were only being true to ourselves, and would ever afterwards have been tortured by self-reproach had we given up too easily.

With the Atlantic between us, I don't expect I shall ever be able to climb with Bob or Dick again. This is inevitable, but I treasure the experience of sharing an expedition with those two humorous and rugged American mountaineers. It is Hamish, however, who is the central figure of this story, for it was he who conceived the expedition while he was in New Zealand, and it is with him I would like to leave the last word.

He is a truly remarkable man, full of contradictions, yet still the most likeable of persons. He is, for instance, utterly indifferent to personal comfort and health, yet amazingly fastidious about personal cleanliness or tidiness. At the height of a blizzard his tent would be spotlessly clean and neat, with every particle of snow, stale food or dirt carefully swept out. He also had the gift of making his own amusements and, during long periods of storm, his mellow baritone would rise above the soughing of the wind, chanting Highland songs or, incongruously, I.R.A. dirges, the latter partly to evoke the inevitable explosion from me, to the glee of the Americans. Then in the evening he would perhaps recite his latest poem before a critical audience. His endurance and energy, too, were remarkable. I have never known anyone walk uphill so fast and with so little fuss; and he is undoubtedly a master climber. Conventional people have often condemned Hamish (and certain of his fellow-spirits in the Creagh Dhu Club of Glasgow) for being rash and suicidal climbers. This is simply not true, for the very valid reason that, if they were, they could not possibly remain alive and unmaimed today. There is much of the canny Scot in Hamish, and before he embarks on any ostensibly madcap scheme you can be sure he assesses the chances very shrewdly and then takes into full account his formidable personal mountain prowess. This admixture of prudence and enterprise makes him the most exhilarating and reliable of companions on an expedition. Nor has he wife, job or responsibilities to burden his spirit. This makes him the truly archetypal Scottish adventurer, with that love and affinity for wild lands, that sort of yearning which might be expressed musically in the majestic yet harrowing theme chords of Wagner's *Flying Dutchman*. May good fortune walk with this happy man as he clanks off to the hills, his rucksack full of jingling pitons and poetry books.

During our several meetings after we returned, my conversations with Hamish have been far more concerned with future expeditions than past. When, however, we did talk of our shared adventure on Rakaposhi, we seemed to crystallize our feelings in the aphorism of: "Well, we had a bloody good try." Or, as the poet put it:

Ah, but a man's reach should exceed his grasp,
Or what's a heaven for?

19. View along the crest of the S.W. Spur to the summit. The great face of the Monk's Head is obscured by the Gendarme, the first rocky protuberance seen after the snowy part of the spur.

0. Flt. Lt. John Sims, R.A.F.

Mr. Sahib Shah, Surveyor.

Capt. Dicky Grant, M.C R.M.

apt. Raja Aslam, Punjab Regt.

Capt. Warwick Deacock, Middx. Regt.

Lt-Cmdr. Richard Brool R.N.

apt. Shah Khan, Northern Scouts.

Capt. Jimmy Mills, R.A.S.C.

Surg-Lt. Tom Patey, R.

Book Two

The British-Pakistani Forces Himalayan Expedition 1958

Patrons:
Field-Marshal Sir Gerald W. R. Templer, G.C.B., G.C.M.G., K.B.E., D.S.O.
General Mohammad Ayub Khan, H.J.

Chairman:
Major-General J. L. Moulton, C.B., D.S.O., O.B.E.

IX

COMBINED OPERATIONS

Soft!—What are you
That fly me thus? some villain mountaineers?
I have heard of such—Cymbeline, Act iv, Scene 11

THERE is a moment in the course of every expedition when you suddenly find yourself looking forward to the end of it. You have had your fill of danger and discomfort; your beard, which has now lost something of its novelty, has been photographed more than enough. A blizzard is no longer a joyous excuse for a joust with the elements but a cause for delay and imprisonment in a tent. The Sybarite in you cries out for the refinements and sensitivities of civilized life, unnecessary though they are. This tremendous contrast between city and expedition life is one of the most deeply rooted reasons why ostensibly soft, contented and urbane men voluntarily undergo such hardships; the very contrast is the attraction. It is not quite a case of hitting your head against a brick wall for the pure pleasure of stopping; rather is it an over-indulgence in turn of both the Epicurean and the Stoic in yourself so that each is thrown into sharper relief and relished the more.

You will vow that the expedition you are just completing will be your last. You are physically very weary (particularly after a Himalayan expedition) and you plan to eat juicy steaks and drink beer, in a cool climate of course, until kingdom come. And then, after a lapse of time, you observe your fingers flicking over the pages of an atlas in a disinterested sort of way; you might even, almost as an eavesdropper, hear yourself discussing the feasibility of some madcap venture in a very analytical and detached vein. The symptoms are unmistakable: you've had enough steaks and beer, comfort and security, and you are seeking contrast like a drug.

When I returned from my Karakoram expedition in 1956 I had, on the face of it, realized my ambition of exploring in the polar regions and mountaineering in the Himalayas. The Marines had made of me a trainer of climbers and snow fighters; the Corps had gone further and had even enabled me to pursue these two activities to their ultimate, for which I was indeed grateful. My Greenland and Rakaposhi experiences in addition to keeping me fully up-to-date in cold weather and mountain techniques, which were useful in my job, gave me a rare insight into my own reactions to the whole gamut of emotions; fatigue principally, boredom, frustration and hardship often, danger occasionally. This self-knowledge, this revelation of the flaws in one's make-up, is the most priceless acquisition a man can make. Only through the recognition of one's weaknesses can strength be assessed. Only when a frailty is acknowledged may it be fought and conquered. In theory, therefore, I should have returned, at least for a while, to the parade ground or office with a deep inner contentment. And so I would have, had not my defeat on Rakaposhi gnawed at me.

Time and again, with increasing dissatisfaction, I turned over in my mind the events of that day when our attack had faltered at 23,500 feet. Had it really been so dangerously cold? Was the summit really so distant as to make our quest hopeless? I still don't know. What really rankled was that events had conspired to prevent me putting myself to the final test with the mountain. If we had gone on, might not one of us at least have succeeded? Surely Hamish, who had the resilience of a young lion, might have got there. In consequence a sense of unfulfilment and of unease was my legacy from Rakaposhi. I still had a score to settle before I could count my experience complete. I started to feel Ahab-ish about the mountain until the very hump of the Monk's Head, and the surging up-sweep of snow beyond, became my Moby Dick. An urge, a need, to stand on the summit snows of a Himalayan giant or at least to participate in a successful expedition, became my prime mountain emotion blurring the more wholesome aesthetic and physical motives. In this turbulent, almost vindictive, state of mind it was probably as well that the Pakistani embargo on foreign expeditions seemed to have put Rakaposhi out of my reach. I ceased to be specific; any great peak would do, but I must not fail on it. Let Ahab beware Ahab!

Then, during the winter of 1956 (by which time I had passed the steaks and beer phase) the first positive incident occurred which was to spark off the subsequent stream of events. At a Climbers' Club meet in North Wales I fell into conversation with a stranger to me, a regular officer in the Army called Captain Warwick Deacock. He broached the subject of a Combined Services Himalayan expedition. I seem to remember discussing this with him in an impersonal, analytical sort of way (not even recognizing my own symptoms at the time) and thinking it was a splendid idea in which I wished him all luck; and then more or less forgot the idea. But Warwick did not. Some weeks later I met him again when he elaborated his plans. He had thought up the idea of the expedition with another Army officer, Captain Jimmy Mills, with whom he had climbed on an expedition to the mountains of Alaska. They wanted an officer with Himalayan high-altitude experience to join them and probably become leader. Captain Tony Streather of the Glosters would have been their natural choice. Tony had already been on three major ventures, culminating in his ascent of Kangchenjunga, the third highest mountain in the world. However, Tony was leading an Oxford University expedition to Haramosh in 1957, which ruled him out for our expedition in 1958. Major Charles Wylie, of the Brigade of Gurkhas, who had been on the successful Everest expedition was another very suitable person. Again, he was going on an expedition to Machapuchare (22,958 ft.) in Nepal in 1957 so he also would not be free in '58. So I became the interim leader. I say "interim" because there was, until quite late in the game, a chance that Sir John Hunt might join us. Sir John had encouraged our endeavor from its inception, and seriously considered taking part in it if his very onerous duties in connection with the Duke of Edinburgh Award scheme permitted. Eventually he was unable to spare the necessary four months and, instead, spent six weeks climbing in the Caucasus as a guest of the Russians. Needless to say, his powerful support was one of the greatest assistance to us.

As a serviceman himself, the idea of a services expedition had appealed to him and I think it was with genuine regret that he had to drop out. We certainly missed him.

In the early months of 1957 we developed our plans assiduously. This phase of the organization is by far the pleasantest. Only the wider issues are decided, usually in fairly broad terms, and one is not pinned down to specific and mundane details. No one is asked, for instance, how many primus prickers will be needed or how much sugar nine men will eat in four months. An outline emerged: we would attempt a major, virgin peak; we would carry out an incidental scientific programme; we would select two officers from each service, and in addition enrol a medical officer; we would climb in the Karakoram Range in Pakistan rather than the Indian Himalayas.

The idea then occurred to us that, as we were going to Pakistan, why not invite the Pakistan Army to participate on the same scale as the British Army and supply two of their own officers to join us, not merely as liaison officers, but as full and equal members? I wrote to the General Headquarters of the Pakistan Army at Rawalpindi and received an encouraging reply. This Commonwealth aspect was most attractive and, what is more, mutually helpful. We would finance the expedition and provide the equipment, which is not easily obtainable in Pakistan and the Pakistanis would help us not only with local knowledge, but also with certain assistance which their Services could provide, the most useful of which was transport. The whole idea was a happy one and we named ourselves the "British-Pakistani Forces Himalayan Expedition". We constituted, in effect, a small but none the less demanding experiment in international and inter-service co-operation.

Now that we had decided the scope of the expedition we were able to choose our peak. As first choice we selected Disteghil Sar (25,868 ft.) in the Hispar Glacier region. It was one of the highest unclimbed peaks in the world and its ascent would be a glittering mountaineering prize which would reflect great credit on the Services. It is a wise precaution these days when so many expeditions take the field each year (I thought ruefully of the Mustagh Tower) to give the Government of Pakistan an alternative objective in case another party has made prior application for your first choice of peak.

We gave Saltoro Kangri (25,400 ft.) in the Saltoro Range as our alternative. In 1935 Hunt had been a member of an expedition which had almost climbed the peak, reaching a point within a thousand feet of the summit; if he managed to come with us Sir John would be delighted to tackle his old adversary.

Our plans were now concrete enough to put them on an official service basis and it was here at this crucial stage that Charles Wylie really managed to get our expedition off to a flying start. Charles was at that time at the War Office. Knowing that the Chief of the Imperial General Staff, Field-Marshal Sir Gerald W. R. Templer, was always ready to encourage a really worthwhile service enterprise, Charles told the Field-Marshal all about our proposed venture. To our delight the C.I.G.S. warmly supported our plan and commended it to the other Chiefs of Staff, Admiral of the Fleet the Earl Mountbatten of Burma and Air Chief Marshal Sir Dermot Boyle, who also added their blessing. Although these very experienced officers undoubtedly judged our scheme on its merits, it is in the Service tradition to support exploration. The Navy and more latterly, the Air Force, have played a dominant part in polar exploration while the names of Army officers, from its first reconnaissance in 1921 to its successful ascent in 1953, have been associated with Mount Everest.

In complete confidence we were now able to get our organization and planning into top gear. We exercised control by a committee on which the three Services were represented. An officer of the Royal Marines, Major-General J. L. Moulton, the Chief of Amphibious Warfare, kindly consented to become the chairman of our committee. This was a very happy arrangement for not only was the General head of a joint Services organization (which fitted in admirably with the character of our expedition), but he was also a mountaineer himself, being a member of the Climbers' Club. He took a very active part in our planning and soon his office in Amphibious Warfare Headquarters in Whitehall became our nerve center. Two very experienced men at the same time joined our committee. They were Pat Pirie Gordon who had been Treasurer of the Everest, Greenland and Trans-Antarctic expeditions and who guided our financial affairs with sagacity and sympathy, even allowing us an overdraft despite the fact he knew us quite well. George Greenfield became our literary agent, as he has done for many expeditions, and handled the extremely tricky business of selling the expedition story, photographs and film. From my 1956 experience I realized only too well that this is a realm full of pitfalls for the amateur.

The General now invited Field-Marshal Templer and General Mohammad Ayub Khan, the Commander-in-Chief of the Pakistan Army, to become our Joint Patrons; they both graciously accepted. Their support, as much in Pakistan as in Britain, was a great encouragement to us and it proclaimed very effectively the international and joint Service character of the expedition. General Ayub Khan, who has since become President of Pakistan, nominated Brigadier Sultan Mohammad, who was serving at the Pakistan High Commission in London, to represent him on our committee, thus providing us with an expert on Pakistani affairs.

As 1957 drew to its close we made our final selection of members. By then Sir John Hunt had finally decided that he was unable to join us and I was confirmed as leader. Our total numbers would be seven British officers, including a medical officer, two Pakistan Army officers, and one Pakistani surveyor attached to the expedition by the Surveyor-General of Pakistan.

From the Royal Navy I invited my oldest mountaineering friend, Lieutenant-Commander Richard Brooke, to join us. Besides having climbed a lot together, we had also been on a summer expedition to Greenland in 1951 and had been fellow members of the British North Greenland Expedition from 1952-4, sharing many climbs and adventures. After Greenland he had gone South to join Sir Edmund Hillary's party at Scott Base on the famous Trans-Antarctic expedition. By the end of our expedition he therefore had an explorer's unique hat-trick by having visited both of the polar regions and the Himalayas. He is of middle height, wiry and athletic, with the clear grey eyes of a sailor. He joined the expedition under ideal conditions: by that I mean he was driving his dog team in the Antarctic while we in Britain were writing multitudinous letters. He returned to New Zealand from Scott Base and was able to do some training climbs in the New Zealand Alps before catching up with the expedition at Karachi. Richard, as well as supervising our survey program, had the distinction of being our Senior Member of the Alpine Club. When we failed to reach agreement on any subject, such as whether to move up to Camp 1, or whether to have Weetabix or Grape Nuts for breakfast, as a final resort we would refer it to the Senior Member, whose word on these occasions would be final. Richard was wise and clear-thinking; he was also a very shrewd mountaineer with a great deal of experience, especially on snow and ice. He was one of the most valuable members of the team.

Captain Jimmy Mills of the Royal Army Service Corps was a founder member of our venture; in fact, I am not sure that the idea was not his in the first place; he had earlier served as an infantry officer in the Queen's Royal Regiment and the Parachute Regiment. Jimmy had wide climbing experience in the Alps, Norway and the Sinai. He had led two Parachute Brigade mountaineering expeditions, one to the Ruwenzori or "Mountains of the Moon" in 1954 and the other to Alaska in 1956. Being a professional at the task, he looked after the expedition food and, in the fashion of professionals, he made a thoroughly workmanlike job of it. He was wise enough to send us all, in good time, a list of the various rations we would be living on so that we could make constructive criticisms at the time rather than bellyache ineffectively in the field. It is impossible to please everyone, particularly as one's palate becomes finnicky with altitude. I think Jimmy's rations, modelled on solid Army fare, were practical and adequate. His thought, like his movement, was deliberate and sure. There was a relentless strain in him and I never saw him, or can even imagine him, giving up. Whenever I had to make a difficult decision, or to sort out a complex situation, I always sought the counsel of Richard Brooke and Jimmy Mills. Their advice, like their personalities, was clear and unselfish. It is an immeasurable advantage for a leader to have such men to lean on in difficult times. Jimmy and I were also keen cine-photographers and between us we made the expedition film.

It is usually a good thing for an expedition to have a "character"; we had Tom Patey. I had originally been put in touch with him when we were planning in 1955 to go to the Muztagh Tower. I had written to my friend, Ross Higgins, the secretary of the Scottish Mountaineering Club, asking him if "he knew of a good man, who was a good climber, and also a doctor—in that priority". I was told that Tom Patey answered to that description. In the event Tom went to the Mustagh Tower with Hartog, and climbed that formidable peak. In 1957 he was due to undergo his National Service. I watched him like a hawk, determined to get him (with his willing co-operation) into the expedition whichever Service he joined. Not entirely by coincidence he joined the Navy and again, not entirely by coincidence served at the Commando School (later called 42 Commando R.M.) where I myself was stationed and where the Commando climbing school is located. Tom is many things: certainly the most gloriously untidy man I have ever camped with; probably one of the strongest all-round climbers in Britain today; allergic to cooking but not to eating; a lover and maker of all music; Bach, grand opera, the blues; a human dynamo, who somehow contrived to look unhealthy. All of which would combine to make him a very unliveable-with person were it not for his delightful sense of humor. In Tom there is a streak of pure eccentricity for although he is a most striking person he does nothing for effect, and is, I am sure, quite oblivious of his impact on people. His energy was, by our standards, superhuman and apparently little effected by altitude. After a gruelling day he would have a cup of sweet tea and then, while we lay exhausted on our air-beds, would kick snow-steps up the next section of mountainside to make our task easier next morning. He was thin and quite tall but his slightly stooping figure somehow made him look less than his near six feet; his features were rough hewn, like a young Victor McLaglan, and his complexion was a trifle unhealthy, belying his iron constitution. We were amused to hear one of the Pakistani members, early in the expedition, remark to Tom: "I shouldn't go above base camp if I were you, doctor, you don't look too strong!" So, despite the fact that the medical kit was strewn between six camps, and one was quite likely to discover the penicillin in a ration box, Tom with his accordion, his humor and his unbounded and thrustful energy, his kit always overflowing from his rucksack, was a powerful asset. He was, of course, a Scot—a race very dissimilar to the English. Aren't they, Hamish?

Warwick Deacock, with Jimmy Mills a founder member, came

from the Middlesex Regiment, in which he was a regular captain, and was attached to the 1st Parachute Battalion. He had started his Service life in the Royal Marines, serving in the Commandos during the years 1944-7, where he (like myself) learned to climb. He went out of the Service for a few years after that, climbing extensively in the Alps and, when broke, taking odd jobs in France such as heavy truck-driving or laboring in Marseilles. He rejoined the Service in 1951, obtaining a regular commission in the Middlesex Regiment. His soldiering took him to Japan, where he enjoyed some ski-mountaineering and to Indo-China where he was attached to the Foreign Legion and also contrived to get some climbing. His luck, from the climbing point of view, held and he was stationed in Austria for a couple of years, making full use of the Alps almost in his backyard. He had been with Jimmy Mills on the Parachute Brigade expedition to Alaska in 1956 and in 1957 went to Finnish Lapland with the British Schools Exploring Society. Warwick Deacock was tall, dark and handsome; to his expeditions he always brought a sense of mission, a crusading spirit, either to prove himself to himself or to set an example to those "gentlemen in England now abed". In other words he was an idealist. To him fell the task (perhaps worse than procuring the food) of organizing the expedition equipment. His duties were never-ending for in Pakistan porters or villagers never stopped asking for one thing—more! Warwick amassed the ton or so of equipment with military thoroughness and it is eloquent of his efficiency that never, at any stage, were we held up for lack of a vital item. He was the expedition's amateur botanist and could occasionally be observed acting out of character as the big, tough parachutist by browsing among the flowers.

Then there was John Sims, a Flight Lieutenant in the Royal Air Force. John had joined the R.A.F. as a University entrant, going to Oxford and later, in 1942, training as a pilot in South Africa. He qualified as a fighter pilot, seeing war service in North Africa, Italy and Yugoslavia. After the war he went back to Oxford where he took a degree in engineering and became a prominent member of the Oxford University Mountaineering Club. He rejoined the R.A.F. and became a flying instructor on jets; he was also, at one stage, in charge of the R.A.F. Mountain Rescue team at Valley in North

Wales. This team spends much of its time recovering climbers, defunct or otherwise, from the foot of the rock faces of Snowdonia. In 1955 he climbed in the Himalayas as a member of the R.A.F. expedition to the Lahul area. John Sims was a very able and competent all-round mountaineer. He was lightly built, almost gnomish, with quick exact movements, tousled hair, and bright laughing eyes. In the mountains he sported a red wool bonnet with a tassel on top and we immediately nicknamed him "Noddy". John's engineering knowledge was most useful and he became the undisputed king of the primuses and was called upon to solve all our mechanical problems, such as cine-cameras that suddenly stopped working. He was a very experienced outdoor man and if suddenly one wanted a needle and thread or a patch for a leaky air-bed at some high camp it was only necessary to ask John for them. He was self-effacing and unselfish—two qualities that often go together—and time and time again John would quietly get on with some unsavory job which everyone else was studiously shunning. These really solid virtues of mountain competence and public spirit deservedly gained for him the unstinted respect of his comrades. In me he always induced a feeling of humility.

The last man to join the expedition was Dicky Grant, a captain of Royal Marines. Dicky, like myself, was a product of the Royal Marine Commandos and had learned his climbing in the Cliff Assault Wing. His experience was limited to his military mountaineering and snow training and he was therefore the only one of us who had not been on an expedition before. This did not deter me one whit for I had known Dicky for a dozen years and had complete confidence in his ability and toughness. As a Commando climbing instructor he had climbed extensively in Britain; he had also climbed in the Mont Blanc area with the crack French Chasseurs Alpins of the Ecole d'Haute Montagne and had spent long attachments to the Norwegian and Canadian armies for cold weather training. He had served in the Commandos almost continuously since the end of the war and had been engaged with the Queen's enemies in Palestine, Cyprus (where he was awarded the Military Cross), and Suez. Dicky was stocky and well-muscled; he became known as "Commando Dick". He had the brightest of blue eyes, blond hair and a fair complexion which proved an irresistible temptation to every biting insect in Pakistan. He coped manfully with the job of Treasurer in the field, which I foisted on him, but I suspect that he was too full of the love of human nature to enjoy the game of hard bargaining. The man who holds the money should be as flint-hearted as an Income-Tax collector. As a climber, traveller, "snow man", beast of burden or general explorer, Dicky compared most favorably with any of the veteran expedition men among us and this, I think, speaks well for his Service training (and for our own Corps in particular) which is sometimes regarded by the untutored as being wooden or inflexible. Dicky achieved remarkable success in handling villagers. Even though he knew not a word of Urdu he would persuade them to conform to his wishes by smiling at them and bellowing drill instructors' platitudes or vituperation. "Get fell in and we'll play a blinder!" he roared, whatever that phrase might mean. And they apparently did.

These seven climbers formed the British contingent. At the same time the Pakistan Army G.H.Q. in Rawalpindi was selecting the Pakistani members, whom we will meet later. I was well content with the team: our pooled expedition experience was formidable, indeed mondial in its catholicity. Three of us had previous Himalayan experience. It is generally accepted, although there have been exceptions, that a man in his early twenties is not yet mature enough to withstand the mental and physical stresses of climbing at extreme altitudes however brilliant he might be on British rocks, or in the Alps and that the thirties are probably the best age. I was relieved to note that all our team were in their thirties except Tom Patey but, as we have already observed, Tom was a proven high altitude man who did not readily conform to any rules. Tom was the youngest at 26 and I was the oldest at 35. Being all of the same generation, much of the same vintage, and therefore of approximately the same mental and physical maturity, there were no barriers of age between us which might occur in a party containing, say, a leader in his late fifties and a member in his very early twenties. I was very interested to observe the effect on our personal relationships, for good or evil, of this uniformity of our ages, experiences and service background.

There are two sorts of objective a Himalayan expedition may

select: either to explore a little-known glacial area or to attempt a major peak. The first is pleasantly vague, conducive to a good scientific program, and very suitable for a small party, even of limited experience. It is usually thoroughly enjoyable. Attempting a major peak is the big show. It is spectacular, expensive, attracts attention, demands elaborate organization and a strong party (in experience at least if not always in numbers), as I knew to my cost, and its outcome is quite final—either you stand on the summit or you don't. Nobody knows exactly what "exploring a little-known glacial area" means; everyone knows exactly whether or not you have succeeded in climbing your peak. Being a strong party of nine climbers we were obliged to select a major peak as our objective; anything under 24,000 feet could reasonably have been classed as taking a sledgehammer to crush a grape. We found ourselves on a finely balanced see-saw. In order to justify the wonderful backing of the Service Chiefs we ought to choose a mountain which offered more than a fair chance of success. For a worthwhile success, and to employ the full resources of our large and strong party, we ought to tackle one of the great unclimbed peaks of the Himalayas. These two requirements were hard to reconcile. Mountaineering history has shown that, with the glorious exception of the French on Annapurna, an oxygenless party very seldom succeeds on its first attempt on a great mountain. When we chose Disteghil Sar (25,868 feet) in the Spring of 1957 it had never been attempted. With my 1956 failure very fresh in my mind I was more sensitive to the implications of failure than most. If only Rakaposhi were available it would meet our requirements admirably. It was a famous mountain, a high one, but without the repution of being a killer peak. On it I would personally be confident of success.

It was then that we heard that in 1957 British expeditions were setting out for each of our alternative objectives, Disteghil Sar and Saltoro Kangri. Alf Gregory, who had been on the successful 1953 Everest expedition, was leading a party to Disteghil Sar at the same time that the renowned British mountaineer, Eric Shipton, was leading a University party to the Siachen Glacier area with the intention of attempting Saltoro Kangri if conditions were favorable. If both expeditions were successful we would have to select yet another objective. There were no reconnoitred peaks in the Karakorams that I knew of and I suggested throwing a dart at the rather lovely Karakoram map produced by the Royal Geographical Society and choosing the nearest twenty-five-thousand-footer to it! We could only wait and see. I tended to wait and worry.

Late in 1957 the reports of these two expeditions filtered in. Shipton had encountered heavy going in the Siachen area and had not attempted Saltoro Kangri. The expedition did report, however, that the route that Hunt had tried in 1935, and so nearly succeeded in climbing, had looked to be in bad condition and heavily corniced. Gregory also failed to climb Disteghil Sar. He encountered difficult and dangerous snow conditions and was forced back at about 21,000 feet.

In the light of this information I began to relish less and less the thought of gambling our money and reputation on either of these two mountains. The theme "Success with Safety" drummed through my head; there would be little certitude of us attaining either. I began to think again of Rakaposhi. Tony Streather, who had been in Pakistan in 1957 attempting Haramosh—two of his party were killed—confirmed that the Pakistani authorities were still keen on keeping foreign expeditions away from Rakaposhi so that, eventually, it could be scaled by an all-Pakistan party. Was this ban on Rakaposhi, I pondered, utterly irrevocable? It was worth a try.

At a subsequent committee meeting the members agreed with my suggestion to alter our objective to Rakaposhi, if this could be achieved. With the help of Brigadier Sultan Mohammed we made a tactful approach to the Government of Pakistan, pointing out the joint nature of our expedition and asking for permission to try Rakaposhi. You may imagine my surprise when I was informed that a German expedition, led by Albert Bitterling, had already been granted permission to try the peak in 1958! I tried to get in touch with Bitterling via the leader of the German Karakoram Expedition, Dr. Pillewizer, with whom I was in correspondence. I received a reply from the distinguished German mountaineer, Paul Bauer, who was writing from the German Himalayan Institute on Pillewizer's behalf. Bauer assured me that: "*There is* no *German expedition to Rakaposhi. Nobody knows anything about it*, *nor our Foreign Office*, *nor the German Alpine Club, nor we, nor the scientific societies.*" He told me to contact a Dr. Schneider, one of Pillewizer's party, on my arrival in Karachi who would help me straighten things out. It seemed that, if we moved to Rakaposhi, Dr. Pillewizer's team would have more scope for movement in Hunza and Nagyr. It all seemed very straightforward; a matter that could easily be arranged either in Britain, or on arrival in Karachi. We had solved much the same sort of problem in 1956 when three parties seemed to be converging on the Mustagh Tower. It did seem a bit odd, though, that no one in Germany appeared even to have heard of Bitterling's projected enterprise.

It was now early 1958: Jimmy Mills, who was serving in Germany, had received our complaints about his rations, ignored or rectified them, and ordered the ton or so of food we would need. Warwick Deacock had procured the equipment and packed the food. Our stores, two-and-a-half tons of them, were then loaded aboard a frigate, H.M.S. *Loch Killisport*, and taken to Aden. From there they were trans-shipped to a cargo boat and conveyed to Karachi. By the end of February most of our arrangements had been very satisfactorily concluded: our leave had been granted (we were given four months, a month of which was our "privilege" leave, which we surrendered), generous donations had been obtained from the Mount Everest Foundation and the Nuffield Trust, and British manufacturers had, as ever, been most public-spirited in helping our enterprise. We were all tremendously grateful to these anonymous Managing Directors or Sales Managers, many of whom gave their product from a pure motive of generosity well knowing that we could be of little or no benefit to them from the advertising aspect. No British expedition could take the field without this generous, in fact traditional, support from industry. Everything was fixed except the one crucial question of which mountain we were going to climb.

In March 1958, with Dicky Grant to assist me, I went to Norway for three weeks to run a Royal Marines' course of cold weather warfare, more simply ski training. In the cold, exhilarating winter sunshine we skied through forests and across foothills, burying our faces from time to time in the snow; we bivouacked in brushwood shelters, slept in snow-holes, igloos and tiny two-man tents. In other words, we got to know each other well, became very fit, and refreshed our technique of snow-climbing and camping. Dicky's performance in all these activities justified my conviction that the elaborate climbing and snow training he had received in the Royal Marine Commandos more than compensated for his lack of expedition experience.

I was lucky enough to meet my old friend, Henry Berg, who had climbed Tirich Mir (25,263 feet) with the Norwegian expedition in 1950. Together we visited the Romsdal mountains and made a winter ascent (quite a rarity) of Venjatind (6,045 feet). With us was one of our best instructors, my good friend Sergeant Jarvis. In the bitterly cold dawn we skied several miles through woods towards our peak. When the snow steepened we abandoned our skis, Jarvis and I changing our ski-boots for rubber-soled climbing-boots. We plugged our way up 3,000 feet of mountainside sinking up to our calves in soft snow. On the summit ridge the snow became harder and steeper. Jarvis and I brought our ice-axes into use but were surprised to see Berg manage with crampons and a pair of ski sticks. Like most Norwegians his balance and confidence on snow was superb. However, after the climb he discovered that his toes, due to the constricting effect of the crampon straps and the tight ski-boots, were quite badly frostbitten, causing him to hobble around in bedroom slippers for a week or so. Later, during our expedition, I was to recall this lesson vividly.

As there were no less than four officers from the naval service in the final line-up of seven British members, giving us quite a salty flavor, on my return from Norway I called on the First Sea Lord, Admiral of the Fleet The Earl Mountbatten of Burma, who from the outset had shown great interest in our venture. In his office (a sweeping glance revealed Japanese swords, models of ships) Admiral Mountbatten told me how much he approved of enterprises such as the one we were undertaking, rapped a few very pertinent questions, and offered any personal help he could provide. Then, his fingertips together, he swung round in his chair to face me and the First Sea Lord was metamorphosed into the ex-Viceroy. He gave me much good advice about the Gilgit Agency we were about to visit and wished us luck.

On the same day I met Field-Marshal Templer for the first time. Crossing Whitehall from the Admiralty I walked into the War Office by the main entrance. A certain mystique seems to be associated with these portals through which normally only a few very senior officers and certain equally illustrious civil servants are vouchsafed to pass. As I entered, the hall porter, by his bearing quite obviously an old soldier, advanced with an expression on his face that indicated that he was going to throw me out—in the nicest possible way. When I murmured the Field-Marshal's name, his already stiff back straightened imperceptibly and I was ushered in. The Field-Marshal, who had taken an intense and personal interest in our doings, was warm, direct and helpful, particularly in the vital matter of changing our objective to Rakaposhi. He also told me that by a coincidence General Ayub Khan was in London and a meeting between our Patrons and the expedition members was arranged to take place a few days prior to our departure. This was a very happy arrangement and the meeting again took place in the War Office. (I was almost blasé as I walked through the famous doors this time!) General Ayub Khan also threw in his weight behind our request to go to Rakaposhi, and this combined support was later to be of the utmost value. The General also told us that, in order to help us get news of our progress to the outside world, he would let us have a Signals Detachment from the Pakistan Army at base camp. Finally, as if this were not enough, he donated two thousand rupees to the expedition funds. This was the first indication of the quite superlative support we were to receive from our Pakistani brothers-in-arms.

This felicitous meeting ended in an orgy of Press photography during which I noted that only the Press may take liberties with the great, herding the Patrons into groups at one end of the room, then the other, here adjusting the position of an arm, there pushing a shoulder into a more becoming posture; enough to make an old soldier tremble.

X

RETURN TO RAKAPOSHI

. . . but surely we are brave
who take the Golden Road to Samarkand.
—James Elroy Flecker.

THE morning of Friday, April 25th was bright but cold. A chill east wind was sweeping Lyneham aerodrome where the R.A.F. Comet was standing on the tarmac, looking powerful and elegant in readiness for its flight to the East. In the passenger reception room the six British expedition members (all of us except Richard Brooke) occupied themselves with desultory talk and last-minute crises. Did anyone really know if the total expedition film stock had been sent to Pakistan? No one could reply, so we consoled ourselves with the thought that it just must have; it was too important not to have gone!

A reporter from a large national newspaper came up and asked me:

"Why do you climb mountains, Captain Banks? What is the thing inside you that makes you do it?"

This, first thing in the morning, when I was well and truly committed to climbing them, and had been for many years, was too much for me.

"Oh, God, I don't know. Can't you ask me something about the equipment. We're taking a baby portable tape-recorder, you know."

I escaped to mumble farewell platitudes to my wife and to read the telegrams of well wishes which had been sent by the Chief of Air Staff, the R.A.F. Mountaineering Association, Sir John Hunt and the Commandant General of Royal Marines, General Hardy. A B.B.C. television team lured us out onto the tarmac, beside the Comet, to record an interview. This was pure misery. A strong and icy wind cut through the tropical uniform we were wearing (El

Adem was only four hours' flying away). After a while the cameras and recorders were set up satisfactorily and we were ready to start. Inevitably at just that moment an aircraft on the tarmac started to run up its engines. We crouched out of the wind and I chatted to the cameraman, Eddy Smailes, who had shared some adventures with me when he had been a newsreel cameraman covering the opening phases of the British North Greenland Expedition. On that occasion someone had almost talked him into crossing a glacier and meeting a ship. It was just as well he declined because in the event the ship never arrived and Eddy would have spent an involuntary year in the Arctic with us. By the time our reminiscences had ended, the aircraft had stopped making a noise and I shivered and stuttered my way through a T.V. interview. At the end of it a very important looking person in a bowler hat came up to the B.B.C. interviewer and asked him to do it again because he had used the expression "raff" instead of the more correct R.A.F. But by then it was too late anyhow.

A last good-bye and we were imprisoned in the luxurious interior of a V.I.P. Comet. What a difference to the familiar bucket-seats of the Dakotas of Transport Command of the old days. As the civil Boeing and Comet jets come into service with the airlines, jet flight will, I suppose, become a commonplace thing. But there is always a first time, and this was my first jet flight. The seat really seemed to push me in the back as we accelerated down the runway, and then we proceeded to climb at an impressively steep angle, nose high, until we were around 40,000 feet and cruising at a silent and comfortable 500 m.p.h.

In little over four hours we landed at El Adem, in Libya, where we stayed the night. El Adem had all the impersonal unfriendliness of any transit camp. The surrounding country, flat, unattractive scrub and desert, looked fit only for war. Somehow we had contrived to get a couple of cases of milk stout into the roomy underbelly of the Comet. We therefore demolished these in the course of a planning session. We allocated jobs and responsibilities to be undertaken at Karachi and somehow learned in the course of the business that Tom Patey was absolutely petrified of snakes. He implored us not even to joke about them.

This was also our first real meeting as a team, even though our two Pakistani members and Richard Brooke were absent. I therefore took the opportunity to expound my views on the form of leadership I proposed to employ. Our party was nine strong, quite large in fact. This implied that people would inevitably become scattered and would have to receive orders which they had had no opportunity to discuss. We would work therefore on the understanding that we were all of much the same age and experience and that no one's personal opinion was more significant than that of the next man. We would make our plans by general discussion with everyone possible available, thereby utilizing the combined experience of us all. I would sum up the substance of our discourses and announce the plan. Members who were absent from these discussions, and received the plan of action in the form of orders, would obey them cheerfully in the knowledge that they were *vox populi*. With a team of individualists of the same age, experience and background this form of democracy, a sort of government by Assembly in the style of the ancient Greek Polis (where every free citizen was a complete man) seemed apposite. Finally, and most important of all, I emphasized that I took neither the job nor myself over-seriously. Shipton might even have approved!

We took off for Bahrein next morning. I spent a few minutes in the cockpit while John Sims, an instructor of jet pilots, tried to explain what the forest of dials and knobs meant. My impression was that jet controls are even more complicated than the ordinary piston aircraft, which are quite incomprehensible anyway. I noted that the outside temperature was minus 55 degrees F., which was a degree colder than I had experienced on the Greenland ice-cap. We landed at Bahrein, with Jimmy Mills still in battledress, looking terribly British and extremely uncomfortable. Dicky Grant and I, the two Marines in the team, managed, without any effort, to maintain the Corps tradition that it is practically impossible ever to get two Marine officers to dress alike, except on rare parade occasions.

Karachi was little over two hours from Bahrein by Comet. Having had a good night's rest, and having travelled for a total of only about twelve hours, we arrived in Karachi fresh. This would certainly not have been the case had we travelled by the usual "milk run" by tourist-class airline. We were given a V.I.P. reception at Karachi Airport. This means, in effect, that the immigration and Customs officials come to you instead of you going to them. Because none of us are V.I.P.s or ever likely to be, we were most impressed by this reception. An official photographer took pictures of us with Colonel Azizur Rahman who was in charge of the civil airport, and then two officers from the Ministry of Defense ushered us through Customs to some awaiting vehicles which conveyed us to the Pakistan Air Force Station at Mauripur, where we were accommodated in fine style in the Officers' Mess. We were absolutely delighted with this warm and friendly (and beautifully organized) reception. As the days passed we were to come to realize that this efficiency and hospitality was typical of all the Pakistani Services with whom we were to co-operate.

I cannot overstress, or be too enthusiastic about, this support we received from the Pakistani Services. For instance, at Karachi not only were we allowed to live in the P.A.F. Officers' Mess, but we were not permitted to buy a single thing in the mess—not even a drink; everything was given free. In addition two taxis were put at our disposal to use in Karachi to arrange the many points connected with our move up to Rawalpindi and on to Gilgit.

Expeditions will normally find that they have business to do both at Karachi and Rawalpindi. We therefore split the party at Karachi. Jimmy Mills, with Dicky Grant, Tom Patey and John Sims, flew up to 'Pindi in the weekly P.A.F. Bristol Freighter on May 1st. At 'Pindi Jimmy fixed up our liaison with the Pakistan Army, welcomed Captain Raja Mohammad Aslam into the team, arranged the many details of food and equipment involved with our signal detachment composed of a *Lance Naik* (Lance Corporal) and two signallers who were to accompany the expedition, ordered the porters' food which we were to collect at Gilgit from the Service Corps, and still found time to do some fitness training with the Pakistan Army team which was training for the Asian Games in Tokyo. In 'Pindi they encountered at General Headquarters exactly the same friendly help which we had earlier experienced from the Ministry of Defense in Karachi.

Back in Karachi Warwick Deacock who, it will be remembered,

was looking after our equipment, and I were having our own problems. We had consigned from Britain 45 crates which had been conveyed to Aden by the frigate, H.M.S. *Loch Killisport*. They had been taken on at Aden by S.S. *Nowshera*. Unfortunately *Nowshera* only discharged 43 of them at Karachi. Warwick Deacock and Dicky Grant had spent some hot and frustrating days in the Karachi docks searching barges and godowns (warehouses) for the missing items. In this they were assisted by the Karachi representative of the Himalayan Club, Mr. W. A. Brown of Imperial Chemicals. Mr. Brown put at the disposal of the expedition one of his staff, Mr. A. C. Collett. Now Collett had been a Customs Officer in Karachi so what he did not know of the intricacies of Karachi docks and shipping was not worth knowing. Some detective work on Collett's part revealed the two crates to be reposing at Bombay in the custody of a branch of the same shipping agents we were using at Karachi. To make things worse the crates contained some survey equipment vital to the scientific program. When this was explained to the agents, together with the fact that the crates had been misdirected by their own inefficiency, we were simply told that the cases would be retrieved at some future date, by sea, and at our expense. I wrote a personal letter to a very famous shipping man in London and handed the Karachi agents a copy. The crates were flown to Karachi from Bombay the following day.

I also called on Air Commodore Maqbool Rabb, the acting Commander-in-Chief of the Pakistan Air Force. He was as charming as he was helpful and indeed could not do too much for us. Through his offices we had our complete expedition stores, two and a half tons of them, flown up to 'Pindi and then on to Gilgit by special Bristol Freighter. Warwick Deacock, who still had the responsibility of stores like an albatross round his neck, flew up to 'Pindi in this special aircraft leaving me in Karachi to cope with the few outstanding problems. One of these was our film which had been shipped from Britain later than the remainder of the stores and in a different ship. The situation was complicated by the fact that there was a grain shortage in Pakistan at the time and extra grain ships had been rushed to the port. The result was that there was a considerable delay and a modicum of confusion at the unloading wharves.

This is where Collett swung into action. He located the ship, arranged with the Chief Officer that a special effort should be made to locate our crate and within 24 hours duly produced it. With staggering *expertisme*, and with a fistful of forms covered with hieroglyphics at all the right places, he slid this through Customs in a matter of minutes. I knew from my 1956 experience that had I been conducting this transaction it would have taken me a very minimum of three days. In all this Collett was assisted by a remarkable little Pakistani. A single glance at this man was all that was needed to disclose that he burned with a bright and gem-like flame. His protruding eyes glowed with keenness and anticipation, his speech bubbled out of his mouth, one word hurrying the next, his thin arms gesticulated. He forced everyone who came within his orbit to do three times as much work, three times as fast, as normal —and most of it unnecessary. Before him the most lethargic of officials was spurred reluctantly into action. To his energy and Collett's experience the expedition owes a real debt. Unfortunately these symptoms of unnatural energy in our Pakistani friend were diagnosed by Tom Patey as probably being an over-active thyroid gland. So our poor little friend was burning the flame of his life too quickly; sadly we reaped the benefit.

The question of the expedition objective was my chief preoccupation in Karachi. We had left Britain under the impression that there was definitely no German expedition to Rakaposhi and that it would be a simple matter of a few days to alter our objective from Disteghil Sar to Rakaposhi. As Paul Bauer had suggested to me in his letter, I contacted Dr. Schneider on my arrival in Karachi. From him I learned the somewhat astounding news that in Germany they had only heard of the Bitterling expedition when I had relayed to them the news I myself had received from the Pakistan Ministry of Kashmir Affairs. It seems apparent that this expedition was organized more or less in secret without the German Himalayan Institute, Alpine Club or scientific societies being informed. If this is so (and on the surface that is how it appears to me) it is a rather sad reflection on the internecine factions and dissonance in German mountaineering: and they address each other as *bergkamerad*!

The situation was that Bitterling definitely had permission for

Rakaposhi, we were given permission for Disteghil Sar and the German Pillewizer expedition to Hunza had permission withheld. We had a three-cornered meeting at the Ministry of Defense, presided over by Commander Hameed, Pakistan Navy, and attended by myself and a representative from the German Embassy. The German representative was asked to find out within forty-eight hours whether or not the Bitterling expedition was in fact coming. On my part I asked that we might try Rakaposhi before the arrival of the Germans in late July or August. The Ministry of Defense was scrupulously fair in keeping to its word and giving Bitterling priority and every chance to go to the mountain if he wished. However, when no answer was received after eight days the Ministry gave us permission to go to Rakaposhi on the understanding that we would withdraw if the Germans ever showed up. As a curious sequel I received a letter from Bitterling saying that he was not coming but that three other German climbers were, sailing from Italy on July 30th. He asked if these three might join us. Three people attempting Rakaposhi in August or September did not seem a very wise plan to me. Because they would arrive after we had left I had to refuse his invitation.

At the Ministry of Defense I thanked Major-General Malik Sher Bahadur for all the assistance he had given us. He had now provided us with all the ingredients of a safe and successful expedition: the rest was up to us—and Rakaposhi. I found it both easy and refreshing doing business at the Ministry of Defense with officers of wide experience who were capable of giving crisp decisions. I hope General Sher Bahadur will not mind if I say that standing in his office before his desk, addressing the trim military figure in uniform very similar to our own, I felt just as if I were at home.

On the very day that I obtained permission to go to Rakaposhi and extracted the precious film from the ship a cable arrived from Brooke saying that he was flying up from Bombay. I went out to the airport to meet my oldest mountaineering and expedition friend. I soon spotted him among the disembarking passengers looking spare and fit after his year in the Antarctic. We exchanged inadequate platitudes over the gulf of the Customs barrier and were soon in a taxi talking expedition shop at a rate of knots. Was the Arctic as cold as the Antarctic? What was Ed Hillary like as a polar man? He too had some kit problems: some of his gear was coming air-freight from Bombay and could not be located. This was chicken-feed to Collett and his small Pakistani fire-cracker and the kit was duly located and sent on to us.

The next morning Brooke and I were away (thanks, I suspect, to Squadron Leader Siddiqi who had been making all the flying arrangements for the expedition) in the routine Bristol Freighter which calls at Peshawar and 'Pindi. Facing me in the aircraft on take-off was the Pakistani champion squash player. I think he was frightened by the terrible din the Bristol engines make, for he broke out into a terrible sweat until we joked him out of it.

I turned to my neighbor, a Pakistani Flight Lieutenant, and asked him if we were to be given breakfast on the aircraft.

"I do not know," he replied, "but in any case you shall have half of mine." This unimportant remark, this small gesture, seemed to me typical of the attitude of the Pakistani Services towards us. They were a new country but willing to show unlimited generosity and co-operation to anyone willing to meet them on equal terms.

In 'Pindi I reported to Brigadier C. H. B. Rodham—or "Roddy" as he is universally known. Roddy had been a regimental officer in the Garhwalis before the war. He had been in the retreat from Burma and had fought his way back in again as a brigade commander. On the partition of the sub-continent in 1947 he, together with a number of other Indian Army officers, had opted for service with the Pakistan Army and had served with them ever since. Now, when he spoke of "us" and "our army" he referred to the Pakistanis and not the British. The Pakistan Army is modelled very closely on the British and these ex-Indian Army officers, working under new masters but in little altered circumstances, continue to render loyal service.

Himalayan expeditions came under Roddy's wing and we found that he had got us splendidly organized. He had already sent the remainder of our party on to Gilgit, again by special Pakistan Air Force Bristol Freighter. Brooke and I, after fixing a few details (Brooke being our surveyor called on the Survey Department in the Murree hills, forty miles away) arranged our own flight to Gilgit.

We were scheduled to fly on May 10th, but a low bank of clouds discernible on the northern horizon warned us that flying conditions over the Himalayan foothills were unsuitable.

Because of the inherent danger of the flight the weather must be perfect at both ends of the hop before an aircraft is allowed to take off. At least that is the theory.

Richard Brooke and I kicked our heels for a day. I awoke at dawn on Sunday, May 11th, and walked outside my room at the Signals Officers' Mess and scanned the horizon to the north. It appeared cloudless but slightly hazy.

Some hours later we were chatting to the pilot, Flying Officer F. Hussain, and his aircrew as the plane was loaded with drums of oil and some of our expedition equipment. I mentioned to Hussain how glad I was that there was to be a flight that day because the whole expedition was jacked up at Gilgit, only waiting for Richard Brooke and myself. Once we arrived we could start the approach march.

We took off and flew north. The Bristol Freighter, as Hussain explained to me, is horribly noisy but gratifyingly reliable and powerful. Having made the flight in 1956 I was looking forward keenly to seeing again the stupendous view of the isolated mass of Nanga Parbat, but as we picked up the great Indus valley the clouds clamped down and I became fairly certain that Hussain would turn back. However we roared steadily on just below the cloud ceiling which must have been at about 13,000 feet. This meant that we could not take the direct route over the Babusar Pass which is 13,690 feet. Instead we followed the sinuous length of the Indus gorge. On each side of us minor Himalayan peaks, up to about 18,000 feet, pushed their heads up into the clouds. Of Nanga Parbat there was not a glimpse. Ahead of us, near the village of Bunji, the cloud was even lower and I marvelled that Hussain was forcing on. I worried a little as well because if he were forced back there was little room to turn in that narrow valley.

We flew through the bad weather and soon I recognized the greenery of Gilgit, many miles ahead, standing out as a livid verdant patch among the uniform brown of the stark and waterless Kara-koram. We ran in, losing height, and I recognized the fort in the

Northern Scouts barracks and a summer-house by the river in which I had stayed.

A strong and gusting wind obliged Hussain to fly up the valley and make his run in from the north over a small hill, a tricky approach unbeloved by pilots. At the moment that he touched down he must have been caught by a powerful gust, for the aircraft made a prodigious bounce. These things, I understand, usually go in threes, and our next bounce again threw the aircraft high into the air. By this time I was sweating. I knew the airstrip very well and the thought flashed through my mind that if we were not firmly on the runway by the time the control building flashed by my window we would be precariously near the cliff-rimmed and fast-flowing Gilgit river. I looked across at Richard; his face was taut. True to form, we stayed down after the third bounce, I glimpsed the control building and heard the wheels grinding into the gravel of the airstrip as the brakes were applied. I hadn't been very keen on a dip in the river, anyway.

"Gawd," I said to Richard, "were you worried too?"

"You bet. Mountaineering's safe compared to this," he replied, now with a relaxed grin.

We all got out of the aircraft and the airport officer walked over towards us.

"I'm going to charge you for three landings!" he joked to Hussain. I thanked Hussain for having flown through such rotten weather.

"I thought you would have turned back near Bunji," I said to him.

"I would have done if it was a routine trip but you said the whole expedition was waiting for you so I forced on," he replied. I thanked him even more. Here was another instance (I will never tire of relating them) when a Pakistani Serviceman went right out of his way, and on this occasion took quite a risk, to help us along. Whether or not we got up Rakaposhi, this Commonwealth co-operation would be a reward in itself. About three or four days of bad weather followed, which stopped all sorties to Gilgit, making us truly indebted to the aircrew of that Bristol Freighter.

A jeep drove up to take us to the Northern Scouts mess where the remainder of the expedition was waiting for us. The drive refreshed old memories: the roads shaded by graceful willows, the water runnels whispering busily, the crowded bazaar with its jumble of Gilgitis, Hunzas, Chitralis, Pathans, refugee Kashmiris and Turkis, the latter almond-eyed with smooth light complexions and, often, beautiful Kashgar silk for sale. This was central Asia; almost Tartary. As I drove along I noticed, without much pleasure, that the snow was lying on the containing valley walls of Gilgit, hillsides which had been dry and brown on our arrival in 1956. There had been some very heavy snowfalls in the late spring, and summer was late in coming, bringing the snow line down to about 11,000 feet. In 1956 it had been nearer 15,000 feet. The implications were grave: we might not be able to get the villagers up to base camp. They could not sleep out in the snow, neither was their clothing suitable for travelling through soft snow.

At the Northern Scouts mess at Gilgit I met for the first time our Pakistani members: Captain Mohammad Shah Khan of the Northern Scouts, Captain Raja Mohammad Aslam of the Punjab Regiment, and Sahib Shah, our surveyor.

Captain Mohammad Shah Khan, or Shah Khan as we called him, was going to be a great asset to the team. He was a Hunza man and in fact was an uncle of the Mir of Hunza. He had hand-picked our six high-altitude porters, all of whom he knew personally. This was going to be of immeasurable value during the expedition for he could speak to them in their own language, keep them fully informed of what was going on and, very important, if they had any grievances or uncertainties, he would hear about them, and settle them at once, before they could assume serious proportions. Trouble between members and porters, which is distressingly common, is almost always the fruit of the language barrier. We would be delightfully free of these worries.

Shah Khan, who was a wiry man of middle height and light complexion, had gained considerable expedition experience, particularly with the German expedition led by Rebitsch which had looked at Rakaposhi in 1954 and then operated in the Batura Glacier area. He had climbed high on this expedition. Also, he had run courses in ski-ing and mountaineering for the Pakistan Army. Add to that the fact that in the course of his duty as an officer of the Northern

Scouts, and also on his numerous hunting trips, he had travelled high and wide in the Gilgit Agency, and it will be realized how lucky we were to have so talented, experienced and influential an officer with us. At Gilgit Shah Khan introduced us to the six Hunza high-altitude porters he had selected for the expedition.

Captain Raja Mohammad Aslam we quickly nicknamed "Raja". He was a strapping officer of six-feet-three and came from the Punjab Regt., where he had been Adjutant of his regimental depot. He had visited Gilgit previously when he had undergone a mountaineering course run by Shah Khan. His mountaineering knowledge was rather scant but he was fit and keen. He was an excellent organizer and was very helpful in arranging the host of details both at G.H.Q. in Rawalpindi, and with the military authorities in Gilgit.

Sahib Shah, a Pathan from Peshawar, was one of the most experienced surveyors in the Department of the Surveyor-General of Pakistan. He had been on several previous expeditions including Rebitsch's in 1954 and Tony Streather's to Haramosh in 1957. He was wise in the way of expeditions and settled in with us very easily. He had a warm and friendly personality, was full of chatty amusing conversation and had long dark eyelashes any girl would envy. We liked Sahib Shah immensely, principally, I think, because he was always ready to muck in with us and share our chores or relaxations. He was really one of us. He also attained a height of over 19,000 feet—which is quite something for an alleged non-mountaineer.

The Pakistan Army signals detachment had also joined us by this time. Lance Naik Zaffarullah, a sturdy and intelligent young N.C.O., was in charge. With him was an operator to work the set and a technician to maintain it.

Finally there was Ashraf Khan, a piratical-looking old orderly with culinary pretensions who Dicky Grant had, literally, popped into the aircraft at 'Pindi at the last moment. Ashraf with his toothless grin, monotonous chiding voice, illusions of past grandeur when he had served with British regiments, with his cooking, occasionally superb usually only just edible, served as the general expedition whipping-boy. All our ills could, with some ingenuity, be laid at his door so that when we reviled him for his latest atrocity (undercooked mutton, overstewed tea) he was probably performing the very useful, but hardly enviable function, of absorbing much of the ill humor we might otherwise have lavished on each other. Poor old Ashraf. In some ways his popularity, or otherwise, was a reflection of the morale of the expedition. We could suffer him best when we ourselves were cheerful.

But on the night of May the 11th at Gilgit these considerations were in the future, a future made exciting by the uncertainties of the adventures inevitably ahead of us. My last-minute packing completed, I made my way over to the mess for supper: whisky followed by curry followed by whisky. I remember sitting out on the lawn, as big tropical stars rose above the snow-speckled black and white of the hillsides and the more distant whiteness of unclimbed peaks obtruded into the sky. Then, through the flower-scented air, came the unmistakable skirl of pipe music. I find this, Sassenach that I am, the most emotional of sounds. These airs, the 92nd's Farewell, the Road to the Isles, so appropriate in a Highland mess were one of the more odd legacies of British India of pre-partition days. In this little frontier station of Gilgit, at the meeting point of Russia, China, Afghanistan and Pakistan, almost the hub of Central Asia, this music suddenly came home to me making the hairs on the back of my scalp tingle. It helped me shrug off memories of tedious desk-bound bureaucratic planning in Britain, hot rounds of offices and docks in Karachi and 'Pindi. It came to me with a jolt that these days were over; ahead was adventure, fatigue, danger perhaps, and above all, Rakaposhi, strong and impassive, huddled there ready to test our puny strength, flaunt our weaknesses or punish our foolishness.

The following morning we said good-bye to Lt.-Col. Muzaffar, the Commanding Officer of the Northern Scouts. This regiment, which was raised after partition, is really a corps of frontier guards organized militarily. Colonel Muzaffar had provided a fleet of jeeps with trailers to take us along the Hunza road to the village of Nomal where we would cross the river by rope bridge and follow the same route that we had used in 1956. At the bridge Shah Khan had arranged for a hundred villagers from Matum Das to meet us and carry our stores up to Jaglot (see map 1, page 34). We proposed to use the same base camp site as before.

One of the less apparent advantages of being a traveller is that you have a steadily increasing number of places to revisit. It is true that going back to a place lacks the wonderment of first sight but this is compensated by the little thrills of pleasure derived from each view, or person, recognized and associated in the mind with past experiences. Hence I refreshed my memory at every turn of the road as it wound round its precipitous rock buttresses high above the Hunza river. We drove without halt past the Rest House of Nomal and on to the bridge, the same one no doubt that we had used before because traditionally these contraptions are only replaced when they break, the economy no doubt justifying the occasional watery demise.

It was noon on a scorching hot day, the sun beating down on the bare rocks and reflecting back mercilessly, when we arrived. We then allocated loads, with the usual prolonged arguments over wages and weights customary in the East. Warwick Deacock had had a hundred or so little metal discs made, each with a number on it and a string attached so that it could be hung around the neck. One was given to each villager, the number and description being noted so that the load could be checked on arrival at the other end. This was a sensible and practical idea which only went awry when the family donkey was used to carry several loads or when Grandfather spread his load round the less distinguished members of the family. These villagers were, once again, utterly honest (a virtue far from universal among the Himalayan hillmen) and we had little to fear. The discs, none the less, were worn with pride and amusement, hanging round the men's necks alongside the Moslem prayers on a similar piece of string. The river was, comparatively, very low, indicating that the snows were only just beginning to melt; later the river would be a raging torrent.

In dribs and drabs the villagers started off towards Jaglot in the late afternoon with the result that darkness caught us on the river bank, in a patch of fields and trees, about five miles upstream just below the hillside which lies below Jaglot. The convoy was hopelessly spread out, so we camped among the bushes after a mere half march. This was probably, in retrospect, not a bad thing. We gently stretched our leg muscles, and exercised our rucksack-carrying shoulder muscles, in preparation for more strenuous days ahead. We also organized our camping and cooking routine.

In the cool of the following morning we zig-zagged up the hill track, passed under a wooden arch and arrived in the green sanctuary of Jaglot. I hurried on to the village where I met many old friends including Sadi Kali, the veteran of Tilman's and Band's expeditions of 1947 and 1954, and our mail runner of 1956, who agreed to do the job again this time. At the village we had to pay off the Matum Das men and take on another hundred Jaglotis. A large field in the middle of the village was used as a parade ground and the business was conducted with expert help from Shah Khan. It turned out that there were not enough Jaglotis available to carry all our stores, so we had to retain about twenty Matum Das men.

While this *bandobast* was being negotiated we rested in the shade of an orchard and made coffee. When the village *lambardar*, or headman, was offered a cup, he replied (more or less) in Urdu: "Thanks a lot, but I won't. I might catch something nasty from the cup. You can't be too careful these days, old man!"

Shah Khan was welcomed in Jaglot where the villagers kissed his hand and called him *Huzoor*, or Lord. He was presented with a young bullock by a village elder. This, by local custom, he accepted graciously and then immediately returned to its owner.

It was a clear day and Rakaposhi was easily visible above an intervening ridge, our first sight of our objective. As soon as possible we started up the valley with the intention of reaching the pine forest of Darbar by evening. From Darbar base camp could be attained in one day—or so we thought. The walk up to Darbar was most enjoyable, at first anyway, as we passed green fields with young crops, then followed a stream, criss-crossing it on rustic wooden bridges. We then walked the length of a flat bottomed valley strewn with the sort of large round stones the size of rugby balls sometimes found on beaches. This was quite tiring to unfit muscles. We then climbed a hillside and entered the pine forest of Darbar. The glade in which we proposed to camp was at the far end of the forest. Evening was advancing and the pines seemed never ending. The altitude, now approaching 10,000 feet, also took its toil, so that by the time I arrived at the forest clearing at the head of the convoy, the villagers were well and truly spread out.

Soon we had a large camp-fire burning as groups of men drifted in, dim shadows sliding out of the darkness, their off-white Hunza hats and *chogas* (homespun cloaks) looming ghost-like against the blackness of the trees. They made their fires in village or family groups and soon *chappatties*, their staple food, were baking. There were about seven absentees, seedy elders of Jaglot who were not quite up to the strain of load carrying. Dicky Grant organized a rescue party and disappeared into the wood to carry the loads in for these unfortunates. This he accomplished successfully.

After supper Shah Khan called some of the Matum Das men round our fire to sing and dance. Their rhythms, beaten out by handclaps to accompany the songs, were sharp, excellently timed and most appealing. Their dances, mostly posturing with great emphasis on exact and significant foot movements, were graceful, dignified and very formal. We were able to retaliate when Tom Patey produced his accordion and John Sims did a Highland Fling. With tired bodies, and breathing the pine-scented air, we slept well that night.

Next morning was cold and rainy. The valley walls, only a few hundred feet above us, were snow-whitened; base camp would be four thousand feet higher and under deep snow. In these conditions base might well be more than a day's march away, and beyond the ability of the crudely clad villagers. We then discovered that the unfortunate Matum Das men had now run out of food. We therefore sent all the villagers home to give us time to carry out a reconnaissance and, if necessary, pioneer a track through the snow up to the site of base camp. The season was late, we were early; there was no reason for haste.

For almost a week we dallied at Darbar, and a very pleasant week too. We walked towards base camp and confirmed that snow was thick on the ground about 1,500 feet above us. We were consoled by the knowledge that a couple of days of fierce Himalayan sun would roll the snow-line back up the hillside with remarkable speed. It was all very different to last time.

One evening Shah Khan pointed out some markhor, a breed of

wild mountain goat, on the rock-face above camp. They would have been a most welcome addition to the pot as well as a prized hunting trophy, but they were gone next morning before he could set out with a gun. We also shook down as a party, this being our first opportunity of really getting to know each other. We made ourselves comfortable, erecting a brushwood shelter as a mess room. Old Ashraf, the cook, walked around wet to the skin and looking miserable, stoutly asserting that he had never been drier or happier. He must have been feeling the altitude and some of us wondered whether he was going to die, if not here then certainly at base camp. He was about sixty years of age and can only be described as scrawny. A medical examination by our doctor, Tom Patey, gave him no grounds whatever to expect longevity. It was during our halt at Darbar that I gave old Ashraf his first lesson with a pressure-cooker explaining, with the aid of Raja as a translator, exactly how the thing worked. I repeated the lesson, with Ashraf setting the controls. He obviously did not understand a word because during the whole time he was with us he abused the gadget, filling it, for instance, almost to the brim with some substance such as porridge which swells to several times its dry volume. The cooker positively throbbed, but Ashraf remained blissfully unaware how often he came close to an ignoble, food-spattered death. He must also have been puzzled why the British from time to time would examine the pressure-cooker, then do a dance of mixed fear and rage, mouthing incomprehensibly.

With Tom Patey and Dicky Grant I walked up above Darbar towards the site of base camp to examine snow conditions. The weather had remained bad and we were soon soaked in a cold downpour of rain. We passed the highest summer pasture and shepherd's hut and climbed the boulder-strewn hillside above it. Here we met knee-deep snow which, obviously, would get deeper towards base. Reckoning that at least two days of sunshine were necessary before the journey to base could be attempted, we walked back to Darbar. Avalanches of new snow were cascading off the hillsides; the mountains were not yet ready for climbing.

For a couple of days fingers of cloud entwined themselves through the trees and there was a steady drip-drip of rain from the pines.

Now that the villagers had gone down we had enough tentage to get everyone under canvas so that despite the storms, this was a pleasant hiatus. There were new toys in the equipment to play with. I started to use a lightweight, battery-driven tape-recorder for a diary instead of a notebook, and found it effective. In the mess-tent I noticed that Raja, with good mess manners, tended to hang back politely when meals were served.

"Raja," I said to him, "there are two sorts on an expedition: the quick and the hungry. Get stuck in!" Which he did.

The Signals Detachment demonstrated its ability to look after itself. They had been quick to notice disused shelters behind some trees and had quickly occupied them thus enjoying roomier, drier living conditions than the rest of us. Lance Naik Zaffarullah was obviously the independent, self-sufficient type who would look after himself and his men in primitive conditions without making a fuss. He got his set on the air and I passed my first message from the field, telling how we were held up and why. They used an American Army transmitter, power for which was obtained by means of a hand-cranked dynamo. The advantage of this hand-crank was that a petrol generator (with its petrol and oil) and heavy batteries were unnecessary. The wireless and generator were easily carried, making a light, mobile and efficient unit. I had assumed that Zaffarullah would pass his messages to the Northern Scouts H.Q. at Gilgit, some twenty-five miles distant. I was most impressed when he told me that he would be sending the messages direct to G.H.Q. at Rawalpindi, about 200 miles away. I am happy to report that these arrangements worked admirably and it was a point of pride with the detachment, even if it took them all night, that they cleared perfectly every message I handed them.

I think we were the only expedition that ever had transmitting facilities to the outside world, although numerous expeditions have had "walkie-talkies" for use between camps and also ordinary receivers for picking up weather broadcasts and ordinary radio programmes. These facilities enabled us to keep the Public Relations Directorate at G.H.Q. supplied with a steady stream of up-to-date bulletins which they in turn released to Reuters and Radio Pakistan. News of expeditions usually reaches the public by runner and airmail so that it is several weeks old, and therefore stale from the press point of view, before it is available to the public. Our news was always "hot". We have General Ayub Khan's brainwave to thank for this.

We also used the wireless to receive weather forecasts. A special forecast was broadcast each day for the benefit of the Austrian expedition attempting Haramosh, our neighboring peak. G.H.Q. kindly obtained copies of this forecast and transmitted them to us. These forecasts, particularly from the long-range aspect, were most valuable.

A fine day lured people out on training walks, the most popular of which was to ascend the caudal end of the North-West Ridge which swept up close by and gave splendid panoramic views of our proposed route, the South-West Spur. A second day of peerless weather sent the snow-line rolling another five hundred feet up the mountain and we sent down for the Jagloti porters to get them to come up to us at Darbar (10,000 ft.) and carry our stores up to base camp (14,000 ft.).

The Jaglotis arrived at nightfall on May 17th. I was always somewhat surprised by the confidence with which these men would travel over rough tracks by night until I remembered how spoilt we Europeans are with our urban habits and ubiquitous street lights. We have almost forgotten what darkness is. It was a lovely night, the pines sharp against a tropical sky big with stars, the glow of the fire playing on the trees and highlighting the faces grouped round it. Two sheep had been brought up and a further regular supply of two each week had been assured by the headman. We had dried all our sodden kit and were fit and keen to go.

That evening one of our spontaneous jazz sessions broke out. Tom Patey must have been in his "New Orleans" mood for he began playing a selection of blues on his accordion. Jimmy Mills, I think it was, took up the rhythm with an aluminium plate and spoon. Dicky Grant and Tom started to sing in their best Alabama accents. Soon everyone was carried away by the music, banging and singing. We had numerous subsequent sessions such as this, which did enormous damage to the cooking utensils, causing Ashraf to look even more funereal. This uninhibited outburst by allegedly

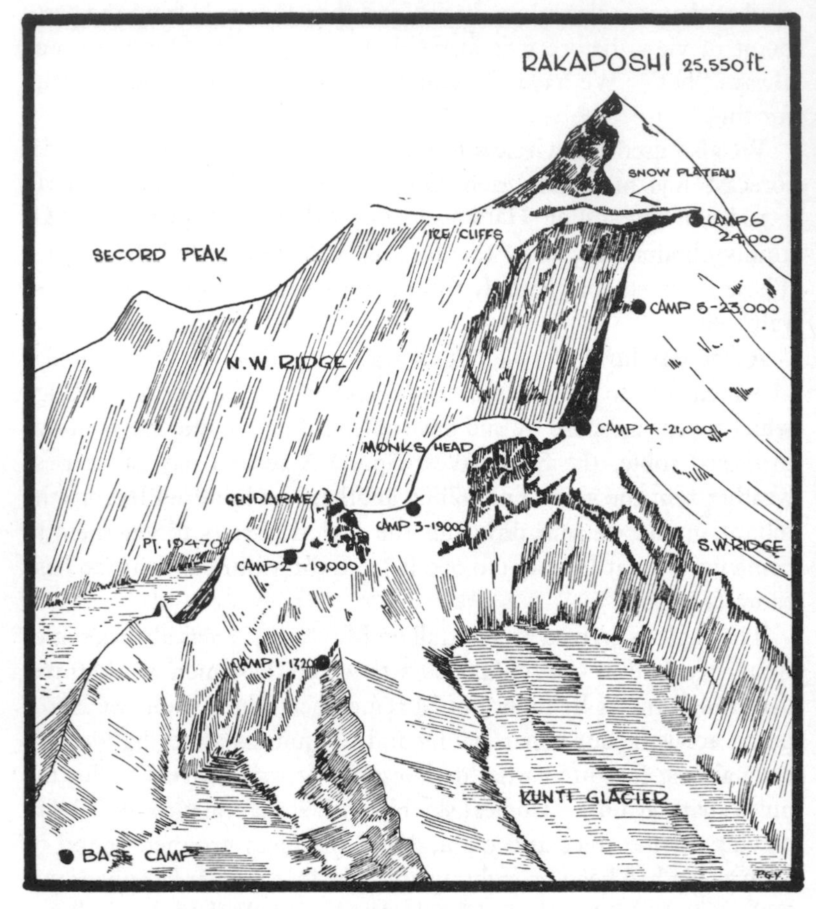

Map III

Sketch of the S.W. Spur of Rakaposhi, showing the main features and the camps of the British-Pakistani Forces Himalayan Expedition, 1958.

straight-laced and conventionally decorous British officers was deliciously out of character.

While Shah Khan, Jimmy Mills and Warwick Deacock organized the move of the Jaglotis up to base, I planned to go on ahead with Tom Patey and two porters to work out a new Camp 1 and a short-cut to the main ridge of the South-West Spur (see Map III, above). It will be recalled that in 1956 we gained the ridge at a col at the foot of a snow peak marked Point 19,470 on the map. It was on the traverse of this peak that almost every member had nearly come to grief as a result of a fall. In retrospect I considered it both a dangerous and an unnecessary peak to traverse. In 1956 Hamish MacInnes and I had spied out a short-cut which we considered a considerable improvement on the old route. It involved an upwards right-slanting traverse almost directly towards the Gendarme. Not only would it be shorter and safer but it would also cut out the switch-back caused by Point 19,470. It is always irritating to have to lose height in the Himalayas after it has been gained with such toil. Equally, it is most unwelcome to have to climb upwards during an alleged descent. So we would be well rid of Point 19,470 and our notorious "Road to Rakaposhi" if we could work out a successful short-cut.

Consequently, on the morning of May 18th while Shah Khan was organizing the Jaglotis and Jimmy and Warwick weighing and arranging loads, Tom and I, with Akbar and Bul-Bul, swept out of camp, feeling full of go. A minute later I swept back again to pick up my hat that I had forgotten, and swept out again. It was a perfect day for travel: clear sky, cool sunlight, fit bodies. We emerged from the forest, noticed as we crossed it that the stream was swollen with the sun-melted snow, and climbed the broad scree hump to the upper pasture and hut. The boulder-strewn hillside beyond which had been deep in snow a few days earlier was now dry and easily passable. We climbed it and followed the crest of a sharp rib of moraine which clung to the side of the rock-covered and crevassed glacier. Stopping now and then for chocolate or photography, and enjoying every minute of our walk, we at last came to the thousand feet or so of loose scree which led up to the site of base camp. This section had half killed us in 1956. Now we took it in much better form although there was a period that was trying, when the wind dropped and the sun beat down.

At length we sighted the tall, slim cairn Bob Swift and Dick Irvin had built. At 14,300 feet snow was everywhere and we had to scrape away at it in order to pitch our two tents. After a cup of sweet tea Tom and I still seemed to possess some surplus energy so we walked another 800 feet up the mountainside to a large, isolated boulder from which we could study the flank of the South-West

Spur and work out our short-cut. We both agreed that it was feasible and thought that we could discern a slight nick in a ridge about 3,000 feet above us which offered a possible site for Camp 1. The ridge itself seemed to lie back at an easy enough angle to guarantee the sort of unexciting climbing desirable on a porter route. Confident that we had solved the morrow's problems we returned to base.

When I recalled how, in 1956, we had all been utterly spent when we arrived at base camp I was most satisfied with our performance on this occasion. It was evident that I was far better acclimatized this time. Tom, also, felt that he was going far more strongly than he had been at a comparable height on his 1956 expedition. This improvement is attributable either to our period of acclimatization at Darbar or to the theory, widely acknowledged, that a man goes much better in the Himalayas after his first season.

Before we set out from camp again next morning we erected a framework of four long poles to show the main body where base camp would be situated and to give them a bit of encouragement. On the top of the poles I hung a pair of Hamish's old gym shoes that I found. It is revealing that when Hamish abandons anything not even the poorest villager thinks it worth recovering!

We took with us the two Hunza porters, Akbar and Bul-Bul. Akbar was the oldest of the porters, perhaps forty or so years of age (there are no birth certificates in Hunza and people guess at their age), and he had been appointed *Sirdar* or headman by Shah Khan. He was a courteous and obliging person, but not quite strong enough a personality for a leader. Bul-Bul was the toughest of the porters. He had a muscular frame, a strong and hard-looking face with a hooked nose, and a great fund of determination. We were lucky in the fact that all our porters had been on previous expeditions.

We got away early and made steady progress, walking on the firm, hard-frozen snow. We soon passed the boulder we had reached the evening before and made for the foot of the ridge on which, higher up, we planned to place Camp 1. We reached the ridge by a col at the snout of a glacier which ran down from the Gendarme, and then we took to the mixed snow and rocks. As we made height we slowly revised our somewhat premature dismissal of the ridge as an easy snow plod or rock scramble. It was much steeper than it

21. Shah Khan and his Labrador, "Rusty" who followed him up to Camp 1 (17,300 ft.) and became the top dog in Pakistan.

22. Descending the second step beyond the Gendarme.

23. The summit of the Gendarme. Note the face mask and the marker sticks in the rucksack. Camp 2 lies in the dip of the snowy ridge in the middle foreground, among pinpoints of rocks.

24. The summit of Rakaposhi from the "Notch".

25. Deacock, followed by Banks, climbing the corniced ridge of the S.W. Spur. Note the long peg in Deacock's rucksack used for securing fixed ropes into the snow.

had appeared and the snow was lying on rock slabs. As the day warmed up we slowed down, the snow softening and becoming unstable. Tom, who had been in the van the whole time, forced on in front working like a Trojan at his step-kicking. The porters, feeling the altitude every bit as much as we did, lagged a long way behind so that I took up the role of connecting link between Tom ahead and them behind, contriving to keep both in sight. When the ridge became steeper, the sun hotter and the snow more treacherous, we were forced to rope up.

We went steadily on for hour after hour, looking desperately but vainly for a patch of snow, a mere five feet by eight feet, at not too steep an angle where we could scoop out a tent platform. Towards one o'clock we were getting extremely tired and the snow was so unstable as to be positively dangerous if we attempted to return over the same route. At last, after seven hours of hard going, we came to the easement or nick in the ridge we had noticed from below. In a snow-bank under a boulder we hacked out a tent platform and brewed a cup of sweet tea to revive ourselves.

We proposed to remain in the camp and investigate the route up towards the crest of the South-West Spur some 2,000 feet above us, on the morrow; Akbar and Bul-Bul we would send down at once. The solution for the descent was easily and obviously solved. From the nick in the ridge where our tent stood pitched, was a snow-gully running down towards the broad snow-basin we had crossed early in the day. This gully viewed *en face* had looked prohibitively steep whereas the ridge, which was foreshortened, looked quite easy. The reverse was actually the case; it is very easy to be misled looking up the great hillsides of the Karakoram. The top section of the gully was indeed steep but we minimized this difficulty by hammering a piton into the boulder under which our tent nestled and suspending a rope from it which reached down the steepest part of the gully. The porters lowered themselves down the rope and slid the next couple of thousand feet down the hillside in a sitting glissade. We watched them until they attained safe ground. The gully was obviously going to become the highway to Camp 1—if the upper part of the route to the ridge also proved satisfactory.

We cooked a meal of meat bar, cheese and butter, all mixed

together, on Tom's primus, which leaked fumes slightly, and we then passed a comfortable and warm night in our double sleeping-bags insulated from the cold of the snow by air-mattresses. I always suffer from sleeplessness when I first try to sleep at a high altitude, so for the first night or two, until I become acclimatized, I take a sleeping-tablet, as I did on this occasion.

Snow fell during the night and was still falling at daybreak. Both of us awoke with agonizing headaches which were much sharper than the common altitude headache with which we were both familiar and which, with me, never persisted more than the first few hours after arrival at a certain altitude. Tom suspected some form of poisoning from the fumes escaping from the leaky Primus, and I think he was right. We were incapable of eating breakfast (porridge and tea) or indeed of moving until about ten o'clock. By then there was about a foot of new snow on the ground, and it was still falling. We ascertained that the route above us, leading up to the crest of the ridge, was more than reasonable and we then descended the fixed rope into the gully in which there was much new powder snow which seemed quite liable to avalanche.

Tom was about a hundred feet below me as we climbed down the gully, facing inwards and kicking our boots well into the under-layer of hard snow. Cloud was swirling, reducing visibility. Then, after a while I looked down but of Tom there was no sign. I shouted but heard no answering shout. I scanned the mountainside far below in case Tom has risked starting an avalanche and had glissaded. There was no little black figure to be seen against the uniform chalk white below me. With a jolt it came to me that Tom must have either been caught by, or caused, an avalanche and he was now probably buried, perhaps suffocating, under several feet of loose avalanche debris somewhere on the snowfield below. The implications drummed through my mind: first, I must be in equal danger so I must quickly move from the center to the side of the gully to get out of the natural avalanche track; second I myself *dare not*, on any account, get caught by another avalanche or there would be no one to bring the tidings and organize a rescue party. I felt half sick with the responsibility.

I crossed to the side of the gully where an avalanche would probably by-pass me and I took from my rucksack a long ice-piton which I used, dagger-like, to stab into the snow to give an extra point of adhesion. I moved slowly and carefully, pausing from time to time to shout, whistle and examine the snow for a black dot. An hour must have passed and I resigned myself mentally to the certainty that Tom had had an accident. What a grisly start to the expedition!

A little lower down I rounded a corner and, with something of the relief of a parent finding a temporarily lost child, spotted Tom toiling up towards me. We exchanged inarticulate bellows.

"Thought you were in an avalanche," I shouted when we got within range.

"Thought you were in a crevasse. Was coming back to find you," he shouted back.

So we had each been quite unnecessarily worried stiff about the other for the last hour. It was amazing how, in my own mind, the character of the slope changed once I saw Tom safe. Until then it had been an evil integument of snow just waiting to disintegrate and hiss under my feet to sweep me so softly down the slope to a cold, gentle and perpetual sleep. Now it was a frolicsome slide down which I slithered carefree on my backside.

"Hell! Am I glad to see you," we said to each other when we were together.

XI

THE SIEGE IS LAID

A land of leaning ice
Hugged by plaster-grey arches of sky,
Flings itself silently
Into eternity—Hart Crane.

TOM PATEY and I continued on down together. We had found a satisfactory site for Camp 1 and it seemed reasonable to assume that the route above Camp 1 up to the ridge crest of the South-West Spur was climbable.

At the site of base camp there was a bustle of activity with porters arriving, stores being sorted and tents being erected. From Shah Khan and Jimmy Mills I learned how the move had been executed. At Darbar there had been something over a hundred loads but only fifty-five villagers to carry them, with an imponderable and quite unpredictable additional number of donkeys, small boys, or heroes who would carry a double burden for double pay. In the prevailing snow conditions base camp was more than a reasonable day's march away and because the porters would be required to make two carries to base it was important that they were not worked so hard on the first lift that they were unwilling or incapable of repeating the performance the next day. It was decided, therefore, to make two short lifts up above Darbar on the first day: this would place all the stores within a reasonable day's march of base. In two lifts these stores would then be carried up to base camp. This plan was agreed to and, in fact, worked.

Thus on the third day, May 20th, the last loads were being carried in to base as Tom Patey and I came down from Camp 1.

Jimmy Mills told me about the more racy and colorful characters among the porters. There was The One-Eyed Riley with a piratical black patch over one eye; "Elvis Presley", with a low sibilant voice and something of a sense of humor; Shylock, a grasping villain with two donkeys surpassed only by Fred the Monster who had three donkeys and was always asking for more and more loads only to find that his unfortunate beasts could not carry them. They needed a bit of urging at times, Jimmy explained to me, but as before they had carried well and, most important of all, had been scrupulously honest. A pay parade with much bargaining followed during which Dicky Grant's fund of rupees and tolerance was strained, but found adequate.

The various military brains in the party sorted out the two and a half tons of heaped equipment and food and by evening a regular little township of ten tents, shelter for no less than twenty-one men, nestled under the brown cliffs of the South-West Spur: the fourth base camp to be sited there. A freshly slaughtered sheep (killed in the Moslem way, its throat slit as "Allah Akbar" (Allah is Great) was intoned) hung from a sheerlegs of poles; neat stacks of food boxes and jerricans of paraffin made their appearance on the moraine; a large mess tent, with a kitchen annex for Ashraf, was put up. Snow was a foot deep on the ground and the many rivulets coursing down the hillside had not yet made up their minds where they wanted to meander. The weather was cold and cloudy and living conditions, generally, too damp and soggy for comfort. None the less, we had arrived intact and in good time. The too-frequent snowfalls brought the snow-line low and did not produce the best of conditions for our climb; one decent fine spell would put all this right.

That evening after our first supper in the mess tent, and assisted by a bottle of whisky which was passed round, I expounded my plan:

"Everyone got a tot? Good. Look, what I suggest is more or less this. We'll do a slow, cautious build-up to the foot of the Monk's Head at 19,000 feet. The old principle of 'carry high, sleep low'. Each camp must have a tent, stove, and a full 16 man/day ration box in reserve in case anyone gets storm-bound there. On this lower part of the mountain I'd like the Hunzas to do the heavy work so that we can save our strength for the top. We'll build-up slowly to the foot of the Monk's Head where we'll gather in strength with masses of reserve food so that even if the whole party is stormbound there for ten days we will be able to sit it out. In other words we will use siege tactics below the Monk's Head. Above it we'll use rush tactics. With six Hunzas carrying loads for us we ought to be able to get eight of us camped at 21,000 feet on top of the Monk's Head with eleven days food and enough tents for three camps. Above the Monk's Head three giant steps of about 1,500 feet each lead up to the summit. We'll need three days of good weather to climb these three great steps. On the first good day eight of us will go up the first step, four of us acting as porters. This will enable four men to camp at 23,000 feet. This is where our top camp was in 'fifty-six. To be quite sure that the summit pair can make it it is essential that our top camp this time should be one step higher, that is at about 24,000 feet. So the four men camped at 23,000 feet will carry up again the next day leaving two of them camped at 24,000 feet. This pair ought to be able to knock off the summit on the first fine day. We've got thousands of feet of fixed rope. Let's use every foot of it. It makes life easier and safer, especially for the porters. On the lower section Tom and I are fairly certain the short-cut will go above Camp 1. One thing I want to emphasize. Once above the Monk's Head we're committed to a 'set-piece attack', to use military jargon. Once we are launched nothing must turn us back. We must bash through to the summit in accordance with the plan—flat out! If we get good weather, who knows, we might even get a second rope to the summit.

"I'm sorry to have inflicted a speech on you all. Unless anyone has any violent disagreement, that's the plan and for goodness' sake let's stick to it if once we agree to it."

There was a murmur of assent.

"Jimmy, you can pick the bones out of what I've just said and work out how much food we'll need at the various camps?"

"O.K., Mike. I'll get together with Warwick on the equipment side and we'll work out exactly how much food and gear has to go to each camp. Logistics, we call it in the Army," he replied.

"Suits me," said Warwick, "good job you've just passed the Staff College entrance exam, Jimmy."

"Shah Khan," I added, "there will be a tremendous amount of

gear to go up to Camp 1. It is the bottom layer of the pyramid, as it were. Something around fifty loads. Do you think you might recruit half a dozen Jaglotis to carry up to Camp 1 and speed up the porterage? We've got some spare boots and windproofs for them."

"I'll see the headman and fix it. I think it will be all right," he replied.

This is the general manner in which we ran our affairs. Once I had crystallized the outline plan, which we had probably been discussing for days, I found myself wonderfully relieved of responsibility. Jimmy Mills and Warwick Deacock, working patiently with pencil and paper, would transform my "masses of reserve food", for instance, into orderly lists of rations and equipment. If the expedition did run "like a military operation" (in its best sense) then Jimmy and Warwick were largely responsible for the behind-the-scenes organization. Shah Khan, assisted by Raja, was absolutely invaluable in seeing that the porters played their part in the plan. He attended to their many wants, kept them fully informed of what was going on and, as often as not, led them himself on the difficult sections. Tom Patey, an almost unbelievable fount of energy, closely followed by Richard Brooke and John Sims, would almost literally hurl himself at the immediate mountaineering problem, his lone figure, with his long-legged stride becoming a familiar sight in the van, usually half an hour ahead of the rest of the convoy.

Without any fuss, or much ostensible delegation of responsibility, everyone took on a key job to suit his experience or personality. Each found that he was playing a vital part of his own choosing in our adventure. By a happy accident there were no clashes of interest or, more unpredictable, of temperament. Personality problems are far harder to solve than mountaineering ones. I thanked my lucky stars that we seemed to have all the ingredients of a harmonious party: that is unless temperament, for some mysterious reason, appeared at altitude.

A few days were needed after our arrival in base to prepare the food and equipment for the six camps we would be pitching. John Sims, for instance, had a field day with the primuses. For some reason I have never been able to comprehend silent burners will operate at any altitude with an ordinary-sized nipple whereas a roarer burner will not. John, therefore, surrounded himself for two days with multitudinous bits of stoves and at the end of it produced the right numbers of the right sort for every camp. Warwick Deacock and Jimmy Mills, having worked out their logistics, proceeded to sort out the correct quantities of stores to implement the plan. And all of us in turn spent about an hour a day trying to tell old Ashraf how to make tea. Water (but not washing-up water) had to be brought to the boil, then tea added, then, almost immediately afterwards, the pot removed from the fire, we explained. Ashraf, that great traditionalist, won hands down. He listened with many a "yes, Sahib", "*accha*, Sahib" and "*thik hai*, Sahib" and then, utterly unperturbed, dished us up with the same brew of black and sour tea that the Colonel Sahib in the 68th Durham Light Infantry had got in 1927. After all, what was good enough for the Colonel Sahib ought to be good enough for this scruffy looking shower. Only Dicky Grant and Tom Patey found favor with Ashraf.

"May Allah grant you good promotion," he said to them, adding to Dicky: "Allah will make you a brigadier general."

We had with us Nadir Aman, a porter who had been with me in 1956. Unfortunately his family was involved in a law case that was shortly due to come up before the Mir of Hunza and he regretfully had to leave us. In his place Shah Khan managed to recruit from Matum Das, the nearest Hunza village, a man called Guliami (immediately nicknamed Gor Blimey!) who had expedition experience.

Our intention was to pioneer the route from Camp 1 to Camp 2 as soon as possible so that, while the Jaglotis carried loads up to Camp 1 the Hunzas, living at Camp 1 should immediately take them on up to Camp 2. Stocking camps is like building a pyramid: the bottom layers are the largest. By this combined porterage we hoped to build the two bottom layers—the two largest layers—of our pyramid in record time. And so it would have been had it not been for the weather. Travellers generalizing about Karakoram weather (a somewhat rash thing to do), say, as a rule of thumb, that phases of four days of storm and eight days of clear weather are the pattern. This had been borne out by my 1956 experience and we now looked forward to alternate storms followed by even longer periods of fine weather. During our two months on the mountain the weather never once conformed to the expected pattern. We had neither long storms nor lengthy fine spells. But we were not to know that at this early stage and Tom and I, the Karakoram veterans, kept assuring the others that a fine spell was inevitably on the way which would melt and compact the new snow, stopping the avalanches and producing an excellent climbing medium. Eventually we resigned ourselves to desultory snowfalls and half-hearted sunshine and made the best of conditions.

Tom Patey and Richard Brooke went up to Camp 1 during the first patch of reasonable weather, planning to prove the route upwards towards the ridge and to find a site for Camp 2. Above Camp 1 they made slow and difficult progress in deep and steep snow. They did not quite gain the ridge but reached a thin sliver of rock sticking out of the hillside which we called the Shark's Fin. They could see the remainder of the way and pronounced it climbable. It was a great relief to me to know for certain that the short-cut was feasible.

Meanwhile the six Jagloti villagers had arrived and we fitted them out with windproof trousers and boots. We gave some of them ice-axes and the remainder made do with wooden staves. The carry from base to Camp 1 was the longest of the lifts between any of the camps, being about 3,400 feet. The route led up the mixed scree and rock hillside above base camp, followed the edge of the Kunti glacier, and then sloped diagonally upwards across a broad snowfield. This snowfield then narrowed into a gully which led in 1,000 feet, to the notch in the ridge where Camp 1 was placed. The upper part was very steep. The Jaglotis felt the altitude on the first day and we let them stop 1,000 feet short of Camp 1 so as not to force them up the final steep section of the gully, which might have frightened them off. They went up again the next day, escorted by Raja who, at the beginning of the difficult part where we had placed fixed ropes, gave each Jagloti one of the doctor's pep tablets. The result was electric. They went up like the clappers, disdaining our assistance even on the last hundred feet which was extremely steep. Shah Khan taught us how to say "Jaglotis are strong men" in the local dialect and we shouted this at them. We took the loads from their backs as they heaved themselves over the lip of snow at the head of the gully and gave them cigarettes and tea. Then with one hand casually on the rope they launched themselves happily into space and slithered down the slope to base.

The build-up of Camp 1 went splendidly for the next five days, Hunzas and Jaglotis working together. On one occasion Shah Khan's yellow Labrador, "Rusty" accompanied his master to Camp 1. How he managed to scrabble up the top, icy section of the gully I cannot imagine. None the less at 17,300 feet he was top dog in Pakistan that day.

While these activities were going on Richard Brooke and Tom Patey were persisting in their attempts to climb up to the ridge and to safeguard the route by means of fixed ropes. In the unsettled weather with its almost daily snowfalls this was a difficult and dangerous task. On May 26th they had fixed ropes up to the Shark's Fin which was about 500 feet below the crest of the ridge. They climbed towards the crest and had reached a point within a couple of hundred feet of it, having taken Dexidrene tablets to counter the fatigue caused by slogging through deep snow at 19,000 feet. They noticed as they ascended that the snow, which was for once hard and brittle, rang hollowly under their feet. Then, without warning or noise, the whole surface of the mountainside for hundreds of feet around them broke and slid with increasing velocity down the mountain. They plunged their ice-axes into the snow up to the hilts and hung on grimly. Luckily for them they were on an ill-defined ridge which served to deflect the snow into channels on either side of them. The avalanche passed and they were left safely clutching their life-saving axes, badly shaken by their escape.

"This place is distinctly dangerous. I propose that we turn back," Richard Brooke enunciated slowly and calmly in his best quarterdeck manner. Afterwards he could not recall having uttered this utterly British remark. But retreat they did, at full pelt.

Down at Camp 1 where I happened to be, we could vouch for the size of the avalanche when two great lobes of avalanche debris the size of a football field came to rest on the glacier a few hundred yards from camp. It had been a "wind slab" avalanche, that is an avalanche composed of the upper crust of snow which had been blown hard and compacted by the wind and was lying insecurely adhered to the firmer snow beneath. Once again we vowed to wait for the ever-imminent fine spell before we again tackled this tricky section. We all retired to base where we paid off the Jaglotis with sincere gratitude for their assistance in accelerating our build-up.

These incessant snow-storms, in addition to making base a cold and cheerless place, would obliterate all the steps which had been kicked in the snow slopes with so much toil, making a repetition of the labor necessary. As an example a slope which might take six to seven hours to flog up in new deep snow could be climbed, once the steps were made and a fixed rope placed, in about two hours.

A blue sky and a favorable weather forecast on June 1st saw a renewal of activity. Richard Brooke, Tom Patey, John Sims and Dicky Grant, a stout quartet, went up to Camp 1 determined to open the route to Camp 2 if it were humanly possible. June 2nd was also a good day, so we assumed they would be successful in their route pioneering and the rest of us, including all the Hunzas, moved up to Camp 1 in anticipation. Our hunch was justified, for shortly after we arrived at Camp 1 we espied the outline of a tiny figure standing silhouetted on a prominent rock island on the ridge about 2,000 feet above us. When the four of them came down they confirmed that the route had been opened, the steps kicked and the ropes fixed. Mild excitement had been caused when a small wind-slab avalanche had broken away at their feet, but the threat was not enough to deter us from using the route.

The next phase of the build-up was for Jimmy Mills, John Sims, Warwick Deacock and myself to establish Camp 2 and rope the Gendarme while Shah Khan supervised the Hunzas as they stocked Camp 2, living the while in Camp 1 ("Carry high, sleep low" again).

Consequently the four of us, accompanied by the Hunzas, climbed up to the ridge in perfect weather on the following day. Had the long-awaited fine spell at last arrived? If so we would force on to the foot of the Monk's Head just as soon as we could.

The route from Camp 1 up to Camp 2 was consistently steep but never very steep. Over a thousand feet of fixed rope led directly up the snowfield. Being able to hang outwards on the rope and use the arms to assist the feet greatly lessened the toil. As we ascended first Nanga Parbat appeared beyond the murk of the Indus valley, then

Haramosh and Dobani popped up their heads above the intervening South-West Ridge. I felt very little altitude effect and enjoyed the day thoroughly. The fixed ropes terminated at the crest of the ridge. The slope here was steep and we tied onto a climbing rope to move along to the isolated rocks we called Rock Island.

Here we started to excavate the snow to hack out tent platforms. There was a layer of ice underneath so that we labored long and hard before we had cleared space enough to pitch two small two-man tents. The porters returned to Camp 1 with the intention of carrying another load up the next day, when we would be climbing along the ridge and roping the Gendarme.

Camp 2 was a spectacular place, with its tremendous views from Nanga Parbat in the South right round to the Hindu Kush in the dim distances to the North-West. The two tent platforms were dug into the side of a respectably steep slope so that the moment a person emerged from a tent he was on a snow climb. This was convenient in so far as one could stretch one's hand out of a tent door and with a flick of the wrist jettison rubbish directly down the hillside. John Sims, to his everlasting shame, while spending a penny more or less suspended in space, relaxed his grip on our one and only toilet roll and saw it career a thousand feet down into the depths trailing a merry white streamer. Luckily I had in my rucksack a copy of *The Times Weekly Review*, printed on thin air-mail paper.

With the help of sleeping-tablets we slept well enough on our first night at 19,000 feet. John Sims and Warwick Deacock both suffered from a certain amount of tooth trouble which can be very jading at any altitude. We dosed Warwick with antibiotics in the hope of dispersing any abscesses.

The following morning we had planned to climb along the ridge and place fixed ropes on the Gendarme which was about a mile distant. The Gendarme, though not a large feature, was, as I well knew, the steepest single step on the whole climb to the summit. It had been snowing most of the night and was still snowing when we poked our heads out of the sleeve entrances in the morning. It is not usually wise to climb during, or immediately after, a heavy snowfall so we bided our time. The weather during that day was extremely odd. The stratus clouds in which we were enveloped would occasionally lift enabling us to see under them all the way to Nanga Parbat, some sixty miles distant. Normally the weather is bitterly cold at this altitude during a snowstorm. Now, however, we experienced the odd combination of a stifling, sultry day with, at the same time, snow falling heavily out of the clouds. The tents were airless ovens. There were periods when the sky was clear and blue above us yet fine particles of snow fell out of the empyrean. I had previously experienced this phenomenon on the Greenland ice-cap and Scott had remarked upon it on the South polar plateau.

If that day was too unsettled for climbing the next was incomparably worse. Visibility was bad, occasionally as low as ten yards, and a strong wind was drifting the snow. Obviously the snow would take several days to come into condition, so we prepared to retreat to base down the fixed ropes (God bless them!) in keeping with our principle of riding out storms at base if possible where we would not deteriorate physically or consume the precious food which had been carried high up the mountain. Imagine our surprise, therefore, when out of the storm emerged the dim figure of Shah Khan closely followed by five Hunzas bearing loads. This was a redoubtable performance on Shah Khan's part, forcing his way up the mountain with loads in weather that we considered bad enough to justify our own retirement to base.

"Good show!" we shouted to Shah Khan, and "*Shabash*" or "Well done" to each Hunza as he lurched over the steep lip of a cornice a few feet below camp.

"I went in front and told the Hunzas that if I thought it was O.K. they were to follow," explained Shah Khan. And, of course, the Hunzas had complete faith in their leader and had followed happily up the ropes despite the dreadful weather. It was so bad that we stuck to our plan of returning to base. I remember our descent very clearly: ten figures groping through the storm, ghostlike in the cloud and drift and whitened by the blowing flakes or by tumbles on the ropes which half covered us with snow. Down at Camp I the Hunzas made us tea and gave us some cold roast chicken. While we continued down to base Shah Khan said he would wait one more day and if the weather did not then clear he also would descend with the Hunzas, and with Raja who was also with him.

So the four of us from Camp 2 slid down the fixed ropes in the gully. This descent from Camp 1 to base offered the longest glissade, or snow-slide, I have ever experienced—a full two thousand feet. Half-way down the gully I let go of the fixed rope and sitting down, with my axe jammed under my arm as a brake, I let myself slide. I swooshed down the first thousand feet in fine style but then the slope grew less steep and I kept stopping. To increase the area in contact with the snow and thus to lessen friction, I placed my rucksack on my chest and lay flat and stiff as a board on the snow. Acting as a human ski I was able to get under way again. This was an odd sensation, lying flat on my back, cruising down the mountain at a steady six miles an hour with my hood pulled over my head and only a soft hissing of the snow and the slow movement of the sky above me to tell me that I was in motion. I could have been stretched out on the beach for all I was doing about it.

A vile night followed, the snow continuing throughout the next day. Avalanches began to fall, making us a little worried about Shah Khan and his party up at Camp 1. We fervently hoped he would not repeat his feat of yesterday by climbing up to Camp 2 again. He would be safe if he stayed put at Camp 1, which was pitched on a ridge and was therefore clear of all avalanche tracks.

We were just finishing a cold and mournful breakfast when we felt the mess-tent buffeted by a sudden and strong gust of wind. We thought the tent was going to blow down and we grabbed the poles and door-flap to stop the whole thing being blown away.

"It's an avalanche," shouted someone, and indeed we realized that this was the wind, loaded with snow particles, that an avalanche drives ahead of it. The air was filled with snow dust and we waited for the deluge of snow to strike us. It never did, but when we went outside we saw that the avalanche debris had stopped a mere twenty yards short of the camp. The force of the gust had snapped several of the guy-ropes of the tent. This made us more than ever apprehensive about the men up in Camp 1, and we prayed that they would not budge from the safety of their tents.

At about eleven o'clock that same morning of Friday, June 6th, someone spotted a figure emerging from the white swirl of snow and cloud on the slope above base, and raised a shout. What had brought them down in this weather? Were they safe? I was half sick with doubts and worry.

"*Thik Hai?*" we shouted interrogatively as the first man came within hailing distance.

"*Sabchise thik*, Sahib"—"Everything is well, Sahib," came the reassuring answer from the leading Hunza.

Soon they were all in and we learned that the whole party had been struck by a heavy avalanche while descending the gully below Camp 1. A certain amount of equipment, mostly ice-axes, had been lost and there were some cuts and bruises, notably Ali Gohar, who in addition to the resident carbuncle on his chin now had a cut jaw, a loose tooth and a broken finger. Tom Patey disappeared into the Hunzas' tent with his medical kit to treat them. They were all wet to the skin and suffering from varying degrees of shock.

In the mess tent we gave Shah Khan and Raja cups of hot sweet tea and listened to their story. I used my little tape-recorder to record my interview with them. The reader will, I am sure, appreciate that these recorded words, which I am going to reproduce verbatim, though vivid, were spoken in a tongue foreign to them by fatigued men who had just had a harrowing experience.

"*Now, Shah Khan, would you tell us what happened to you?*"

"*There was quite a heavy snowfall all night. We didn't really want to come down but when we saw this heavy snowfall we made up our mind to come down—as soon as quick. So we came down the gully and reached the platform* [this was about 400 feet down the gully]. *A few chaps were ahead of me: Johar Beg, Ali Gohar and Sep, I was fourth and Raja was fifth, Akbar was last. All of a sudden—we didn't hear any noise—but something hit us and then, with the first hit, I felt the* [fixed] *rope come round my neck so I thought it might kill me. But thank God it came off and I was going down . . . and all of a sudden a big thing came and hit me in the face and then I don't know what happened to me.*"

"*Could you see anything, Shah Khan?*"

"*No, it was mist, very poor visibility, we didn't see anything. We didn't see the avalanche coming down. Only we felt it hit us. So I came down—I mean for a long time. I didn't know what was happening. All of a sudden I could feel I could breathe. I was quite happy that I would be safe now, but even then I was again under the snow and I was feeling suffocated. But when I came down near Tilman's old Camp 1 I came out of the avalanche and I was actually worried about the others."*

"*Now, if you had arrived at Tilman's Camp 1 you must have fallen over 1,000 feet, about 1,300 feet. Terrific fall, isn't it?*"

"*Yes, a terrific fall. But anyhow it was a new experience—because I am alive now I can say I enjoyed it! So, I was worried about the others. I shouted to everybody behind me. They replied to say 'everybody O.K.—they're safe'.*"

"*What did the Hunzas say when they came out of the avalanche, to find themselves alive?*"

"*Only one chap was a bit worried, Johar Beg, because he was hit and didn't come far down.*"

"*There was a lot of blood on his anorak. Did he cut himself with his ice-axe?*"

"*No, that was Ali Gohar. I think he also got a hit in the teeth and will be ill.*"

"*How far was everybody separated when the avalanche stopped? Were you all together?*"

"*No, we were all spread out. Only three chaps, Johar Beg, Gohar and myself were together, the others were quite far from each other.*"

"*I think you were very fortunate when you felt that rope tighten. It could have broken your neck very easily.*"

"*Yes, I was very lucky.*"

I then turned to Raja, who at that moment was examining somewhat ruefully a cut thumb and a rope burn on his arm. He was still shaken and, holding the microphone, spoke carefully into it, rather as if he were giving evidence at a court-martial.

"*On the afternoon of the 5th Shah Khan was worried especially as it was snowing so heavily. He called a conference of everyone of us and told us that we should move by evening. But I was a little reluctant thinking that the next day being Friday we would have better weather* [Friday is the Moslem holy day, hence Raja's expectation of fine weather]. *Then we decided to stay until next morning. But today the weather was no good and it had been snowing throughout the night. We decided that we must leave immediately. So at about ten we started leaving. The Hunzas were in front of us. I was last but one and Shah Khan was in front of me. I had just come down about a thousand feet from Camp 1 when suddenly something hit me hard. Well, I knew it was an avalanche but I didn't know whether it was a minor or a big one.*"

"*You were holding on the fixed rope, then, were you Raja?*"

"*Yes, I was holding the rope. So I tightened my grip and in that grip used a lot of force but it was no use to me. My gloves went off; ice-axe hit me in different places, but after about three minutes of this struggle I could not hold the rope. I started 'swimming', sometimes my head downwards, sometimes my head up, you know, all over the place. In this I lost my rucksack too. Then it took me about three minutes down the slope. I was all the time thinking what was going to happen to each one of us. And, really, when I could not breathe I knew that was the end—probably. But suddenly I came up and for about half a minute stayed up, 'swimming', and that was a great thing for me to breathe again. Well, again I went down. I don't know what happened then. Suddenly I found my neck sticking up and I was almost buried. Looking around I found everyone in the same condition.*

"*At the same time I saw Shah Khan looking towards me and shouting if I was all right, so I gave him the signal that I was all right and at the same time I started counting everyone of us. So I was very happy that we were complete in number and everyone was trying to move. I was so exhausted and tired that I could not move an inch. Well, I moved a bit but the snow had come so loose I just couldn't walk. So I was thinking probably if an avalanche comes that will finish us completely, because we were very exhausted. And it did come but this time it was a very minor one and it stopped just a few yards ahead of me. Then I rolled because I was thinking when I was rolling I had learned it in the Infantry School and I could do it so well, because there was no other way of getting out of the loose snow. In the meantime the Hunza who was nearest to me came up and he was quite happy because he was out of it. Then I started to look for my rucksack and found it a few yards from me. I was very happy to have it because there were so many things in it.*"

"Thanks, Shah Khan and Raja," I *concluded,* "*and thank God you are all safe after such a lucky escape.*"

Thus ended the first phase of the expedition, a period mostly of storm with infrequent and short spells of reasonable climbing weather. We had little to show, other than a fully stocked Camp 1, for seventeen days of effort and we were a trifle depressed by the incessant procession of snowfall, avalanche, snow plod. I was privately worried lest the Germans should suddenly burst upon the scene when we should be ordered off the mountain. But what had happened to the fine spells? The weather was cold and snowy enough for it to be February instead of June.

We were sitting round the mess table one evening after supper, the ground deep under snow and the wind blowing white tongues of it into the tent under the door flap, when Ashraf's flat monotone broke through our conversation:

"My Major Sahib he climb Rakaposhi long time ago."

The import of this remark sank in; a respectful silence followed. Ashraf, surprised perhaps at the success of his opening gambit, warmed to his theme.

"Major Gory-Doone Sahib, officer of very high family. He was my officer in 68th Durham Light Infantry on the frontier. Pathans shoot at us. If I smoke cigarette at night, Pathans shoot it 'pit-pung'. Major Gory-Doone very brave man. He wear steel jacket and hat and take knife go kill tigers. Like that!" Here he made a few strokes in the air, felling, maybe, a brace of tigers. "Major Gory-Doone, old man. No teeth. His wife more old. No teeth. Before the war Major come here, climb Rakaposhi."

"What, in his armor?" asked a sceptic irreverently.

Ashraf ignored this rudery.

"All my officer Sahibs were very high family," he said meaningfully surveying the unkempt, bearded ruffians squatting on ration-boxes round the table.

"Very high family," he repeated dolefully.

It looked that even if we battered our way through continuous snowstorms to the summit it would only be a second ascent!

XII

BUILD-UP

. . . but to recall the step, and pass out to the upper air—this is the toil, this the labour—Virgil, Aeneid vi, 126.

WHILE Shah Khan, Raja and the Hunzas rested after their near-escape in the avalanche, Richard Brooke, Warwick Deacock and I walked up the mountainside the next day to see if we could retrieve any of the ice-axes or other bits and pieces which had been lost.

When we arrived at the isolated boulder which was our usual first halting place we had a clear view of the snow slope which led into the gully and on up to Camp 1. We were appalled by what we saw. A truly enormous avalanche had thundered down the hillside from the very crest of the South-West Spur. It had travelled with such momentum that its debris had reached the Kunti Glacier. Furthermore, instead of being the usual new, soft snow it was composed of great hard lumps of snow varying in size from cannon balls to snow boulders as big as armchairs. So hard were they that a blow with the ice-axe barely chipped them. The avalanche had cut great troughs in the snow six feet deep and the whole area had something the appearance of a ploughed field after an armored division had run amok in it. We wandered over this huge devastated area looking forlornly for anything black protruding through the snow with that same hopeless air of bomb victims in a town like Cologne looking for remnants of their homes.

Again Rakaposhi had been a merciful mountain. Had the Hunzas been caught in this holocaust, instead of the gentle soft snow slide, they would have perished, their bodies broken and buried, the expedition ending in a tragic shambles. It being Friday, perhaps Allah had been merciful.

Boredom soon overcomes fear, and after two days of reasonable weather we resumed our build-up. The four of us who had recently been at Camp 2, Jimmy Mills, Warwick Deacock, John Sims and I, again set out to rope the Gendarme, a task we had been prevented from doing by bad weather a few days earlier.

On June 8th, therefore, we four climbed up to Camp 1. For much of the way we were able to walk on the rock-hard avalanche debris. The gully, however, made very heavy going, the surface alternating between bullet-hard semi-ice and deep soft snow. We found an ice-axe and half a tent-pole on the way up. The journey took us five hours whereas it would only have taken us half that time had we been climbing on previously kicked steps.

Camp 1 was half buried by the recent snow falls and it took us two hours to dig it out. The weight of the snow on the tents had ripped them. It is prudent, and less trouble in the long run, to collapse tents when a camp is being temporarily evacuated. It entails less labor to erect a tent than to dig one out.

We got up early the next morning, for we knew that we had a hard day before us with new steps to be kicked up 2,000 feet of snow. I was cook and got up at 4.30 a.m. Breakfast consisted of porridge, tea and Army "hard-tack" biscuits, if anyone was hungry enough to want them. I remember crouching in the tent trying to boil water with two defective stoves which took turns in spluttering out. Before the heat of the sun warmed the world it was cold and miserable. Two hours later we commenced the climb, that snow treadmill which is Himalayan mountaineering. First a long slanting traverse which carried us up 800 feet to the foot of the fixed ropes. This was horrid. The sun came up and started to fry us; there was little wind to counteract the heat glare reflected from the dazzling snow. We took it in turns to flounder in the lead, cutting a trough rather than kicking steps. Life became easier when we gained the ropes.

Climbers often assume that fixed ropes are only necessary, or useful, on very steep ground where the actual climbing is difficult, but they have other, less obvious, advantages. They can lead the way up, or down, a mountainside in the worst visibility. They constitute a continuous belay, a rope anchor, which not only protects a climber against a fall but might also prevent him being swept away by an avalanche. Finally they greatly assist the climber even on slopes that are not prohibitively steep. It is far easier to grab the rope, lean out and haul up than it is to walk up without its assistance when much attention has to be paid to correct balance. A fixed rope also permits a climber to climb slithery, unstable snow which would otherwise be impossible, or very toilsome, to ascend. In all we used about four thousand feet of fixed rope, every inch of it being of good value. Had we had more we would, no doubt, have used it too.

We made better progress once on the ropes, our eyes fixed on the Shark's Fin, a thin pencil of rock elegant against the rich blue sky. We took it in turns to go in front and kick the steps and in due course the Shark's Fin was reached. Here we stopped and ate chocolate while we admired, as we never ceased to do, the huge mass of Nanga Parbat. From the top of the rope, 500 feet higher, we had to traverse along the ridge for several hundred yards, being careful not to venture too near the corniced edge which overhung the Biro Glacier thousands of feet below. This traverse was on soft, steep snow which did not compact well. Realizing our danger somewhat belatedly we roped up and reached the steep snow-wall and cornice on the top of which Camp 2 was perched. This needed careful climbing and then we were safely at camp—if that precarious camp can be described as safe.

The weather seemed to have assumed a rhythm. Absent were the alternate spells of storm and shine which had typified 1956. Instead there was almost a monsoon sequence although we were not in the area affected by the monsoon. It was usually fine in the morning until noon or one o'clock when the clouds, which at ten o'clock had been isolated wisps, thickened over our heads and at the same time snow started to fall. This would continue until evening when, once again, the sky would clear. In consequence we abandoned hope of the snow ever becoming hard and granular and resigned ourselves to a knee-deep plod, the whole way to the top if necessary.

The sky cleared before sunset, giving my companions their first view towards Chitral, Tirich Mir and the Hindu Kush. It is curious yet pleasant how a wonderful view, particularly when seen for the first time, lifts a man's morale. Perhaps it is one of the reasons we climb, even though we would hardly admit that we had come half-way round the world merely to admire the scenery.

That night it was very cold; the water froze solid in the cooking-pot and my feet felt icy. At all camps above 19,000 feet during cold nights our breath would condense on the roof of the tent which would be covered with an icy rime by the morning. When the tent was shaken, the stove lit, or when the sun impinged on the canvas, the occupants would be subjected to a cold shower. This was most irritating, a single freezing drip falling on the tip of the nose having an effect on temper far beyond its meagre importance.

Warwick chose this particular morning to inflict his "brose" on us. He had already expounded its advantages:

"All you have to do is to heat one pot of water. You pour some of this on porridge to make brose. I'll add some chocolate to it. The rest of the water is then all ready for tea. Makes breakfast dead simple—and much quicker."

"We'll give it a trial," we had replied apprehensively.

We did. After the customary waking curse from the next tent, followed by the hiss of a primus as Warwick commenced his culinary short-cut, mugs were handed across to the tent John Sims and I were sharing. I delved into mine with my spoon. The glutinous mixture of warm water, coagulated oats with occasional lumps of broken chocolate (which had suffered badly passing through the tropics) quite repelled me. I reached out through the tent door and sent the contents of the mug on a 2,000-ft. journey. Camp 2 was handy in that respect.

"Never again," I called across to Warwick.

"Nonsense. Wonderful stuff. I could live on it," replied Warwick, and indeed he could, having an iron digestion, and was "a man of an unbounded stomach"—a most valuable asset to an explorer.

We set off to the Gendarme laden with fixed rope. As we climbed through deep snow along the ridge we stopped from time to time to plant marker sticks, with little red flags tied to them, along the route. They would be invaluable if we had to pass this way in cloud when they would act as a safeguard against our wandering over the cornice. We reached the foot of the Gendarme in two hours.

The four of us remained roped together for the climb, which John Sims was to lead. He was also the lightest, and therefore the easiest to hold, if he fell off the unstable snow. The second man concerned himself with John's safety, the two rear men carrying and securing the fixed rope. From the bergschrund the Gendarme is only about 200 feet high, but it is as steep as anything on the mountain, its flanks sweeping down to the glaciers far below, lending it a rare sense of airiness and isolation. The rocks which had helped us in 1956 were now so deeply plastered in snow that they would clearly be of little use. The climb this time was going to be a precarious "swim" up deep, steep avalanchy snow, which was probably overlying ice.

John Sims crossed the bergschrund without trouble and started to plough his way forwards and upwards. Spread out on the rope we followed. There were no rocks to which we could anchor ourselves so we had to use ice-axe belays. But here the snow was so soft that the axe plunged in without resistance until it hit ice, when it bounced off. Our belays were therefore "theoretical", for the benefit of morale mostly. I was third on the climbing rope and it was my particular job to attach the fixed rope to this surface of fluffy snow. I would scoop the new snow away and get down to the ice. I would then hammer in an ice-piton which is a sharp spike about the size and shape of the blade of a carving-knife. Sometimes this was wobbly so we would pack it with snow, stamp it down and irrigate the area with that limited supply of warm fluid that every man carries. The resultant freezing produces a firm area of "snowcrete". We used half a dozen pitons in this manner and fashioned a safe rope handrail.

Out in front John Sims was doing wonders. The snow was knee-deep on his downhill side and thigh-deep on his uphill side. There was a tremendous and sheer drop down to his right which must have made his progress an unnerving business. He climbed steadily, having to lift his feet high out of the snow troughs before he could pass them forward to the next step. His left shoulder was pressed against the slope, his left leg buried thigh-deep, his right leg almost dangling over the abyss. It was a fine lead.

Eventually he arrived at a rock—in which I later hammered a

smaller rock-piton to secure the top of the rope—and climbed a narrow and vertiginous ridge to a small platform at the very summit of the Gendarme. This was no larger than a medium-sized dining-room table and we huddled together in a close quartet. The top of the Gendarme was only half-way between Camps 2 and 3 but we had taken a long time to wade through the snow and fix the ropes, so we called it a day and returned to camp. From the summit I had scanned the snow at the foot of the Monk's Head for any sign of the two tents we had left pitched in 1956. No speck of black broke the even whiteness of the snowfield.

Two activities now progressed concurrently: while we were working on the Gendarme and beyond the remainder of the expedition was concentrated at Camp 1 and engaged in carrying loads up to Camp 2. They usually arrived at Camp 2 while we were ourselves out, so for three days Richard Brooke and I exchanged written messages on a small cleft stick stuck in the snow outside one of the tents at Camp 2. During this period Tom Patey had been treating the new porter, Guliami (Gor Blimey), for some minor chest trouble. This became worse and Tom, then at Camp 1, suddenly became worried as he pondered Guliami's symptoms. Acting on an impulse Tom suddenly raced down to base camp one evening and gave Guliami a most thorough check. Pneumonia was diagnosed and treated. Guliami was then, for his own health's sake, sent back to his village. When he came to descend his eyes were streaming with tears at the thought that he was letting the expedition down and bringing discredit on the Hunzas—which of course he was not. He had been a cheerful and willing porter and we were very sorry to lose him. In retrospect Tom reckoned that we worked a fair exchange with the Hunzas: they gave us stomach upsets and we gave them colds, to which ailment they were very prone and from which they suffered far worse than would a European.

Our surveyor, Sahib Shah, had been busy plane-tabling lower down in the Jaglot Nullah while we were building up our camps. By climbing the containing walls of the Nullah he had been able to survey a considerable area and fill in a mass of detail as well as correct certain errors on the existing map. For instance, until Sahib Shah put it right the map of the area around base camp showed little resemblance to the ground: a whole glacier was missing. When he was satisfied with his work in the valley Sahib Shah came up to base camp with the intention of climbing to the crest of the South-West Spur whence he would obtain a splendid view in all directions. It would be an ideal spot to make a survey station. A snag arose: the crest of the ridge was a good 19,000 feet high, some of it tough going. Would Sahib Shah, who had no pretensions to being a climber, make it?

"You see, Leader Sahib," he had said to me, "I want to go higher than I have ever been before and to make one of the highest survey stations made by a Pakistani surveyor."

"We'll help you—all we can," I replied, "but we must organize some Hunzas to help carry your survey gear."

"Thank you. I will see you on the ridge, *Baba*," he assured me, using the friendly Pathan "*Baba*".

As good as his word, Sahib Shah, accompanied by Richard Brooke, who was wise in the ways of survey, climbed up to the ridge and completed his survey. This was a splendid effort when it is recalled that, in the first instance, Sahib Shah was not a climber, and that in addition he had had no acclimatization but went straight up from base camp. I am happy to report that his survey work was most fruitful and, by the end of the expedition, he had covered 300 square miles of territory with his plane-tabling. But over and above this he was a charming and amusing man to have with us.

At this juncture Raja fell sick with either malaria or kidney trouble—we never really discovered which. On Tom Patey's advice he went down the valley to recuperate for a week or so. This was most unfortunate for Raja because he left us just as we pushed on high up the mountain and there was no subsequent opportunity for him to catch us up.

The day after we had roped the Gendarme we set out to complete the route over to Camp 3. This would entail a descent of the two steep snow steps on the far side of the Gendarme, both of which would require to be roped. We climbed to the top of the Gendarme with little bother, the steps we had kicked on the day before now being frozen into firm buckets. The fixed rope made the ascent of the Gendarme itself quite easy.

Near the summit we found a rock sticking out of the snow to which we were able to tie the fixed rope. I then led down the first snow-step. This was quite straightforward except for a small crevasse which I discovered by suddenly finding that my foot was in air instead of on snow. We then walked a couple of hundred yards over some snow humps to the top of the next step, this time a longer and steeper one. We were now faced with the problem of attaching the fixed rope to snow. We could not reach under the snow to any ice in which we might have driven an ice-piton. Instead we removed the thick cardboard cover from a ration box we were carrying. This we filled with snow, tied our rope to it, and buried about three feet down. We then stamped snow hard down on it, irrigated it, and found it to be a perfect anchor. This descent was about 300 feet to a col. I climbed down first, checking that the route was free of crevasses. Warwick Deacock came down last, facing inwards and carefully kicking closely spaced steps which would be invaluable when we came to climb back up the slope on our return journey.

We now had a goodish way to go, in deep snow, under the ice cliffs and seracs we nicknamed the "Notch" and then on across a broad snowfield to a level area where we proposed to site our Camp 3 at about 19,000 feet. It will be observed that Camp 2 was also at 19,000 feet, so this section of the climb was a switchback with the Gendarme in the middle. Clouds had been drifting across the sun and the wind had been rising and falling. The result was that we were overheated one moment, half-frozen the next.

Taking it in turns we waded through the deep snow of the Notch. Whenever a crevasse was suspected, and there were some enormous ones around, we used ice-axe belays while the leader advanced cautiously, prodding the snow in front of him. After we had been going for about six hours, John Sims was the first to feel the strain. The exertion, aggravated by a painfully fitting rucksack, took its toll. He could barely move one foot in front of the other and, a symptom new to me, he was virtually unable to speak. Warwick, also very tired, led up a final steep corner of about 30 feet, having first jettisoned his rucksack. This I picked up and followed him. He was then fairly spent, leaving Jimmy and me the only fit ones. The site of Camp 3 was not far away so I forced on, repeatedly telling my friends that it was only about 50 yards away until they ceased to believe me.

At last we reached our old camp site where John and Warwick needed reviving. We pitched the Army 8-man tent and prepared several pots of that incomparable life-saver, hot, sweet tea. We also opened some tins of stewed steak and ate some chocolate. Warwick and John each took a Dexidrene tablet and Jimmy Mills handed round some glucose tablets to be eaten on the march as a source of quick energy.

Immensely fortified by the food we prepared to leave. I scouted round and prodded here and there for the two tents we had left in 1956 but I think we must have been standing on twenty feet of new snow. Our previous camp therefore joined the forty man/days of Cambridge food in this gargantuan refrigerator. We left camp briskly, like new men and reached Camp 2 in about two hours. We were entertained on the way by a splendid sunset which we over-photographed. Not knowing the exact effect of a pep tablet on a tired man at this height we remained roped up in case either John or Warwick were victims of over-optimism, which these drugs are alleged to be able to cause. We were well pleased with our work: Camp 3 was now properly established.

A couple of days later the lift from Camp 1 to Camp 2 was completed and it was time to occupy Camp 3 and tackle the Monk's Head. On June 14th a large convoy of us moved over to Camp 3. Tom Patey, Richard Brooke and Dicky Grant came up from Camp 1 and continued over to Camp 3. This was a long and tiring day for them. When we arrived at Camp 3 we had to re-erect the tent which we had collapsed before we left lest it should have become drifted over with snow. Dicky Grant then suddenly seemed to be seized with soldierly ardor for he attempted to get us to erect the tent in strict military sequence under his supervision. The inevitable result was that we acted the goat as he played the sergeant-major. "Commando Dick" was subsequently teased every time he put a tent up.

The occupants of Camp 3, Richard Brooke, Tom Patey and Dicky Grant, now had the task of roping the Monk's Head while, at the same time the remainder of the expedition ferried loads over the Gendarme from Camp 2 to Camp 3. It will be recalled that it was at the Gendarme that the Hunzas had turned back in 1956. Would they make it this time? I asked the expert.

"Shah Khan, what do the Hunzas really think about going over the Gendarme?"

"I think they are not very happy," Shah Khan replied. "You see, that Nadir Aman chap who was with you before, he said it was very difficult."

"I see. But I think we'd better have a go."

"O.K. Mike, but with no loads, or very light loads, first time," he advised.

On June 15th we tried them out. I must admit that, seen from Camp 2 the Gendarme looked most formidable, the thin line of our steps seeming to hug the sheer face of the snow above a frightening drop. The drama was heightened when we issued each porter with a rope sling and a karabiner, or snap-link, so that he could use the sling as a belt and clip onto the fixed rope. A fall would then be impossible.

Carrying only token loads we trailed out of camp and followed the heaving switchback of the ridge to the foot of the Gendarme. The first few feet of the fixed rope, up and over the filled-in bergschrund, were respectably steep and I had a hushed and apprehensive audience as I swung up. Shah Khan, appreciating that it all depended on him, quickly followed me concealing any misgivings he might have had. The moment he did this the issue was settled. The Hunzas immediately followed, chatting happily and shouting to each other how difficult and dangerous it all was, and what splendid porters they were! Once again we had good cause to be grateful for Shah Khan's splendid influence and leadership.

When we had congregated on the far side I turned to Shah Khan.

"Will you tell them *shabash*—well done—and that the Monk's Head is much easier than what they have just done?"

Shah Khan explained this to them, which they accepted and thereby set the seal on our success.

"Gendarme *thik*; Monk's Head *thik*," they chorused.

We carried our light loads down to the top on the second step beyond the Gendarme from where we saw a figure on the col about about 300 feet below us. It was John Sims who had been ferrying some loads from the col through the Notch to Camp 3.

"How did the Monk's Head go?" I bellowed down to him against the wind.

" 'Bout two-thirds up. Deep snow. We want more fixed rope," he shouted back.

"Good work. How much rope?"

"At least 500 feet."

I promised to procure this and we waved to each other and returned to our respective camps.

The only way we could produce the necessary extra length of rope was by removing the top section of fixed rope between Camps 1 and 2 in the hope that from now on we would be concerned with going up the mountain, not going down to Camp 1. Jimmy went down to collect this rope at the same time keeping his eyes open for one of the special double-skinned terylene tents we had earmarked for the top camps but which he had accidentally dislodged down the mountainside from the eyrie which was Camp 2. In all, two tents and someone's hat were to follow John Sims's toilet-roll.

A day of bad weather followed. We were now committed to the climb and unable to scamper for base whenever a storm came up. We needed a long fine spell to see us up to the very summit; it did not look like coming. The day started miserably enough for me. Being cook I spilt all the milk, over which I did not cry, but swore.

The following afternoon the snow eased although we remained wrapped in dense cloud. All roped together, the five Hunzas, Shah Khan, Jimmy Mills, Warwick Deacock and myself, we waded out of camp and along the ridge. The old steps, path almost, were now completely obliterated forcing us to peer through the ubiquitous blank of white to catch sight of the little sticks with their red flags we had stuck along the route at intervals of about fifty yards. A few feet on our left huge cornices overhung the void. In these conditions it would be just too easy to walk over one of them in the uniform whiteness. To aggravate the situation people have a tendency, when walking along the side of a slope, to edge uphill—in our instance towards the cornices. The flags always appeared just when we had thought ourselves lost and the visibility improved as we crossed the Gendarme.

We lowered the loads down the second step and walked under

the green veined ice cliffs of the Notch to Camp 3. When we arrived at Camp 3 as usual I noticed the "railway compartment complex" or "camp schism". Just as the average man takes an initial dislike to newcomers who enter his railway compartment during a journey, so the inhabitants of one camp will soon find reasons to heap vituperation on the occupants of other camps.

"Those tired whatnots down there, breathing all that good oxygen and eating all the eggs instead of sending them up to us who're doing all the work," or "Those glamor boys up there, who've got all the mutton, and hogging all the interesting leads, leaving us to be beasts of burden."

So, for an hour or so, the quartet at Camp 3 glared at us and suggested that we put up our tents near by and cook separately. I moved in with the "old guard" and very soon we were our usual homogeneous and harmonious selves heaped together in the happy slum of the big octagonal tent.

The following day Richard Brooke, Tom Patey, Jimmy Mills and Warwick Deacock assailed the Monk's Head with the intention of placing the extra 500 feet of rope we had brought over from Camp 2. From Camp 3 we watched the four tiny black dots, apparently stuck to the sheer face of the Monk's Head, as they climbed. The smallness of a man's figure on that great expanse of snow made us realize how huge the feature was. We knew that they would be climbing as hard as they could go yet the little black dots seemed hardly to move.

On the same day John Sims and Dicky Grant went back to Camp 2 to supervise the move of the Hunzas over to Camp 3 where the whole party was to foregather. They had an unexpectedly hard day due to tricky snow conditions. Beyond the Gendarme a small wind-slab avalanche broke away at their feet. They took the hint and roped up. This was as well, for in the course of the day they encountered no less than five wind-slab avalanches. The largest, which also broke away at the line of their feet, was at least 400 feet wide and went roaring down into the valley below them raising a great cloud of "snow vapor" in its career.

I occupied myself with the cine-camera and in collecting, with Shah Khan and Sep, some loads we had left near the Gendarme at the col. Sep was a sepoy in the Northern Scouts and was Shah

Khan's personal orderly, or batman. He had been on Rebitsch's 1954 expedition which looked at Rakaposhi and then went North to work in the Batura Glacier area. The Germans had given him the nickname of Sep, which was easier than his long Pakistani name, and it had stuck. Sep had joined that expedition ostensibly as cook but he had been such a good all-rounder that he had ended up as a high-altitude porter. He was a cheerful, willing and tough man. He impressed us immensely on one occasion when he swarmed up the fixed ropes, carrying a heavier load than anyone else, and then found the breath to sing the whole way! He had really joined our party as Shah Khan's orderly in base camp, but we had soon appreciated his talent and, while still looking after his officer, he more or less joined the ranks of the Hunza porters.

By afternoon everyone had returned to camp, our numbers now swollen by the Hunzas who joined us, escorted by John and Dicky, after their avalanche-ridden trek from Camp 2. Here we were, no less than thirteen of us, besieging the Monk's Head. No previous expedition had been able to gather in such strength for the assault. All that was now required was for the Hunzas to do one good lift up the Monk's Head and our attack could be driven home at full tilt. Thank goodness the tiresome period of load carrying, of building the bottom layers of the pyramid was over.

That evening, after a technical inquiry as to whether we were collecting our cooking-snow from the same place that we were spending pennies—after all, snow is not usually yellow—I interrogated the Monk's Head party, having suddenly lost interest in my tea.

"What was the climb like?" I asked them at large.

"Two feet of new snow and ice beneath," Dicky Grant replied.

"It was a very tiring slog, quite steep enough in those conditions, and putting the pitons in was difficult. We really need some of those big aluminium stakes of Warwick's," Richard added.

"I got myself into an odd situation up at the top, near that ice-cliff, or serac, or whatever it is," said Tom. "I climbed up round the corner on ice, damn' slippery without crampons in vibrams, with canvas overboots, and to my surprise found myself on a knife-edge ridge. There was the drop of the Monk's Head sort of on the outside and an enormously deep crevasse running uphill giving me another big drop on the *inside*. No good at all for porters—or for me—so I went further right and found a decent snow route."

"We used all that extra rope you sent us, and we still need at least another hundred feet or so," Richard told me.

"Is it going to be O.K. for porters?" I asked.

"Should be," was Tom's opinion, "it's not so steep as the Gendarme but it's more open and exposed; gives you more sensation of height. The steps are fine. We've kicked great buckets all the way. There might be a bit of wind-slab avalanche up there, near the top especially, though it seemed stable enough when we were there."

"Some of the ropes aren't anchored too well. Someone will have to fix them a bit better before the porters heave themselves up on them. The top one is only secured by Tom's small axe being buried there," said Dicky.

As always when I wanted some detailed logistical planning to be done I conferred with Jimmy Mills and Warwick Deacock.

"Now that Johar Beg is sick, and Guliami paid off we've only got five Hunzas, counting Sep. If the members carry their own personal gear as usual can we still carry out the original plan and get all the stores and food for the top three camps up in one big lift? The weather's so unpredictable I hate the thought of losing the extra day if we had to do two lifts up the Monk's Head."

"We'll get down to detail, Mike, but it's going to be a tight squeeze. The porters will have to carry about 40 lb. And every ounce that goes up the Monk's Head has really got to be essential," Warwick answered.

They calculated that the lift was just possible and thereupon transformed their written lists into five packed kitbags, each of about 35–40 lb., for the five Hunzas.

Snow fell heavily during the night forcing us to spend the next day, June 19th, in camp. Warwick and Jimmy made their final estimates and rearranged the Hunzas' loads. Tom lost his tea-mug somewhere in the snow wilderness outside and used a bully-beef tin in its place. The snow was knee- or thigh-deep, the weight of it caving in the sides of the octagonal tent in which we congregated, each person drinking as much tea as anyone else cared to brew. The

26. The "Notch".

27. Looking back towards the summit of the Monk's Head (21,000 ft.).

28. Looking down on the Gendarme and "Notch" from the Monk's Head. Note two figures on the plateau, level with the big crevasse on the right. They are leaving the camp below the "Notch". The tents may be seen one inch above the left end of the big crevasse.

29. Tom Patey climbing a fixed rope at the foot of the Monk's Head. A wind-slab avalanche has just broken away in the foreground.

bad weather seemed local, specially made for us by Rakaposhi, the upper air remaining unclouded and the distant views not unpromising. All the same much snow had fallen and it would be a tiresome wade over the flat dome above the Monk's Head to our next camp, Camp 4.

Jimmy Mills, who was preparing the current brew of tea chose this moment to ask: "Does anyone know where there's any snow?"

Poor Jimmy! He meant unpolluted snow, but after a short pause someone inevitably told him to "put your something head out of the something door and you'll find some something snow".

That same evening I reiterated our plan of campaign for the assault. The Hunzas would make one big carry up the Monk's Head which would establish the eight climbers in Camp 4 at 21,000 feet on top of the Monk's Head. We would need two camps, 5 and 6, above this. All eight of us would carry up to Camp 5 which would be at about 23,000 feet where four of us would remain. These four would then carry up to our assault camp, Camp 6, two of them remaining. These two would, of course, be the summit pair. Camp 6 ought to be at about 24,000 feet, that is within 1,500 feet of the summit. Just as it was a vital part of the plan on Everest to place one camp above the South Col to bring the summit within range, so I considered it absolutely vital to get our Camp 6 established on the top of the second of the three great steps that lead to the summit of Rakaposhi from the dome of the Monk's Head. With the summit only 1,500 feet above our top camp it could probably be climbed in a day despite deep snow or bad weather.

As we were all service officers, and most of us military, I used the convenient analogy of a "set-piece attack" for our plan of assault. In other words we had a pre-set plan for the ascent of the Monk's Head and the three steps beyond. Up till now we had just built up our camps as time, weather and energy permitted, but from now on each man would have a set and individual part to play—and every man was counted on for our success. Once our attack was launched we were well and truly committed to go flat out at the mountain to force a decision one way or the other. I knew from bitter experience that once the flush and *élan* of a first assault is over it is extremely difficult, quite apart from the practical problems of food supplies and so on, to find the physical strength and mental determination to renew the attack. Just as in war turning one's back on the enemy is an almost irretrievable psychological loss, so on a mountain is turning one's back on the summit and surrendering that precious height which has been so laboriously achieved.

"I'll announce who the summit pair and support pair are when we get to the top of the Monk's Head," I told the team assembled in the octagonal tent. "And if the weather is O.K. for us to go tomorrow, then this is the big show. Hundred per cent effort from everyone. Fair enough?"

XIII
ASSAULT

Somewhere above the ice, unwitnessed storms
Break in the darkness on the summit ridge
And the white whirling avalanche
Blends with the storm, the night, the driven snow.

—Michael Roberts.

ON that morning of June 20th when we made our general exodus from Camp 4 the weather was not good, but it was good enough. As usual snow fell during the night (that could have been our mournful expedition chorus: "snow fell during the night") obliterating all the steps we had kicked round the great snow basin beneath the Monk's Head. Clearly there would be a full session of snow flogging that day, across the basin at the foot of the Monk's Head and over its tonsured pate.

Things went badly that morning. Shah Khan woke up feeling unwell. Tom discovered that he had a slight temperature and advised him to stay put if he was in any doubt about his fitness to undertake what was obviously going to be a gruelling day, most of it above 20,000 feet. This put Shah Khan in a most unenviable dilemma: if he came with us and fell ill he might jeopardize the whole show; if he stayed behind he knew full well that we would have to stick to our plan of a "set-piece attack" and he would never be able to catch us up. Shah Khan chose wisely and unselfishly: he elected to stay behind. We respected his decision and knew that we ourselves and the Hunzas would miss him sorely. They always looked to him for leadership and encouragement and we had been counting on him personally for our climb on the upper mountain. He had put such a tremendous effort into our enterprise so far that he richly deserved the reward of getting high on the peak. It is not difficult to imagine how disappointed he himself must have been feeling.

A hundred feet or so of rope still had to be placed at the very top of the Monk's Head so four of us, Tom Patey, Dicky Grant, Richard Brooke and myself went ahead to arrange this in advance of the porters and at the same time to re-kick the steps up the line of the ropes. Just as Richard Brooke and Dicky Grant reached the bergschrund, about sixty feet or so below the tail of the first rope, a windslab avalanche broke away and slithered down into the basin. Tom and I joined them to discuss the whole question as to whether the face was safe to climb or not. Tom took off his rucksack and said that he would give it a good testing. While we belayed his climbing rope he climbed up onto the questionable snow slope and hopped about for a few minutes like a demented frog to see if it would slide. It held, so he climbed up to the foot of the first rope and attached the climbing-rope to it so that the porters would have a rope to help them from the moment the face became steep. We then slowly hauled ourselves up the ropes taking it in turns to go in front and kick the steps.

Despite the fixed ropes, and despite the fact that I had climbed it three times in 1956, I still found the Monk's Head an intimidating place. The steepness was unrelenting, there was a tremendous drop on our left down to the Biro Glacier from the ill-defined ridge we were climbing, and on our right the bland face of the Monk's Head swept down without a break or ledge. There was an unmistakable feeling of scaling a major feature on which a slip would bring disaster.

By the time we had reached the serac quite near the top the Hunzas, who were in fine fettle, were closed up behind us. Unfortunately the top section, which yet had to be roped, was not only steep but composed of deep, unstable snow. It took some considerable time before Richard and Dicky between them had led the ropes to the very crest and given the signal for everyone to follow.

It was by then afternoon and the customary bad weather was closing in. Soon snow was falling on a rising wind. This snow on top of the Monk's Head was, as we suspected, thigh deep. In order to accelerate our progress I gave orders for one person at a time, members and porters alike, to go flat out for thirty paces and then step aside, picking up the tail of the convoy until his turn came round again. As there were twelve of us a man was quite well rested between bouts of feverish kicking. Thirty paces seemed to be about as far as the average person could manage flat out without having to take too long a rest to regain his breath. Even so, at the end of this bout a man would collapse into the snow, his lungs pumping like bellows.

The visibility clamped down, the snow fell more heavily, the wind rose; it was getting late. Periodically I looked at my watch: 3 o'clock, 3.15—we must stop at 3.30 I promised myself in order to give the Hunzas time to get down—3.30 passed, 3.45. We were still nowhere near our proper camp site at the foot of the first great step on the upper mountain, but I did not dare press on. When we reached the flat top of the Monk's Head I called a halt. We would camp here. I was worried about the Hunzas going down by themselves. Old Akbar, the Sirdar, was not only incapable of taking charge, he was half-dead on his feet. I turned to Sep, who as usual was full of strength and good spirits.

"*Asti jao. Aramsi jao*—go slowly, go carefully," I told him. By sign language I indicated that they must clip on to the ropes for the descent.

"*Accha*, Sahib," he assented with his usual warm and confident smile.

The Hunzas left us, their dark and dim shapes merging, then disappearing, into the swirls of cloud and snow. We put up our tents and crawled into them to pass an uneasy night of storm.

Next morning the storm had not abated so we slept on. Some time later there was an easing so we decided that as it was quite out of the question to attempt the first big step, which was a good 2,000 feet, we would at least shift camp a mile or so over to its proper site at the very foot of this great step. This we did, descending a gently sloping ridge, crossing a wide crevasse with much prodding with the axe, and then walking over a rounded whaleback of snow to the camp site. Again there was no sign of the camp we had left pitched in 1956. To get all the stores across we had to do a double journey. This meant that at some stage or other we had to break the golden Himalayan rule of never getting separated from one's sleeping-bag, especially in bad weather.

By the time we had put up a tent at the new site and returned to the old one the blizzard was blowing again. We collected the remaining stores and started back. I noticed that the steps of the person, John Sims, I think it was, who was a mere fifty yards in front of me were completely drifted over by the time I came to use them. With our earlier steps covered we were now faced with the problem of finding our camp in this white void. Tom took the lead, working on a hunch, and like a dog on the scent, he plunged unhesitatingly ahead. He must have a highly developed sense of direction, because he led us unerringly to the little tent which would have been so easy to miss in that almost non-existent visibility.

Another rough night was followed by an equally stormy dawn. In the tumult of wind and snow cooking became a near-impossibility. By mid-morning I was in an agony of physical and mental discomfort. I badly wanted to spend a penny but could not steel myself to go outside into that maddened world of driving snow beyond the skin-thick canvas of our tent and lower my pants. As my discomfort grew some lulls began to occur. Unable to stand the strain any longer, I emerged to perform my task, encouraged from within the tents by the ribaldry of those with happier intestines.

The morning improved (I should have waited half an hour longer) and Tom, filled as ever with restless energy, went off to try the snow on the slope above us. He returned fairly soon to report that he had been able to discern two black dots on the summit of the Monk's Head in the area where we had camped two nights previously. The dots were too big to have been the garbage of our camp. Consequently four of us walked back that afternoon to investigate while Tom and Dicky Grant kicked steps up the next snow slope in preparation for our ascent the following day.

When we arrived at the old camp site we found that an octagonal tent and some rations had appeared. They must have been carried up by a party during yesterday's blizzard. The visibility had been so rotten that we could have been a hundred yards away from them and we would not have seen each other. Why had they been brought up? We were to wait for a week for the answer to that question. As we returned to camp, carrying the food with us but leaving the unwanted tent behind, we could see the black dots of Tom and Dicky who must have climbed nearly a thousand feet up the slope of the first step. That would be an enormous help on the morrow—if no snow fell during the night.

I now had to announce the summit and support pairs. I had

rather assumed that nature would have been a natural eliminator and that by this stage some of us might have been slowed up by altitude or sickness. Not a bit of it. The whole party was in excellent health and I am quite certain that every man was capable of attaining the summit. This speaks well for our program of acclimatization and also indicates that our rations until then must have been adequate despite our grumbles. After a chat with Tom Patey, in his capacity both as doctor and as a climber with previous high-altitude experience I chose the men. Not without some misgiving I placed him and myself in the summit party. We had both proven ourselves previously above 23,000 feet and were both going well. The support pair were Richard Brooke and Dicky Grant. Richard was not only going strongly but his experience of snow mountaineering was second to none on the expedition and was of great value. The other three, Jimmy Mills, John Sims and Warwick Deacock were all going strongly, but it was just a case of someone having to take on the vital task of porterage between Camps 4 and 5.

This selecting of parties was no easy task but it was made much easier for me by the complete loyalty and support with which my friends received my decision even though they themselves might personally have been bitterly disappointed.

"Getting one rope to the top is all we're interested in," Warwick had voiced most unselfishly on behalf of the trio who were to carry up to Camp 5 the next day.

It was a great relief, rather like coming out of the dentist's chair, to have got that decision off my chest. I went into my tent and, in a wave of careless optimism, blew up the primus in my face, burning off my eyebrows in the process. Richard Brooke was in the tent with me and as I had singed his nose and ears some years previously when I had burnt down our tent in Greenland with the aid of a petrol cooker, he made some suggestion, I think, about my joining the fire brigade.

The next morning dawned clear. Excitement was in the air as we rolled up the two lightest tents and packed the assault rations and equipment. Dicky Grant, Richard Brooke, Tom Patey and I were carrying our personal gear only. This consisted of two sleeping-bags, or one sleeping-bag and down clothing, an air-bed (which was rather heavy and weighed about six pounds), some spare clothing, particularly gloves and socks, first-aid kits, rope-slings, camera and film (we did not carry the heavy cine-camera above Camp 4 because we were so short of "coolie-sahibs"), knife, spoon and plate. Forks, it will be noted, are considered quite unnecessary implements, as indeed they are. This, with the weight of the frame rucksack, totalled about thirty pounds—a light load, admittedly, but equivalent to double at that altitude. Our three "porters", Jimmy Mills, Warwick Deacock and John Sims, carried the tents, food, stoves and fuel, making their loads about thirty-five pounds each.

In crisp, bright sunlight we crossed the snow basin on which Camp 4 was sited and started up the broad slope of the first step. Tom's and Dicky's steps of yesterday were a great boon, and we got away to an excellent start. The slope led into a scoop between rock walls and some ice-cliffs. For about a hundred feet it steepened considerably, but on this section Tom had fixed a rope secured at the top by a buried ice-axe. How is it that Tom always seemed to have a spare ice-axe handy? A very useful habit.

We had gained about 800 feet so we stopped for a rest and a bite of food on a convenient platform. Everyone was going well and spirits were high. A few yards further on we passed through a cleft in some ice-cliffs which framed Nanga Parbat most effectively. As each person reached this point he stopped and took a photograph. A snow slope, and a long haul, led upwards to the ribbon of scree and boulders which are so prominent a feature when this step is seen from below. Tom tried to climb the boulders but they were snow-plastered and he gave it up when he saw that the remainder of us were making better progress on the hard snow. We gained height steadily but slowly on the very long ridge which swept up for fully a thousand feet. We became weary and wished only for the torture to cease. The upper section, where the ridge narrowed, was appreciably steeper and more exposed. One by one we trailed into the camp area, a flattening of the ridge at the top of the giant step. I had high hopes of locating the camp we had left here in 1956. The area was a limited one and I thought that I would be able to remember the exact spot where our little tent had been left. In that tent was my camera with some precious exposed film in it—and the banner of our Anglo-American venture, a pair of girl's leopard-skin panties! I searched but in vain, for the wind had sculped the snow into long hummocks, like sand-dunes, which were similar yet subtly different in configuration to the ones I remembered.

We put up the two tents and brewed a warm drink for John, Jimmy and Warwick, to fortify them on their descent. They had performed a gruelling and thankless task knowing that they would have to sacrifice the height they had so laboriously gained on our behalf. After they had left, the indefatigable Tom, muttering "I'll have a look at the start of the route for tomorrow," plodded out of camp, crossed a crevasse and disappeared out of sight over a snow bulge. I was a little worried, knowing that there were crevasses above. Some time later Tom reappeared to tell us that the route above was very straightforward, all the crevasses being completely obscured by the winter snows. We ate a supper of bully beef, soup, biscuits and tea, took our sleeping-pills and wriggled into our sleeping-bags to pass a warm and comfortable, but, as always, fairly sleepless night. I have never met anyone who can sleep really soundly at a great height.

A shower of hoar frost told us, as if we did not already know, that it had been a very cold night. Water left in a pot froze completely solid. My estimate of the temperature was about minus 10 degrees F. As the stove warmed up the air in the tent we were subjected to an unwelcome cold shower.

It was a fine, clear morning only slightly marred by a chilling wind. The view was magnificent. We were now getting on more equal terms with Haramosh and the 23,000 feet peak in the Rakaposhi Range, which until then had been towering over us, was now a brother.

We dismantled the double-walled terylene tent which Tom and I were going to use for Camp 6, and this together with a stove, fuel and six days of food for each of us disappeared into Richard's and Dicky's rucksacks.

We followed Tom's steps out of camp, grateful for them as ever. The snow he had compacted on the small crevasse was now as hard as iron and led us across in perfect safety. The huge crevasses that had menaced us in '56 were not in evidence and we made for the tail of the ribbon of boulders which led almost to the top of this second great step. For some reason these boulders had been blown free of snow, whereas the ones on the step below, which Tom had tried to follow the day before, were covered with snow. We climbed these boulders. I found this a welcome change from the never-ending treadmill of a snow slope, where every step is the same, with nothing to relieve the tedium. On rock each foot has to be placed accurately and each step is different, requiring thought, keeping boredom at bay. I was feeling fit and going very strongly, experiencing a thrill of achievement when I passed the big boulder under whose lee we had crouched despondent and defeated in '56. There was no comparison in the physical and mental condition of the party this time. We paused to hammer some warmth into fingers and toes, and continued on up.

Towards the top the boulders steepened into a mixed rock and snow face. Tom and I, who were in front, missed our footing and slithered down a few feet at almost the same instant, coming to the immediate conclusion that we ought to be roped. Richard suggested that the snow slope on the left offered the best route so, agreeing with him, we roped up and he led off. As he slowed with the effort we took turns in kicking steps up the final hundred feet where the step gave up onto a snow wall. One by one we heaved ourselves over the lip to land ourselves on the rim of the feature we called the Snow Plateau. This part of the route was the only section which was concealed from view from below. We could see a great line of ice-cliffs sweeping in from the North-West Ridge to be lost in the Snow Plateau. Would these ice-cliffs bar our path? Would they constitute a belt of crevasses difficult or impossible to cross? These questions were racing through my mind for the last few feet until I scrabbled over the top and saw the vista before me. A huge snow basin, half a mile wide, ran to the foot of the final slope which then steepened to the summit in a mixture of rock and snow. The ice-cliffs petered out a long way to our left.

There were no insuperable mountaineering difficulties between ourselves and the summit; we were in good health; the weather was fine and ought to remain so on the morrow. It was in the bag—or so we thought.

It was one o'clock when we pitched Camp 6 at about 24,000 feet.

I was greatly relieved that we had been able to carry out my original intention of getting our assault camp at this altitude. There was no doubt now that a fit pair could attain the summit which was 1,500 feet above us and could be glimpsed through drifting curtains of cloud. It looked quite close.

"Well, there it is," said someone as the summit emerged momentarily from the misty clouds.

"You know, it does look close. What about having a bash at it straight away?" suggested Tom.

"I'm with you. It's one o'clock, that gives us nearly seven hours till dark," said Dicky Grant quickly. "What d'you think, Mike?"

"It's a temptation, but it's a gamble. I'm not gambling now I've got this far. It might take a darned sight longer than it looks. Things do at this height. I'm going to get a night's rest and be sure of knocking it off tomorrow. Have a bash if you want to but I'm sleeping here and one other of us must stay with me," I replied.

"Even if two got to the top today, they wouldn't have time to get right down to Camp 5. That would mean four of us in this little tent for the night. And if four of us stay here it means we have only half the reserve of rations if we're caught in a storm," said Richard.

We continued discussing the problem but in the end Richard and Dicky returned to Camp 5 with the intention of coming up again the next day and pushing through to the summit. They would be climbing without loads and would be able to use the steps that Tom and I would have kicked. All four of us, therefore, had a reasonable chance of attaining the summit next day.

Tom and I settled in for the night. We drank mugs of tea but I found that I could not stomach my full ration of our staple supper: bully beef and biscuits. During the night the wind rose alarmingly, which kept me awake despite three sleeping-pills.

By morning a full-blooded blizzard was blowing. The tent was being drifted over, the weight of snow piling up on the sides of the tent was hollowing them in, decreasing the already small area of floor space. One guy had broken and, at this point, the tent bulged in alarmingly. The double terylene walls of the tent were drum tight and the hard-driven spatules of snow spattered angrily against them, shaking the ice hoar-frost inside the tent down into our faces. We ate a cold and miserable breakfast of tea and dry oatmeal biscuits, the hoar-frost shower being more unwelcome than ever that morning. I put my head out through the sleeve entrance, glimpsed the summit through the moving wall of drift, saw that the sky was cloudless, and received an icy faceful of cold snow for my trouble.

"There's a lot of drift, but I've sledged in weather like this in Greenland. It's not too bad once you're outside," I lied to Tom.

"Aye, I'm game to give it a go. I've climbed in blizzards in the Highlands," replied Tom who, I suspect, knew I was lying. The truth of the matter, as we admitted to each other later, was that we had both had such a wretched night that we could not bear the thought of passing another one in that camp.

We were under no illusion as to how bitterly cold it would be outside. Not only would the blizzard suck the warmth out of our bodies, but at 25,000 feet our circulation would be so bad, due to the oxygen lack, that the pure effect of the cold atmosphere (and it was cold that day not counting the effect of the wind) would be much increased. We therefore piled on every shred of clothing we had. Next to my skin I wore a string vest, over which I pulled a thick woollen shirt, a Shetland wool sweater, a heavy Norwegian jersey, and a down-filled jacket. Over my lower limbs I was wearing long woollen underpants, battle-dress trousers and down-filled trousers. Over all this I wore a windproof anorak and trousers of double Grenfell cloth with the hood covering my head, which was also protected by a woollen balaclava helmet and the hood of the down jacket. On my feet were our specially designed vapor barrier boots, while my hands were protected by two pairs of woollen mitts worn under thick, fur-lined gauntlets. We squeezed out through the sleeve entrance of the tents almost hermetically sealed and as bulky as the Michelin Man.

Outside the tent we were in the grip of the storm. The sky was cloudless but a howling wind was tearing across the surface of the snow raising a cloud of drift which was trailing out into the otherwise clear air one of those characteristic streamers or pennants of snow that look so attractive from the valley and cause the Swiss peasants to remark that the mountain *fume sa pipe*. Undeniably the effect is pretty from a distance; within, it is a killer wind. My taped diary later recorded that, seen through the drift the "skyline was ragged, lurid, unfriendly, cold, beastly".

Everything seemed to be fighting against us: the snow was deep, covering our boots always, coming up to our knees sometimes. The effort of balancing in this deep snow while, at the same time we were being buffeted by the storm, was considerable and began to sap precious energy. Tom was in front—his typical position for the whole expedition—and we were crossing a wide snow plateau which slowly steepened until it became a snow face studded with ribbons of rock and isolated boulders. We had a considerable horizontal, or near horizontal, distance to go before we started on the final slopes of the mountain. We had crawled out of the tent at 8.45 a.m. and seemed to have been going for hours. The wind tore at us but the summit seemed to get no closer or our little camp much further below us. Slowly, very slowly, some detached rocks on our right came level with us, then slipped below. Our bodies were warm, but I felt my feet becoming alarmingly cold.

"How are you feeling?" I asked Tom at one of our frequent stops for a breather and bite of rum fudge or glucose.

"I'm all right but my hands are damn' cold," he told me. I then noticed that he was, and had been, banging his hands together and, when we were stopped, holding them in his pockets near the warmth of his stomach. From what I could see of his face under his goggles and hood, it looked drawn. No doubt I looked equally grim with a rime of ice on my beard where my breath was condensing.

"We're getting there," I replied.

We were indeed making steady if slow progress. The snow had become considerably firmer as the slope steepened. Soon it became very hard so that it would have been helpful to put crampons on. However, our feet were so cold that we dared not risk the tightening of the crampon straps worsening the effect of the cold to our feet. I remembered the lesson of my winter climb in Norway. Instead we kicked nicks in the snow.

Looking back, I seem to have no recollection of time during this period, which in fact must have lasted nearly four hours. My mind was numbed but sustained by the transcending knowledge that "we were getting there". This realization, drumming in the back recesses of my brain made our dumb suffering bearable and even, somehow, induced from time to time a feeling of excitement, exultation almost. I felt my feet becoming more wooden but I calculated coldly and methodically that, even if I lost a toe or so, it was a fair bargain for Rakaposhi and one I was very willing to pay. We began taking it in turns to go in front and pick the route which now led over a mixture of rock and hard snow. We stopped, individually, when we felt like it. For several days now our main food intake had been sugar or sugary things. On this final climb I lived from hand to mouth in the true, literal sense of the phrase. I would stop and cram some of my carefully rationed glucose tablets or rum fudge (the rum was flavouring only—I was not too eager to hit the bottle at exactly this juncture!) into my mouth and seconds later would feel a little spurt of energy run through me which would sustain me for another session of uphill plodding until I drooped over my ice-axe gasping, to refuel with sugar again.

We looked back towards our tent, an orange blur in the wind wrack.

"If the viz goes rotten and that tent disappears, we've had it," one of us said. Caught tentless we would not have survived a night in these conditions.

The view above us was now encouraging. We were just below the summit ridge which came in from our right and curled up to the top of the mountain which was in sight and quite close on our left. We therefore had to climb upwards and leftwards converging the whole time on the ridge which was coming in from our right. With the rocks covered with grey-white snow crystals, and with the hard corrugated snow, the scene was quite Highland; we might have been on Ben Nevis in February. But beyond the ridge on our right we caught occasional, exciting glimpses of vast new horizons and mountain chains stretching far away towards the Baltoro Glacier and K2.

"How far, d'you reckon?" I asked Tom.

" 'Bout five hundred feet. It's in the bag," he replied.

"If it's in the bag I could use a pep tablet. Got one?" I asked.

Tom gave me a dexidrene, which I took. In due course it produced a supply of energy and I felt my legs become stronger, the slope less steep and the summit nearer. I was careful to delay taking the dexidrene until the top really was in the bag, for while I consider it usually safe to take these drugs to help the descent, they are potentially dangerous on the ascent when they can easily reduce a man's natural reserve of strength to a perilously low level and induce premature exhaustion. Or, more simply, they enable a man to take more out of himself than is safe.

We were getting very close now and, as we clambered up to the summit ridge itself, the ground steepened and we decided to use the rope. After a couple of hundred feet of roped climbing, but moving together, we came to a little snow rake near a big, sheltering boulder. We were very nearly there. A couple of leads on the rope and we were on the ridge itself with the summit perhaps forty feet away. We were now traversing leftwards and ascending slightly. On our left was the broad slope we had just climbed. On our right was the very crest of the rock ridge, a sharp knife-edge of grey-green rock. I peered over. With a gasp I found myself looking down a dizzy rock wall which fell plumb for hundreds of feet. I was looking down the north face of Rakaposhi, a face which tumbles down, down, down, in a chaos of snow, ice and rock to the bed of the valley 19,000 feet below—the greatest mountain face in the world—and I was looking down it! Through the snow spume I could just see the terraced fields of Hunza or Nagyr and a glacier writhing along the valley floor like an enormous white snake. The ridge steepened a little to an outcrop of rock fifteen feet away. Beyond that the ridge dipped again until it descended and became the North-West Ridge. It was the summit.

This was the great moment. A snow and rock scramble of a few feet and we would be on the summit we had come half-way round the world to tread. These minutes would live with me all my days. Tom and I looked at each other. At this instant when time stood still, when the spirit had triumphed, we ought to utter something ennobling, something appropriate at once to the dispatch of a noble adversary and to the triumph of two Davids over a dispassionate Goliath. It was an inspired moment. Our imaginations ran riot:

"After you, Tom."

"No, after you, Mike!"

XIV

THE WAY DOWN

Great winds blow upon high hills.
—Sixteenth-century proverb.

"GO on, go ahead. It's your mountain," Tom added.

He jammed himself against a rock and paid out the rope as I climbed without difficulty the final fifteen feet to the summit. I kicked a few steps, swished off some snow from the rocky handholds, and I was there. It was a dizzy place and I was being buffeted by the storm which was still at its height, blowing great ragged spume pennants high into the air over the lip of the ridge. Balance was difficult standing up so I sat down and gave Tom a happy wave with my ice-axe.

I have found from experience that blizzards occupy my physical body so fully that they need such a concentration of mental and bodily effort to combat them, that my mind is placed in blinkers and can dwell only on the storm and my means of overcoming it. So it was on Rakaposhi. Until I crouched down on the summit and relaxed my mind, I had been completely absorbed with the immediate problems of ascending the next few feet in front of me and of keeping my body fuelled. Now at last I was able fully to comprehend the situation. Here I was, really on the top of Rakaposhi. I seemed to realize it for the first time. We were there!

I felt wonderment and relief. Wonderment that we had pulled it off and that I really was on the very summit we had all been striving for for six weeks and that I had been thinking about for over two years. Relief that the burden of suspense and responsibility, the unbearable possibility of a second defeat, was now banished.

Storm-lashed though I was, this was a moment of attainment and achievement when my whole heart's desire was just to be there, crouched on the little rock platform with the orchestra of the blizzard loud in my ears.

I opened my camera, a Reid, and tried to take some pictures. The cold was intense and the shutter, instead of moving with a brisk "glop" made a hiccupping "ger-lop" noise, just as it had in Greenland on the colder winter days. We then discovered that neither of us had any of the British or Pakistani flags we had so carefully procured so we were unable to take the customary flag-waving photographs. If I looked down over the sheer north face I had to put my face over the edge and I caught the spindrift blown into the air by the up-draught. I tried to identify Disteghil Sar but I could not be certain that I was not looking at the twenty-five thousanders of the Batura Range. I took some photographs, working the camera with my leather gauntlets on, and tried to take in as much as I could of the view to store my memory with. I then rooted out of the snow two pocketfuls of rocks to give the other members as momentoes of the summit. Tom and I then changed places.

Neither of us lingered for more than about five minutes on the summit. Never, to my knowledge, has a major Himalayan summit been climbed in such vile weather. We were now thoroughly worried about frostbite. We returned to the friendly boulder we had stopped at earlier and rested for a while out of the wind. I could feel that both my big toes, and the toes next to them, were wooden. I could feel them move but I was not deceived by this sensation of movement which was caused by the action of the ligaments in the calf muscles and can easily be confused for a feeling of sensation in the toes themselves. Tom's hands were more serious. When I had been on the summit he had scratched the expedition initials "BPFHE" on a large stone. Trying to put this stone upright he had dropped it on his hand and I saw blood on his gloves. Three fingers of his right hand were wooden and completely without sensation. He had been wearing down-filled gloves, which were too tight, over woollen gloves. I therefore lent him my pair of big, fur-backed leather gauntlets and he gave me his down gloves. Almost immediately a gust of wind whipped away one of these light-weight down gloves from my hand and we watched it scud across the snow and disappear over the abyss of the north face. Luckily I had a spare pair of woollen mitts in my rucksack, which I put on.

Reticence, inbred in our race, is traditional in British mountaineering and was splendidly demonstrated some half-century ago by the three Englishmen who fell to their destruction in the Alps together with Tairraz, their guide. We read that "Tairraz screamed but, like Englishmen, the others met their doom without a word of exclamation." The summit of a mountain, particularly a Himalayan giant, is an overwhelmingly emotional place. It is only too easy, carried away by the moment, to do something un-British which, if it gets out (as these things do) will earn you for the rest of your days those sidelong, embarrassed and reproachful glances in the Alpine Club usually reserved for people wearing made-up bow-ties. True we read of embraces, kisses and hints of tears on the summit of Cho Oyu; hearts overflowing with unspeakable happiness on Annapurna; tears coursing down behind oxygen masks when the Swiss trod the summit of Everest. These were all the acts of splendid people, but, of course, they were not British and are therefore excused. It is therefore with something of a lump in my throat that I recall that black and unforgettable day in British mountaineering when Tilman and Odell climbed the then highest summit ever ascended, Nanda Devi (25,645 feet). So intoxicated was Tilman by altitude and emotion that, as he himself freely admits, *he shook Odell by the hand.*

Knowing the Scots to be an excitable people under their crust of dourness, I was alarmed lest Tom Patey should forget himself in any way. Fortunately, as I have explained, we could only stand on the summit one by one, so we avoided any exhibitionism there. There still remained this dreadful business of shaking hands. Then I remembered. Thank God for Tom's frostbite! I mean, you can't wring a man's hand when it's frostbitten, can you?

Still roped together Tom and I started the descent. After a while the rope became irksome, and we coiled it up. Tom, realizing that his hands needed speedy treatment, plunged down ahead of me towards the yellow dot in the drift which was our tent. I followed at a leisurely pace but found that even walking downhill was an effort. I tried putting on my crampons, wasted much valuable time, and found that they came off after a few paces. I paused now and again to sit in the snow and look at the view, or back towards the summit. Tom was by then half an hour ahead of me and, when I came to the flat snow basin, I heartily wished I had kept up with him, for his steps were filled in by drifting snow. The effect of the dexidrene had worn off and I felt an almost unbearable weariness as I sank knee-deep into the soft snow. As my strength drained away I crammed the last of my glucose tablets into my mouth in an attempt to squeeze the final dregs of vitality out of my drooping body. At first I could manage fifty paces at a time, then thirty, then twenty, and finally only ten. The last hundred yards were the worst. I could just walk for ten paces before I half collapsed over my ice-axe. I would then eat a glucose tablet and press on for another ten paces, lurching uncontrollably sideways when my balance was bad. I must have looked like a very drunken man. I thought that hundred yards would never end.

When at last I staggered up to the tent I saw that the front poles were collapsed, the tent partially buried and the canvas bulged out by the outline of Tom's back.

"You all right?" I called to him.

"Yes, except my hands," he replied.

"Got any tea ready?" I asked forlornly, not hearing the friendly hiss of a primus. Sweet tea was the thing I most wanted in the world at that moment.

"Daren't touch the cold primus with my hands," he explained.

I fixed the front of the tent, dug some snow away from the sides and crawled in. It was chaotic and sordid inside. Tom was crouched half in his sleeping-bag, shaking and juddering like an aspen leaf in the wind. This rigor was caused by his having taken two Priscol tablets which have the effect of driving the warm blood to the extremities and the surface of the skin. This helps get the blood back into frostbitten extremities at the price of lowering the general body temperature. It would have been disastrous had he taken them while still outside, fighting the blizzard. In the warmth of his sleeping-bag (when he got into it) his loss of body heat would be checked.

"The tent was almost flat and half-buried when I got here," he explained. "I had quite a job to dig it out."

"You get into your bag properly and I'll get cracking on the tea," I replied.

The heat of the stove warmed the tent and, while the water was heating, I took my boots off and with some trepidation examined my toes. They looked black at the tips and bloodless and the big toes, particularly, were without sensation. I massaged them for half an hour and took one of Tom's Priscol tablets. Four fingers of Tom's right hand looked bloodless down to the second joint, a far more serious state of affairs than my toes. We drank several pints of tea, by which time it was getting dark and we turned in for the night. Neither of us had felt much like eating nor, so far as I can remember, did we eat anything more than a biscuit.

A storm blew all night and we slept little, if at all. The snow was drifting up against the sides of the tent, encroaching on the already limited floor space. To aggravate conditions Tom's air-bed had gone flat, so we huddled together on mine for warmth. We spent an utterly miserable night.

Drift was still blowing hard and high next morning and, to make things worse, we were in cloud which reduced visibility to about fifty yards. We were both reluctant to move, but we could not face the prospect of another night in that ghastly tent.

"It's bound to clear up," one of us muttered without much conviction. "We'll give it an hour."

We waited for the agreed hour, then another, then another. Still the wind blew and thick cloud swirled round the tent. We decided to make a deadline of one o'clock and then go down whatever the weather. We could just not stand the thought of another night at Camp 6. If we found the correct exit from the Snow Plateau we could descend to the long ribbon of rocks which would guide us safely down through the cloud. Below the rocks we would be more likely to encounter route-finding difficulty. We had to descend a snowfield, which would be featureless for about two or three hundred feet, locate a vague snow ridge, descend it, cross a flat area where there were huge, covered crevasses, descend a short but steep slope and then cross the open crevasse to Camp 5. We hoped that, if we attracted the attention of Richard Brooke and Dicky Grant in Camp 5, they would help us find the way in. Perhaps they might even come up and guide us.

We decided to leave the tent standing at Camp 6 in case Richard and Dicky, or any of the others from Camp 4, were tempted to have a go at the summit themselves—though this did not seem very likely in the prevailing weather. We put on our crampons inside the tent in the warm and then emerged, again with every stitch of available clothing on. I was feeling extremely tired even before we started. We roped up outside the tent and Tom set off in front kicking the steps. Soon we had left our tent behind us and were in a blank white world with a strong wind blowing stinging drift into our faces. Tom had my warm gloves and gauntlets to protect his hands and I felt the cold wind biting my own hands. Tom seems to have an unerring sense of direction (he had found the tent in the blizzard when we were setting up Camp 4) and as he plunged on ahead, a dim figure, I let the rope pay out between us in case he plunged over a cornice. A shout from him told me that, not only had he found the lip of the Snow Plateau, but he had struck it at exactly the right exit. Using the ice-axe for an anchor we climbed down to the rocks, moving one at a time. Facing out and keeping the rocks on our left we continued down, sometimes moving together but mostly one at a time for safety. The snow was either very hard or slithery and uncertain. When we reached the bottom of the rocks we were completely without landmarks but we set off hopefully in what we considered the right direction. The rocks disappeared into the cloud behind us and we were alone in the whiteness. Suddenly we encountered some crevasses which we had not crossed on the ascent. We cast around vainly in all directions to try to pick up some familiar contour or feature in the snow. We were lost. Occasionally the clouds would thin out slightly revealing alarming views of what appeared to be ice-cliffs or snow valleys but which were in fact merely minor dips or hummocks distorted by the mist.

I was now feeling very tired indeed, almost dangerously so. I remember sitting disconsolately on the snow paying out the rope to Tom. I saw him sit down and wave an arm to me. Wearily I waved back. A shout told me that he was waving to me to tighten the rope as he had half fallen into a crevasse. He came back to where I was sitting and we discussed the situation. We reckoned we had no alternative but to find a small crevasse and spend the night in it, out of the wind. It was then 3 p.m. and there seemed little chance that the day would clear up. Mercifully the wind had dropped and we were warm, except for our feet which were feeling very cold due to the effects of frostbite aggravated by the tight straps of the crampons we were wearing. We had sleeping-bags and air-beds in our rucksacks so we would survive the night in a crevasse, even if it were a cold one. The greatest danger was not an obvious one. We had no stove and so we would not be able to melt snow. We were probably getting dangerously dehydrated and another day without water would weaken us seriously. We would emerge from the crevasse on the morrow in a sadly weakened state. Our frostbite would hardly be improved. In the hope that Richard and Dicky might be able to help us we shouted and blew whistles, but received no reply. We then resigned ourselves to a night in a crevasse which would be infinitely worse than our last two nights at Camp 6.

Just then we caught a glimpse of the ridge through the clouds, before they closed in again. It was enough to raise our hopes. We waited and then suddenly the clouds were drawn aside and we found ourselves standing at the top of the little slope which ran down to the crevasse just above Camp 5. Tom's bump of locality had been as faultless as ever, which was a very good job, because there was a sheer drop on one side of us and vertical ice-cliffs on the other.

We then saw the reason why no reply had come from Richard or Dicky: the tent was flat and abandoned. Inside the tent we found a note from Richard saying that the tent had ripped in the storm, the weather was so rotten that they had given up any hope of the summit, and they were short of food. They had therefore descended earlier that day.

I was then so tired that I doubted if I could carry on down to Camp 4 with safety. Tom, however, was getting more worried about his fingers and wanted to give himself an intravenous injection of Heparin at Camp 4 without delay. He asked me if I was game to continue if I took a dexidrene. I agreed, took the pill, and we left Camp 5 and started down the ridge. We followed some excellently cut steps in which, from years of familiarity, I recognized Richard's craftsmanship. The reason for these elaborate steps, which we in crampons found hardly necessary but none the less pleasant, was that Richard and Dicky had left their own crampons at Camp 6 all ready for their summit attempt that never came off. Without crampons on the steep hard snow they had to cut many hundreds of steps. When the steep section of the ridge, with its long and dangerous drop right down to the Biro glacier, was safely passed, we unroped. Tom, as usual forged ahead, gained the length of fixed rope about five hundred feet above Camp 4 and approached the camp. His shout brought out little black figures from the tents.

I half slid, half climbed down the final slope to be met by a smiling Richard who relieved me of my rucksack and escorted me in to camp. I was by then very spent and was grateful when some other kind person removed my crampons for me and yet another handed me the ever-welcome cup of sweet tea.

I have vivid memories of that evening and of the warm friendly atmosphere of the camp. Warwick Deacock and John Sims very kindly let Tom and I crawl into their tent while they walked the mile or so to the octagonal tent which had been left on the summit of the Monk's Head. After a meal Tom prepared a hypodermic syringe, cotton wool, surgical spirit and sterile needles with which to puncture the several blisters which were making his fingers look like so many drumsticks. There was some talk of his losing the top joints of three of them.

"That would ruin your chances as a surgeon, wouldn't it?" I asked him.

"I suppose so, but I was worrying about not being able to play my accordion!" he replied.

Dicky Grant came into the tent to act as medical assistant. First Tom cleaned his hands, then punctured and drained the blisters. He then prepared to give himself an intravenous injection of Heparin. This drug has an anti-coagulant effect on the blood, which it thins, enabling it to penetrate frostbitten and bruised extremities. We had also taken some more Priscol because our feet had become extremely cold again during the descent, partly due to the restricting effect of the crampons we had been wearing. We each had a job to do: lying in my sleeping-bag next to Tom, I held the candle; Tom pushed the needle in and Dicky slowly pushed the plunger of the hypodermic home once it was in. On the first attempt Tom missed his vein and had to try the other arm. This time it was successful and Dicky pressed the plunger home. I can still in my imagination see Dicky's face, candle-lit, blond-bearded and concentrated; Tom, bearded and rugged, taking the needle without wincing.

I had always hoped that we would be able to stage a second assault and get a second rope to the summit. However, not only was there no reserve of food at Camp 4, but no one really had a sufficient reserve of strength left. Richard and Dicky had done quite enough and next morning, when John and Warwick came back from their night in the octagonal tent on top of the Monk's Head we were quite alarmed to observe how utterly spent they were after an hour of plodding through snow. A second assault was quite obviously out of the question and we prepared to descend, happy that the main object of the expedition had been achieved.

Tom, Dicky, Richard and I went on ahead. When we arrived at the octagonal tent on the dome of the Monk's Head we lashed it up very securely as we intended to throw it down the Monk's Head to save carrying it. When we got to the top of the fixed ropes Dicky let it go. It whizzed down out of sight, accelerating madly and bouncing. I hate watching objects, even stones, fall down a hillside because I always identify myself with them and feel myself hurtling down to eternity. It was fortunate that none of the Hunzas saw the black bundle fall or they might well have mistaken it for one of us.

There was deep snow even on the steep face of the Monk's Head and this turned our descent down the ropes into an absolute circus. We would never have got down safely without those ropes: soft snow was covering an underlayer of ice with the result that we climbed down one step and slipped down three, arresting ourselves by grabbing the ropes. Dicky Grant had the worst of it because he was carrying a five-foot tent-pole, which kept throwing him off balance, head over heels, or it would stick in the snow as he slithered and he would have to climb back up for it. Our descent was very tiring in addition to making us feel rather foolish, rolling down the slope like so many drunks. At the bottom I was so fed up with the whole

30. Camp 4 (21,000 ft.) with Haramosh (24,270 ft.) on the left and Dobani (20,126 ft.) in the center.

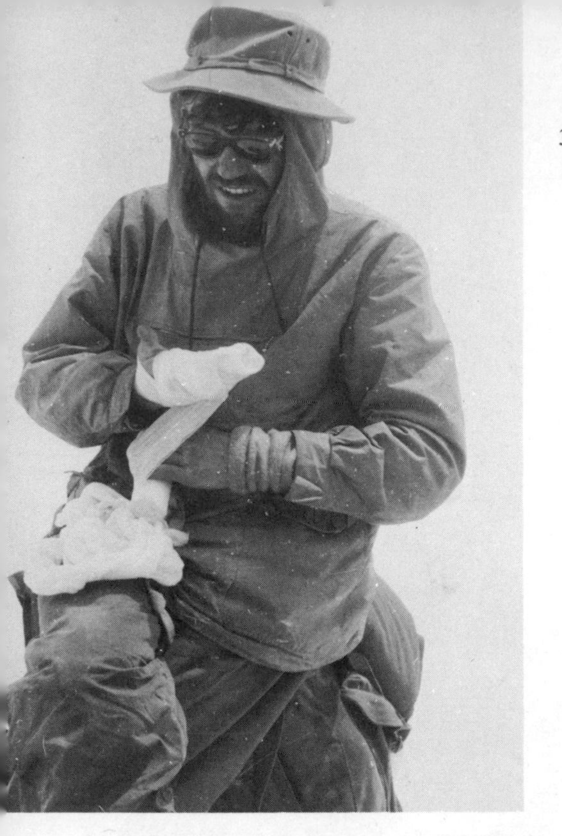

31. Tom Patey bandages his frost-bitten hand during the descent.

32. The summit pair: Mike Banks (left) and Tom Patey.

business that I let go the ropes for the last twenty feet and did a sitting glissade which enabled me to take off and sail clean over the open bergschrund to land on the easy slope beneath where a grinning Hunza was waiting to take my rucksack.

We picked up the tent which had stopped very conveniently near our track, and we all congregated in Camp 4. The Hunzas were delighted to see us, and I remember Ayub massaging our feet in a very expert manner to warm them up.

We broke camp next morning with the intention of going right down to base if we had the strength to kick steps the whole way. Just as we were about to leave we noticed that three black dots had appeared on the summit cone of the Gendarme. It was Shah Khan bringing with him Sep and Johar Beg. This was a very cheering sight because, not only were we pleased to see them and to have some extra help in carrying our over-heavy loads, but we now knew that steps would have been kicked back along the ridge.

Soon Shah Khan was in camp telling me his story. It will be recalled that, on the day that all the members and Hunzas climbed the Monk's Head to start the assault, Shah Khan had, on Tom Patey's advice, stayed behind thereby missing his chance for the summit. On the following day, however, he felt much better and determined to catch us up. This was the day we had shifted camp from the summit of the Monk's Head to the foot of the first step, perhaps a mile away. It will be recalled also that we were caught by a fierce blizzard half-way through this move and had only located our new camp site with extreme difficulty in almost non-existent visibility, thanks mostly to Tom's excellent sense of direction.

On that same day Shah Khan had actually climbed the Monk's Head with the intention of joining up with us. The blizzard struck him as he arrived on the summit but he pressed on following the flags and shouting to attract our attention. He found our deserted camp site and went on beyond to the last of our flags. In the end he had to return, having no cooking equipment with him. The utterly frustrating thing about it all is that Shah Khan might have approached within a hundred yards of us without our being able to see each other. We missed him and Sep very much during our final climb. I personally was also very disappointed that, due entirely to sickness in the first instance, followed by sheer bad luck, Shah Khan was not able to join us in our summit attempt. Shah Khan had perhaps done more than any of us to deserve a shot at the summit. It was certainly due to his splendid influence that the Hunzas gave us such wonderful support. But Shah Khan, being a big-hearted man, shrugged off his misfortune with a friendly smile and an "insh'Allah".

We were a big caravan, therefore, as we left Camp 4 for the last time and trudged back through the Notch to the Gendarme. The snow was far from stable and the Hunzas with their heavy loads found the descent of the Gendarme very trying. Poor little Ayub, the youngest of the porters, was ill with a bronchial trouble and could only just walk. Jimmy Mills therefore escorted him down, keeping him on a fairly tight climbing-rope. Richard and I escorted the remainder of the Hunzas. The top five hundred feet of fixed rope below Camp 2 had been moved over to the Monk's Head, so we had to climb down without it, carefully safeguarding the Hunzas. Down towards Camp 1 the snow became very soft and deep. We would occasionally get stuck in up to the thighs and require a heave from a friend to extract ourselves. By the time we arrived at Camp 1 we were very tired indeed, so we stopped for the inevitable, but none the less welcome, brew of tea. My frostbitten toes were by now becoming painful as I plunged downhill, ramming them forward into my boots.

In a carefree mood I lowered myself down the gully below Camp 1 for the last time. Quite high up, where it was still steep, I let go of the ropes and descended in a standing glissade, sweeping past the Hunzas with a happy shout. They were encouraged to be daring themselves, also infected by an end-of-term feeling, and soon the whole slope was covered with careering figures.

A delightful surprise was sprung on us at base. Raja had organized a most touching reception. A triumphal arch had been constructed from poles. Over it were the words "WELL DONE—BRAVO" fashioned by sticking colored papers cut out from magazines to a white background. From the arch Pakistani and British flags fluttered together with, surprisingly, a dozen or so balloons, giving a gay and festive air. For some completely inscrutable reason Warwick

Deacock had popped these balloons into the stores, which he had been packing just after Christmas. As I approached the arch Raja came forward and in traditional Pakistani fashion put a garland of sweet-smelling mountain-flowers round my neck. I will long remember this sensitive and charming little ceremony. Old Ashraf was ready with tea and the signallers were lined up, beaming with pleasure and sharing the joy of our success. Tired but happy we had a drink to our victory at supper in the mess-tent and then crawled into our sleeping-bags.

The first thing I did next morning was to give Lance Naik Zaffarullah signals addressed to our two Patrons, Field-Marshal Templer and General Ayub Khan telling them of our success. I then drafted out a long news communique for the Army Public Relations staff at G.H.Q. Rawalpindi, to release to the news agencies. In this manner the news of our ascent was announced on the B.B.C. on Sunday, June 29th, the same day that the signal had been cleared by Zaffarullah. The news appeared in the newspapers on the Monday morning. No expedition has ever been able to get its news out to the world so speedily and we are particularly indebted to General Ayub Khan for his brainwave of having a transmitter at base—and supplying us with the wireless and operators.

While we were waiting for the Jaglotis to come up to carry our stores down we passed a very pleasant few days, eating chiefly but also collecting or photographing the wild flowers which were now growing in profusion all around base—rhubarb, primulas, gentians, edelweiss. We feasted on sheep and chicken, and either Ashraf's cooking had improved or we were in a more tolerant mood because Ashraf-baiting seemed to have lessened, with the possible exception of an occasional howl of anger or alarm as he continued to experiment with the pressure-cooker which, for no reason I can fathom, still had not blown up.

On July 4th the Jaglotis appeared, eager for loot. In 1956 they had become nail-crazy, pulling them out of packing-cases for all they were worth. On this occasion our left-overs were chiefly packets of food of which the coolies were half-suspicious but at the same time tortured by the thought that they might be letting something good slip through their fingers. There was a rustle of excitement when we gave away a few pairs of tattered climbing-breeches.

We had estimated that we had thirty-five loads, but when we came to lay them out we discovered that we had fifty-five. We had only asked for thirty-five coolies. The affair resolved itself in a very satisfactory but typically oriental way when forty-five coolies materialized together with a number of donkeys and grandfathers who were left out of sight 1,000 feet down the hill below the steep and troublesome scree. With a last backward glance at the tall, slender cairn, and the summit shining above, we turned our backs and walked down to the forest glade of Darbar, enjoying the profusion of green on the way down—a color our eyes had become unaccustomed to on the arid rock and snow of the upper mountain.

At camp that evening, with the lovely mountain smell of pine in the air, I could see through the gently waving tree tops the ridges of Rakaposhi joining in their summit climax. High, high up in the air; an impossible-looking place for a human to have trodden!

At Darbar Tom held a sick parade. Some genuinely sick villagers were treated by him, with Raja acting as interpreter. Soon, however, the rumor spread that the doctor sahib was giving away medicines and Tom was surrounded by an eager crowd. The procedure was soon reduced to a drill: a man would come up and grasp either his head or his stomach. Tom would then give him a stomach pill for his stomach or a vitamin tablet for his head (he had run low on Codeine for headaches). When a man clutched his head this clearly meant: "I have a headache, or my wife has one. Or, further, at some future date I might get a headache, or, of course, my wife might get one." Anyway, from their point of view it was something for nothing and an occasion to be enjoyed. After a while one man, I think it was our old friend The One-Eyed Riley, pointed to his head, received his pill, and then with a look of enormous cunning, pointed to his stomach and obtained a second pill. One poor old chap lifted up his shirt to reveal a huge tumor on the middle of his spine. It was the size of a grapefruit.

"What on earth's that?" I asked Tom.

"I'm afraid it's T.B. The tumor is caused by his vertebrae more or less disintegrating," he explained.

"And he was carrying a double load of over a hundred pounds! Can't have been doing his back much good."

"Aye, poor old chap. He probably hasn't long to live, but there's nothing I can do," said Tom.

We had a splendid log fire that night with singing and dancing by the Hunzas and Jaglotis. The following day we walked down to Jaglot, stopping on the way at Barit, where the flies had been so insufferable in 1956. Sahib Shah explained to me why the flies were so thick in that particular spot. "This is their hill station. They come up here for the hot season!"

We slept by the side of the river in Jaglot. Just before supper I performed my last hysterical dance around Ashraf's pressure-cooker, which I was certain was on the point of detonation but which he was regarding with both passivity and confidence. I think that pressure-cooker prevented Ashraf and me really becoming friends. In the village we also received a bag of mail which contained many congratulatory letters and cables—indeed we were all surprised but delighted with the interest our success had raised. We were particularly pleased with the congratulations of our two Patrons whose support and confidence we had, I hope, justified. On a lower, but equally pleasing level, the villagers had all called "*Mubarak*" (congratulations) to us as we entered Jaglot.

The next day was horrid. We were pitchforked from the cool temperate mountain climate straight into the unrelieved heat and glare of a desert as we walked down to the Hunza valley and followed the desolate bank of the Hunza River. Had we been wise we would have started well before the dawn. Instead we set off at about eight o'clock and met the full blast of the day's heat as the sun beat down onto the dry earth and the glare reflected back into our faces.

The Jaglotis seemed to like neither the heat nor carrying through the territory of their neighbors from Matum Das. They tried to dump their loads before they reached Matum Das, which was no good to us because the bridge and the jeeps were about a mile the other side of Matum Das. We told them that they would not be paid unless they carried to the bridge. When they reached the bridge they declared that they would not cross it because it was dangerous —and looking back I am not sure they were not right. The water was now much higher in the river and it was frothing and roaring along at a frightening speed. Dicky, who was known to be the man who carried the money and paid the villagers, then made a short but telling speech from the bridge to the effect that he was about to cross with the money and would be pleased to pay anyone who delivered his load to him on the far side. This is called applied psychology. It worked.

A string of jeeps was drawn up on the far side of the rope-bridge waiting to take us to the Northern Scouts mess at Gilgit. I found this reverse crossing of the rope bridge or *jhula* far more intimidating now the river was in spate. I remember that Richard Brooke was crossing just ahead of me and a wave from the river lopped right over his feet. With the heat of the day the volume of water was rising, and we conjectured whether the bridge might not be swept away as the snows were now melting at their very fastest, bringing the water up to its highest level of the year. In fact, had we been three days later there was a high chance that we would have been unable to cross.

So as not to impose too heavy a strain on the rickety-looking bridge only two people were allowed on the bridge at the same time. This was a wise precaution because, had the bridge broken, a man would have had small chance of surviving in that torrent. The crossing took several hours during which time Dicky waited under the meagre shade of his umbrella on the far bank to pay the Jaglotis as they crossed. The rest of us took a jeep to the Rest House at Nomal, a mile away, and waited. Dicky compensated himself somewhat by eating all the chicken cooked for the whole party—a reward he more than earned by his long and hot riverside vigil.

Raising clouds of dust the jeeps were driven off towards Gilgit—a distance of about eighteen miles. Major Sarjayal, Second-in-Command of the Northern Scouts, made us extremely welcome, and at the same time summoned two barbers who removed our beards and gave us army haircuts.

That evening, after a peg of whisky on the lawn, we retired to our rooms to rediscover the pleasure of sleep in a bed. The Rakaposhi adventure was over.

XV

JOURNEY'S ENDING

In a hundred ages of the gods I could not tell thee of the glories of Himachal where Siva lives and where the Ganges falls from the foot of Vishnu like the slender thread of the lotus flower—Hindu text.

THERE was a fortnight for us to while away in Gilgit before our plane was due to take us back to Rawalpindi. In the cool of the evening we would saunter through the bazaar looking at, and occasionally buying, lengths of fine Kashgar silk. Twice we turned out for the Northern Scouts' officers hockey team. The games were unremarkable except for a small band which struck up a merry tune whenever a goal was scored. I noted that the band was quickest and loudest (very properly so!) when the Colonel, who was an excellent center-forward, scored.

We also enjoyed a two-day walking tour to the south of Rakaposhi. We passed through villages where it was customary to give visitors a thorough massage on the assumption that they were tired after a long walk; we attended a village wedding with dancing and music. Richard Brooke and I came back over a 13,500-ft. pass, walking through fragrant pine forests and flower-strewn uplands. Nanga Parbat was revealed in its full glory as three great birds, lammergeiers possibly, cruised overhead.

And then back to the mess in Gilgit where our serenity was only broken by the arrival of Dennis Kemp, a member of the Minapin expedition, to tell us that the leader, and our friend, Ted Warr, had been killed high on the mountain with Dr. Hoyte.

Then we were saying good-bye to our friends in Gilgit and flying to Rawalpindi on a perfect day with clouds dancing about the summits of Haramosh and Nanga Parbat. For a long time we could see

Rakaposhi astern of the aircraft. She was standing up, a proud and solitary column of gleaming snow, the three tremendous steps of the summit ridge now diminished to a mere three kinks, hardly discernible. We skimmed over a ridge which then blotted out our view of the snows, and losing height we flew down the Kagan Valley to the plains. The countryside became a uniformly dull brown and the Karakoram from that instant took on the fabric of a memory.

The staff of G.H.Q. in 'Pindi were most pleased with the outcome of the expedition and we received many congratulations and kindnesses. On one memorable evening a dinner was given to commemorate our success which, it seemed to me, every senior officer in G.H.Q. honored us by attending. Lieutenant-General Musa, the officiating C.-in-C. (General Ayub Khan was at a Baghdad Pact meeting in Istanbul) was our host. I particularly recall a long and pleasant conversation with the Adjutant-General, Major-General Shahid Hamid, who was an authority on the history and customs of Hunza. He it was who told me of the position that Rakaposhi holds in the culture, and particularly in the traditional songs, of Hunza. There was a folk lore, he explained to me, attached to the mountain, much of it of Hindu origin. Rakaposhi was the abode of Shiva, a mountain-god, who had burnt the god of Love on the mountain as a punishment for disturbing him there. The elephant-headed god of Wisdom, Ganesh, was born in the Rakaposhi range. Another legend that General Shahid Hamid recounted to me was how, about three hundred years ago, a dragon was imprisoned in the ice high up on the peak and how, each spring, he tried to break out of his captivity. He was only kept there by the local people lighting great fires at the appropriate moment.

Soon we were in Karachi waving good-bye to Raja from the civil aircraft which flew us home. There was a blistering hot delay at Bahrein—115 degrees F.—while the engine was mended, a delay made terrible by a crowd of elderly female American tourists who were "doing" the world in six weeks and already seemed to be hating each other. At London airport we landed with something of a bump.

"What are all those fire-engines doing racing up the runway?" I asked Richard, who was sitting next to me. "An aircraft must be in trouble somewhere." In fact they had turned out for us as we had burst a tire landing and there was a fire danger. After that it was a matter of surviving two television interviews and then I was driving towards London with my wife, who had tied to the bonnet of the car a replica of our 1956 expedition banner—a pair of leopard-skin "briefs".

Every expedition has, in its nature, a foreground, a middle distance, and a background. The foreground is the planning and preparation, the hopes and frustrations, those utterly insuperable obstacles which are always overcome just at the moment of desperation and abandonment. The brawny adventurer finds himself secretary and drudge, his idealism and athleticism foundering in a flood of paper. These preliminaries to action, though they make dull reading, are part of the very fabric of expeditioning. They put the organizers, good rough hillmen, to a harsh test when they find themselves on trial as businessmen, diplomats, photographers, linguists, scribes, travel agents, caterers. They must also find time to guess—it is with regret that customers are informed that errors cannot be rectified after they have left the country—and to dream. This foreground of preparations which quits the mind so easily once action is joined, is in truth the very bed-rock of the venture.

The action of the expedition is the middle distance which catches the eye—and fills the book. It is the season when a man is given the chance of showing the strength of his convictions. It is an unrealistic interlude outside his urban experience when he applies his strength and skill, his cunning and technique, every practical trick of his trade, to a most palpably artificial end: that of crouching for a few moments on one of the most unproductive points on the earth's surface—the summit of a great peak. The important thing is that he arrives there not by dint of the excellence of his equipment, or the efficacy of his rations, but by the strength of his dream. And in the proper fashion of dreams this whole experience melts and dims and blurs into the twilight of memory; it becomes an insubstantial pageant.

Retrospect is the wide and hazy background, the haunt of inspiration and mystery. The more a man offers up to the mountain the more will remain with him. It is an odd legacy: a few names to add to the list of friends who are to be sent Christmas cards; a finger or toe, frostbitten once, which feels prematurely the first nip of winter; an ambivalent experience which at once brings present content and future restlessness.

When we returned to base camp, and afterwards, we held many a post-mortem on our actions. General Buller I think it was who, when asked how to win wars, growled: "More men." From my 1956 experience I had seen the solution to the problem of the ascent of Rakaposhi as "More men"—and a higher assault camp. I think this strategy was justified, for although a heroic, oxygenless climb of 4,000 feet is possible on the final day, as on Cho Oyu and Nanga Parbat (both of them a thousand feet higher than Rakaposhi) this feat can only be achieved in fine weather. Consequently the ascent becomes a gamble. As I have explained, I am no gambler (no Hermann Buhl either!). When, on June 20th, no less than twelve of us climbed the Monk's Head we had good reason to think that the peak was well and truly in the bag and that several ropes might attain the summit. In the event Tom and I made it by the skin of our teeth, and had we not climbed in the blizzard the subsequent bad weather might well have forced us all to retreat to the foot of the Monk's Head, where our nearest reserves of food lay. We would then have faced the always dubious proposition of a second assault by a tired party. Thank goodness we did what we did. I know that I was spurred on to the summit on that ghastly day by my sense of failure in 1956. Tom, I suspect, needed no such urging; his great hill love combined with his formidable physical and mental strength were more than adequate to the occasion. And again, thank goodness for that.

For the statistically minded, Rakaposhi at the time of its ascent, was the sixth highest mountain in the world to be climbed without oxygen. Three mountains higher than Rakaposhi have been ascended by British parties: Mount Everest (29,002 feet) in 1953, and Kangchenjunga (28,146 feet) in 1955, both with the assistance of oxygen; Nanda Devi (25,645 feet) in 1937 without oxygen. The climbing difficulties on Rakaposhi were probably harder than on any of these other mountains. With its long history of previous expeditions, mostly British, with the long drag from base camp to summit, which made our logistics of food and camps and movements formidably complex, with the fame that attaches to a mountain when even Tilman pronounces it an unhopeful proposition, with all this we might reasonably dub Rakaposhi the "Poor Man's Everest".

While I was visiting Tom Patey some months after our return he showed me a couple of letters he had received from our piratical old cook. Ashraf's English was only very rudimentary, so these letters must have been written at some expense to himself by a scribe in the bazaar in Rawalpindi. In the first letter, after a few polite preliminaries Ashraf came down to business, saying: "Further I hope that you must have received a big reward for your expedition and hope you will not forget my share in your reward as you have been very good to me . . ." His second letter, more peremptory, reflected a certain pique. "Please send me a parcel of those tablets which I shall be thankful to you," he ordered Tom, adding: "I hope you have received your rewards, if so, please send me my share. Salaam to you and your family and pray for your long life." And finally: "P.S. Kindly send me the photos of Rakaposhi also."

Poor old Ashraf! But how could we communicate to him the fact that we had already received, each of us in his own measure, his "big reward". We were given our reward on the mountain, where we worked for it. The most important part of it, the part that could be least accurately predicted or taken for granted, was the genuine and sustained sense of harmony that grew up in our team. I think it is difficult, just about impossible, to judge in the planning stage whether the apparently cheerful and competent crowd of climbers who have been drawn together for the expedition will weld themselves into a team or whether they will degenerate into a bunch of bickering individualists. Much depends on any unavoidable clash of personalities, which happily we were spared. I think our own healthy spirit might be attributed to three main factors: we were all going the same way, with the same aim, to get to the top. This sense of common interest is the strongest bond which, none the less, has on occasions not been strong enough to hold together expeditions containing members whose personalities or ideas are at variance. The second influence that motivated all of us was that of our common service background. Being service officers we were accustomed to discipline and accustomed both to receiving and giving orders in the right spirit. This, I am sure, was a steadying influence. Thirdly, despite our military background we eschewed any form of Prussianism and ran our affairs by open discussion in public council. As leader it was my pleasant and easy task merely to announce the general consensus of opinion in the form of a plan for a particular phase of the expedition. I would then find all the work and responsibility taken out of my hands: Warwick Deacock and Jimmy Mills would work out the details, Tom Patey, with Richard Brooke in close pursuit, would almost literally rush at the next slope; Shah Khan would look after his Hunzas and completely take care of the vital build-up.

Some misguided detractors labelled Hunt's successful Everest expedition a "military operation"; no doubt our own expedition is even more liable to be so described. It is difficult to crystallize the exact implied criticism in this remark. Military operations are, I am sure, just as likely to be either good or bad as business negotiations, football matches or anything else man turns his hand to. If by a military operation it is inferred that we made a firm plan within our resources of men, food and equipment, that we worked all this out in advance, in detail, and we then stuck to our plan, then we did run our expedition like a military operation. If by the expression military operation a person conjures up thoughts of a music-hall Sergeant-Major with waxed moustaches bawling at the men and forcing them to do idiotic things, then that person really needs his head looking at. Certainly Jimmy Mills, with his R.A.S.C. training, arranged his food dumps in neat lines of boxes, with instructions stating where each box was destined; I failed to observe him burnishing the metal head of his ice-axe or teaching the porters how to "Slope Axes". The military, for some reason which utterly evades me, are thought to have a lack of sensitivity, especially where appreciation of the aesthetic is concerned. Perhaps, then, a non-military expedition is one where the members read Rupert Brooke to each other on the lower slopes (where the view is usually best) and admire sunsets. The truth of the matter is that a big peak is a big undertaking and a great deal of organizing is required if it is to be climbed either with certainty or with safety. We were a happy, bearded, scruffy lot, glad to be away from ship, air station, parade ground or office for a few months, but sensible enough to ensure that we were adequately organized along the only lines we knew—military ones. We found time to enjoy sunsets and blue distances, to read prose or poetry, to collect and photograph flowers, to criticize, compare and reorganize to our complete satisfaction the three Services. (I did *not* pass these little gems of military wisdom on to Field-Marshal Templer when we met after the expedition!) We all of us also found time to try to teach Ashraf to use the pressure-cooker. Most important of all, however, we liked each other's company.

In this technological age, when machines in the Services, as in Industry, tend to supplant people, any human experience which develops personal qualities, particularly leadership, is of heightened value. The Army, for instance, runs its own school for Outward Bound training; in the Navy "expedition training", as it is called, was personally introduced by Admiral Mountbatten into the Mediterranean Fleet. In fact, the Admiral described our venture to me as "the ultimate in expedition training". I am confident that, in an intangible way, we are better officers for our experience. We shall rest content if our success (both in the plains and on the summit) points the way to future joint-service enterprises.

I would be indeed ungracious if I did not pay full tribute to our Pakistani friends and the tremendous help they afforded us. Everywhere we encountered only sympathy and kindnesses. We must start at the very top with our Patron, General Mohammed Ayub Khan, who blessed our venture and encouraged us throughout. In Shah Khan, Raja Aslam and Sahib Shah we have made three companions for life. I hope they enjoyed our friendship as much as we enjoyed theirs. The Hunzas, who had least to gain, proved their fine qualities as independent hillmen, and served us wonderfully well under the natural leadership of their own trusted Shah Khan. No expedition ever received better or more loyal support from their Hunzas. The three Pakistan Army signallers worked their wireless set admirably, often up to the knees in snow and slush, with the happy sequel that I hear that they are all now *lance naiks*.

In the way of the Services we were soon scattered around the world: Warwick to the jungles of Malaya with the Special Air

Service; Richard Brooke to the Mediterranean as Number One of a frigate; John Sims somewhere in that fanciful region beyond the sound barrier in his jet.

For myself, if I had faltered in bad weather in 1956, I had forced on in infinitely worse conditions in 1958, and the score was settled. My long pilgrimage to polar ice-cap and Himalayan summit was over. Then, one morning in the bath both my big toenails, black with frostbite, chose to come off seeming to indicate that Rakaposhi had finally worked itself right out of my system. Perhaps my storm years were now over enabling me to make a new approach to the hills with a milder philosophy, a more fitting humility. The mellow words of Conrad Gesner, written over four centuries ago, seemed to come down over the years to me:

> **I have long made up my mind, most learned Vogel, that hence forth, as long as it shall please God to let me live, I shall every year climb a few mountains, or at any rate one, at a time when the flowers are at their best.**

What admirable advice, gentle Conrad; only grant me the wisdom to heed it. But this flower-strewn mountain, it will have snow on it? Good, crisp snow? And rock, Conrad, firm, clean and sheer? Let us arrive at the snows with the sun, just at dawn, when the air is sharp and all life exciting. Our axes will arc in a glint of steel sending the ice chips flying. Then the rock, Conrad. It will be warm and rough in the sun when we reach it; and as we grope for the handholds we will somehow express the ecstasy of our spirit through the strength of our fingertips. Weary after the summit we will come down, perhaps in the calm of evening alpenglow, perhaps through storm-wrack, back at last to the flowers, pausing a while to enjoy them. And look, Conrad! They are edelweiss—our own mountain edelweiss.

APPENDIX A

SURVEY WORK

by Lieutenant-Commander F. R. Brooke, R.N.

THE original survey plans for the expedition were made in the expectation that we would be going to Disteghil Sar. We hoped to carry out a survey of this little-known peak and surrounding glaciers using photo theodolite technique (calibrated 35 mm camera mounted on top of a theodolite) similar to that used in the Everest region and more recently in the Antarctic by the New Zealand party of the Trans-Antarctic Expedition. This method is very suitable to mountain and polar surveying as most of the work is done in the office afterwards and time spent doing fiddly jobs with frozen fingers in the field is cut to a minimum.

When, in Karachi, our objective was changed from Disteghil Sar to Rakaposhi, we found ourselves going to a comparatively well-mapped area, which due to topographical features was of very limited extent. In Rawalpindi the expedition was joined by Mr. Sahib Shah, a plane-tabler from the Pakistan Survey. It was soon apparent that there was very little survey work that could be done in the neighborhood of our base camp and that in the interests of the survey it would be best if Sahib Shah acted quite independently of the expedition. This was done.

His work mainly consisted of making minor corrections to the existing quarter-inch map, obtaining additional height control, and checking the location and marking of existing trigonometrical points. He started with stations on either side of the Jaglot Nullah and then came up to base camp. In a lucky spell of weather he was able to come up to Camp 1 and Camp 2 and do a survey station at each. It was a particularly fine effort to reach Camp 2 at about 19,000 feet—his own altitude record. This was necessary to fix the peaks on the east side of the Kunti glacier and to draw in the glaciers at the head of the Jaglot Nullah which are shown quite erroneously on the existing map. He then worked along, and on the flanks of, the Hunza river between Matum Das and Tol, not far from Hunza. His work covered an area of about 300 square miles.

33. Highest point reached in 1956: Irvin at 23,500 ft.

34. Highest photograph taken in 1958. Patey a few feet below the summit.

35. The banquet to celebrate our victory.

APPENDIX B

PROVISIONING

Captain E. J. E. Mills, R.A.S.C.

INTRODUCTION

There is no doubt that catering for an expedition of service officers has its problems. On the one hand years of plain food, often indifferently cooked, have dulled their palates, and made their approach to food philosophical. In other words, they are prepared to eat most things that they are given. On the other hand, if not connoisseurs of food, they are expert at grousing about food, which can make life for the provisioning member a little difficult. One member, a Scots doctor, even complained about the weevils in the porridge. The sissy!

I cannot complain, however, as I volunteered for the job. Having planned the rations for two previous expeditions, I was eager to experiment on a third. It seems that some people never learn!

During the early stages of the planning, the members of the party were given the chance of criticizing the proposed rations, and to state their own special likes and dislikes. As far as possible, the expedition diet was made up to conform with the wishes of individuals.

Apart from these considerations, the rationing of the expedition was conditioned by two important factors. Firstly, limited money, and secondly, the leaders' wishes to keep weight to a reasonable minimum, so that the carrying of stores on the mountains could be successfully done by the climbers alone, should the porters fail us.

There were three types of packed rations: the main ration; the assault ration; and the luxury ration, as well as fresh food bought in Pakistan.

THE MAIN RATION

Packing and packaging

This was packed in an incredibly short time by Warwick Deacock and his wife, with a few helpers. The ration was arranged in two 8 man/day layers in a fibre-board box of the same type as that used by the army to take 10 man/day rations. The box and slide, which goes over it, are extremely tough, weatherproof and light. When emptied and flattened out they provide good insulation between tent-floor cloths and snow. The containers, with but a few exceptions, are normal sizes available in shops or issued to the army in composite rations. To save weight, packaging was kept as light as possible, and there were only four tins in the whole ration.

Criticism of the ration

Owing to factors and considerations to which I have already referred, the ration was light and in comparison to those taken on some Himalayan expeditions, somewhat austere.

At the end of the expedition members were invited to answer a questionnaire, and to give their criticisms. The completed questionnaires were enlightening, informative and deflating to my ego. In general terms, the members felt that the ration was adequate, and had fulfilled the main requirements. That is, it was sufficient, it kept them fit, and they did not suffer from too much loss of weight. It was not surprising, however, considering the austerity of the ration, that they were unanimous in their desire for more variety in all meal elements, and for tastier foods. Meat bars were not popular, and there had been too much chocolate and sweets, but not enough sugar. Another must was glucose tablets.

Suggested ration

From these criticisms and my own observations, I have evolved the ration shown below. It is a little heavier than the one we ate on Rakaposhi, but when the appetite has constantly to be tempted these extra few ounces are essential.

All container sizes would be standard, and the cost would not be expensive. Packing could be done by the expedition members:

8 MAN/DAY PACK (1 COMPO BOX LAYER)

ACTUAL RATION

Item	Man/ Day Ozs.	Container Weight Ozs.	Container	No.	Remarks	Average amounts actually consumed per man/ day (ounces)
Meat	4 2·5 (meat bar)	8 5 (meat bar)	Tin (meat bar in metal foil)	4	Corned beef, Stewed steak, Meat bar	4 (2 only for meat bar)
Sweets	2	2	Roll	8	Toff-o-Luxe, Boiled sweets	1
Oatmeal	2	16	Card Packet	1		1·5
Cheese	2	8	Tin	2		1·5
Chocolate	4	4	Wrapping	8	Milk, Plain, Fruit, Fruit and Nut, Nut Milk	2
Biscuits Service Plain	3	6	Packet	4		2
Biscuits Sweet	4	8	Packet	4	Digestive, Ginger, Shortbread	3
Sugar	4	1	Packet	32		4
Tea	0·5	0·25	Packet	16		0·5
Milk	1·75	7	Tin	2		1·75
Orange or Lemon Crystals	1·5	12	Polythene bag	1		1
Soup powder	0·5	2	Foil packet	2	Onion, Pea, Beef, Asparagus, Vegetable, Oxtail, Chicken Noodle, Mushroom	0·5
Butter	2	16	Tin	1		1·5
TOTAL WEIGHT	31·25 or 29·75					24·25 or 22·5

Gross weight of 16 man/day rations including box: 38 lb.

SUGGESTED RATION

Item	Weight Ounces	Remarks
Cereal	1·5	Oats, Grapenuts, Sugar Puffs, Farex, Weetabix
Bacon	2	
Condensed milk	1	
Dried egg	1	
Sugar	6	
Dried vegetable	1	Including dried potato
Vita Wheat	3·5	
Nestea	0·375	
Sweet biscuits	2	Digestive, ginger, shortbread, assorted
Butter	2	
Jam	0·5	Plum, strawberry, blackcurrant
Orange/lemonade crystals	1	
Chocolate	2	Plain, milk, fruit and nut
Drinks	0·5	Nescafé, drinking chocolate
Glucose	1	
Sweets	1	Boiled sweets, Kendal mint cake, toffee
Sardines	1·25	
Soup	0·625	
Fruit cake	1·25	
Meat	4	Corned beef, pork luncheon meat, tongue, salmon, dehydrated meats
TOTAL WEIGHT	33·5	

THE ASSAULT RATION

Packing and packaging

This was also packed by Warwick Deacock. Each four man/days were packed into a light cardboard box, six of which fitted into the same type of fibre-board box used for the Main Ration. Later the smaller boxes were transferred to kitbags. This was a mistake, for they were not strong enough and several broke open. Others broke up inside rucksacks, which was not popular. A more substantial carton or stout polythene bag was certainly required. There was only one tin, and the orange and lemonade powder was repacked by Warwick Deacock into alloy extruded tubes or polythene bags.

The ration

ASSAULT RATION—4 MAN/DAY PACKS (IN CARDBOARD BOXES)

ACTUAL RATION

Item	*Man/ Day Ozs.*	*Container Weight Ozs.*	*Container*	*No.*	*Remarks*	*Average amounts actually consumed per man/ day (ounces)*
Corned beef	2	8	Tin	1		2
Oatmeal	2	1	Wrapped	8	In block form	2
Chocolate	2	2	Wrapped	4	Milk and plain	1
Toff-o-Luxe	2	2	Roll	4		1
Biscuits Service, plain	1·5	6	Packet	1		1
Sugar	6	1	Packet	24		6
Tea	0·75	c·25	Packet	12		0·5
Milk	2	4	Tube	2	Condensed	2
Orange and Lemon crystals	2	8	Tube or Polythene bag	1		1
Soup powder	0·5	2	Foil packet	1		0·5
TOTAL WEIGHT		20·75 (1 man/day)				18
GROSS WEIGHT (including Container weight)		6 lb. (4 man/day)				

Criticism of the ration

The ration was based on the 19-ounce diet used successfully by Waller on Saltoro Kangri in 1936. For a party which was expecting to do its own portering over 21,000 feet, it seemed to me that the experiment was well worth repeating.

We arrived at Camp 4 well acclimatized and fit, with good appetites. From this point we grew weak very rapidly until after seven days at this height and above, the feebleness of the party was quite pronounced. The ration was insufficient and lacked interest.

Criticism by the members was again very similar to that of the Main Ration, with an insistence on a heavier ration.

Item	*Weight Ounces*	*Container*	*Remarks*
Cereal	1·5	Polythene bag	Oatmeal blocks, Grape-nuts, Sugar Puffs, Weetabix, or Farex
Milk	1	Tube	Condensed
Sugar	6	Packet and Polythene bag	Lump
Nestea	0·375	Metal foil sachet	
Drinks	0·5	Metal foil sachet	Drinking chocolate, Nescafé
Jam	0·5	Tube	Strawberry, blackcurrant, plum
Biscuits	3	Paper packet	Vitaweat
Sweets	2	Polythene and foil wrapping	To include 1 ounce glucose tablets
Chocolate	2	Foil and paper	Plain, milk, fruit and nut
Soup powder	0·625	Metal foil sachet	Tomato, chicken noodle, asparagus, oxtail, beef
Orange or lemonade crystals	1	Polythene bag	
Meat	4	Metal foil packet	Corned beef, tongue, salmon, pork luncheon meat, dehydrated meat
Marmite	0·125	Tube	
Dried potatoes	0·5	Polythene bag	
Sardines	1·125	Tin	
TOTAL WEIGHT	24·250		

Suggested ration

An assault ration must be light, especially if the expedition cannot afford to employ a large number of high-altitude porters. The question is how much can the weight be pared down? Our experience suggests that at least 24 ounces is necessary. On Everest the average consumption of the 33 ounces assault ration was between half and a full ration; roughly 24 ounces. Band, in writing of the diet on Kanchenjunga in 1955, suggests a 32-ounce high-altitude ration. His plan is to give the climber, with his jaded appetite, a wide variety of choice, based on the assumption that a "little bit of what you fancy does you good".

I have tried to suggest a ration for future expeditions to high mountains. The sort of party I have in mind is a small private one, whose limited finances preclude a large team of high-altitude porters.

LOCAL PURCHASE

Forty pounds of rice were bought in Gilgit. It proved to be far in excess of our requirements, for we had become a little tired of curry-and-rice dishes by the time we started the approach march.

With Shah Khan's help we negotiated a contract with the *Lambardar* at Jaglot to provide us with one, sometimes two sheep a week and as many chickens, potatoes and eggs as the village could spare. These were brought up to Base Camp once a week.

This fresh food, together with other luxury rations, supplemented the main ration, not only in Base Camp, but higher up the mountain. In consequence we were able to eat chicken at Camp 1, and eggs up to Camp 2 at 19,200 feet. There is no reason why eggs packed in alloy containers should not go to the highest camps. Small quantities of chicken, pre-cooked at Base Camp, could also take the place of some tinned meats on the mountain.

"LUXURY" FOOD

An inexpensive selection was presented to each member. These foods were then modified according to their wishes. The total list was:

Food	*Pack*	*Number*
Condensed milk	7 oz. tins	24
Nescafé	2 oz. tins	48
Nesquik	8 oz. tins	12
Corned beef	8 oz. tins	24
Stewed steak	16 oz. tins	20
Blancmange powder	16 oz. tins	6
Orange powder	2 lb. tins	5
Lemonade powder	2 lb. tins	5
Sugar	16 oz. pkts.	32
Golden syrup	16 oz. tins	4

Food	*Pack*	*Number*
Tea	4 oz. pkts.	20
Chocolate wheatmeal	7 lb. tin	4
Chicken noodle soup	2 oz. pkts.	8
Oxtail soup	2 oz. pkts.	7
Pea soup	2 oz. pkts.	6
Asparagus soup	2 oz. pkts.	6
Vegetable soup	2 oz. pkts.	6
Beef soup	2 oz. pkts.	6
Onion soup	2 oz. pkts.	6
Mushroom soup	2 oz. pkts.	6
Mustard	1 oz. tubes	12
Bounty bars	1 lb. pkts.	3
Salt	1½ lb. tins	16
Marmite	2 oz. tubes	24
Potato strip	12 lb. tins	2
Dried onion	4 lb. tins	1
Dried cabbage	4 lb. tins	1
Baking powder	8 oz. tins	4
Bisto	8 oz. pkts.	6
Vitaweat	1 lb. pkts.	10
Tinned peaches	Large tins	2
Tinned pears	Large tins	2
Tinned pineapple	Large tins	2
Mint cake	8 oz. slabs	40
Jams various	2 lb. tins	6
Weatabix	1 lb. pkts.	12
Sage and Onion	4 oz. pkts.	6
Plain flour	3 lb. pkts.	12
Pepper	1 oz. drums	4
Dried fruit	1 lb. pkts.	20
Curry Powder	8¼ oz. tins	8
Tomato ketchup	12 oz. bottles	4
Worcester sauce	Large bottles	2
Pan Yan pickle	Bottles	4
Green Label chutney	Jars	4
Dried yeast	2 lb. pkts.	2
Butter	1 lb. tins	12 tins
Cheeses		2
Rice	1 sack	40 lb.
Fudge	Pkts.	50
Energade tablets	Pkts.	50
Whisky	Bottles	3

Food	*Pack*	*Number*
Rum	Bottles	3
Beef suet	4 oz. pkts.	6
Raisins	12 oz. pkts.	8
Grapenuts	10 oz. pkts.	20
Oxo	6 cube tins	50
Lard	2 lb. tins	4
Cake mix	14 oz. pkts	6
Peanut butter	12 oz. jars	6
Potato mash powder	8 oz. tins	10
Blancmange powder	1 lb. tins	12
Ostermilk No. 2	1 lb. tins	24

Criticism of the ration

In general the luxury ration met with everyone's approval. A greater variety of tasty meats should have been taken. The quantities of jam, tinned fruit, Vitaweat, pickles, sauces, suet, lard, peanut butter and yeast, were all inadequate, and could have been increased fourfold. The omission of tinned fish was a serious error. Dried fruit and cereals should have been doubled. We had twice the quantity of blancmange powder required, and tinned fruit-cake could take the place of at least half the cake mix. Dried soups could be cut out completely.

These foods were not eaten only at Base Camp. Small quantities of most items were taken to the three lower Camps to add interest to the main ration. These were always eaten in preference to items in the main ration.

Some bread was made in Base Camp, and as was expected it proved extremely popular. More bread could have been made had the cook or a Hunza been taught the process.

These extra rations are not essential. Some are advisable, but they are costly, and if money is short the quantities can be reduced without any hardship.

PORTERS' FOOD

The Field Supply Depot of the Pakistan Army Service Corps at Gilgit provided local food for the Hunza porters, as they do for all expeditions. These rations are the same as those issued to Pakistani troops in the loftier frontier outposts. The meat element was provided by the mutton and chickens brought to Base Camp.

In conjunction with Shah Khan, the porters decided on what they would require at Camps 1, 2 and 3. Quantities of the following foods and drinks were also added at each Camp:

Soup powder	Orange and lemonade powder
Tea	Oxo
Coffee	Chocolate
Sugar	Sweets
Milk	

EMERGENCY RATIONS

Each climber and Hunza carried, for use in emergencies, a block of Horlicks Rum Fudge, and two packets of the same firm's "Energade" glucose tablets. Together they provided a source of food and energy sufficient for forty-eight hours. Their total weight was about 8 ounces.

THE RATIONING PLAN ON THE MOUNTAIN

From Camps 1 and 2 Base Camp could be reached in a few hours, and on long sections of the route ropes were fixed. It was therefore only deemed necessary to leave reserves of 16 and 32 man/days food, respectively, at these two Camps.

Camp 3 was in reality the Advanced Base, and here we intended, if necessary, to sit out any storms which might come upon us. Fourteen day's food for eight climbers was stocked here. The Hunzas had ten days of their own food and four days of packed rations. Ten days' assault rations for eight climbers were carried to Camp 4. In theory, Camps 4, 5 and 6 were to be established on consecutive days with the attempt on the summit, and return to Camp 4 being made on the fourth and fifth days. We would therefore have, again in theory, five days reserves. In practice, because of delays by bad weather, and the abandoning of food at the two top Camps, the only edibles at Camp 4 on the morning that we left, were several packets of Toff-o-Luxe, tea and lemonade crystals.

INDEX